Poet of Civic Courage
The Films of Francesco Rosi

Poet of Civic Courage

The Films of Francesco Rosi

Edited by
Carlo Testa

PRAEGER

Westport, Connecticut

Published in the United States and Canada by
Praeger Publishers, 88 Post Road West, Westport, CT 06881
An imprint of Greenwood Publishing Group, Inc.

English language editions, except the United States and Canada,
published by Flicks Books, England.

First published 1996

The Library of Congress has cataloged the hardcover edition as follows:

Poet of civic courage : the films of Francesco Rosi / edited by Carlo
    Testa.
        p.   cm. -- (Contributions to the study of popular culture,
    ISSN 0198-9871 ; no. 59)
        Filmography: p.
        Includes bibliographical references and index.
        ISBN 0-313-30278-2 (alk. paper)
        1. Rosi, Francesco--Criticism and interpretation. I. Testa,
    Carlo. II. Series.
    PN1998.3.R66P64   1996
    791.43'0233'092--dc20   96-28759

A hardcover edition of *Poet of Civic Courage: The Films of Francesco
Rosi* is available from Greenwood Press, an imprint of Greenwood
Publishing Group, Inc. (Contributions to the Study of Popular Culture,
Number 59; ISBN 0-313-30278-2).

Library of Congress Catalog Card Number: 96-28759

ISBN: 0-275-95800-0

Printed in Great Britain.

P

Contents

Acknowledgements

Apart from its indebtedness to its contributors, this book also owes a great deal to a number of people who did their utmost to locate and procure elusive material. Among these, I must gratefully mention my father Alberto and my brother Fabio back in the Old Country; the staff of the Interlibrary Loan office at the University of British Columbia; and, last but not least, Francesco Rosi, who generously helped in every way he could – and kindly accepted to debate issues related to his filmmaking and filmmaking in general with both the patience of the master and the enthusiasm of the novice.

Patience and enthusiasm throughout this project are qualities for which I must also thank my wife, Daniela.

Carlo Testa
University of British Columbia, Vancouver
September 1996

Introduction

Carlo Testa

In *The Pleasure of the Text*, Roland Barthes provokingly suggests that the enjoyment derived from things such as intellectual and speculative pursuits – conventionally held to appeal only to a drab, sublimated rationalism – may in fact spring from an entirely different source. By subverting, at the dawn of the postmodern era, ideas previously received and accepted without criticism, he formalised a liberating suspension of boundaries, which Western culture has followed through ever since.

The long overdue resolution of entrenched dualisms – both political and aesthetic – propounded by Barthes, his questioning of the polarity established, in all fields, between that which is "good" and that which is "pleasurable" contributed to shattering a mental habit that could be called either a legacy of our Judaeo-Christian heritage and of its sense of duty, or a consequence of the systemic dualism that characterised the entire history of Western metaphysics. As Barthes states:

> An entire minor mythology would have us believe that pleasure (and singularly the pleasure of the text) is a rightist notion. On the right, with the same movement, everything abstract, boring, political, is shoved over to the left and pleasure is kept for oneself: welcome to our side, you who are finally coming to the pleasure of literature! And on the left, because of morality (forgetting Marx's and Brecht's cigars), one suspects and disdains any 'residue of hedonism.' On the right, pleasure is championed *against* intellectuality, the clerisy: the old reactionary myth of heart against head, sensation against reasoning, (warm) 'life' against (cold) 'abstraction': must not the artist, according to Debussy's sinister precept, '*humbly seek to give pleasure*'? On the left, knowledge, method, commitment, combat, are drawn up against 'mere delectation' (and yet: what if knowledge itself were *delicious*?).[1]

If Barthes's statement is transposed to the realm of cinema, the consequences are clear: the time has come to proclaim that being an

1

engaged film-goer is, in fact, a *pleasure*. The obvious attendant corollary is that in the post-ideological era being an engaged, courageous citizen is a (supra-partisan) *delicious* affair. If we believe that this is the case, we vindicate notions espoused by Francesco Rosi almost a lifetime ago.

As early as the 1960s, Rosi's blending of aesthetic and civic categories was especially innovative in questioning the assumptions generally held during that period of European high culture. Existentialism, whether characterised by Heideggerian or Sartrian overtones, and conceptually stretching as far afield as Ionesco and Beckett, was a particularly serious offender in opposing enjoyment to engagement and aesthetic pleasure to civic virtues: one could only strive for beauty *or* for seriousness, but not for both simultaneously.[2] More concisely, during Rosi's formative years and throughout the earlier part of his career, aestheticism had for many years seemed suspicious.[3] Nor were things to improve later. In Italy, in particular, the socio-political debate had by the 1970s absurdly opposed to each other two equally improbable cultural bogeypersons: an individualistic hedonism of the reactionary type, on one hand; on the other, a society-conscious, but inflexible, denial of the prerogatives of the individual self.

In his own contribution to this volume (pages 155-158), Rosi aptly reminds us that the ultimate outcome of this polarity was the long years of terrorism, which virtually blocked serious debate and open, constructive political confrontation in his country. It is not surprising, therefore, that the implications of postmodernism were recently absorbed by Italian society with some relief: they allowed Italians to break away from what had been the *impasse* of the 1970s and early 1980s. While the practice of erasing a conflictual past from one's consciousness is, in the long term, a pathological way of dealing with it, in the short term at least it may be an understandable one.

Is there a more permanently successful alternative? A solution can perhaps be found if we accept and develop the non-dualistic Barthesian premise: knowledge – even knowledge about a sorry past – is delicious; engagement – even engagement on painful subjects – is aesthetic; that which is good is the same as that which is pleasurable. This is precisely the artistic terrain that turns out to be Rosi's very own. The marriage of beauty and morals, which Barthes so timely and so liberatingly recognised and theorized, had been alive since the earliest of Rosi's cinematic works.

If one were to identify some major cultural artefacts representing what I should like to call a non-dualistic trend in Italian, and perhaps pan-European, cultural history, it would be difficult to think of examples more appropriate than Rosi's films. In his work, civic courage, rising above specific political banners, blends with a poetic, artistic eye and creates a world of many facets, in which intellectual rigour comes to fruition as aesthetic enjoyment against the backdrop of sceneries as varied as those of the Sicily of *Salvatore Giuliano* (1961); the Amazon forest of *Cronaca di una morte annunciata* (*Chronicle of a Death Foretold*, 1987); the Spain of *Carmen* (1984); the Alps of *Uomini contro* (*Just Another War*, 1970), inspired by Emilio Lussu's war memories; the crumbling, inefficient (but humane and lively) Naples of *Le mani sulla città* (*Hands Over the City*, 1963); the ancestral Apulian fields and villages of *Tre fratelli* (*Three Brothers*, 1980); and many more.

Our collection opens with Ben Lawton's essay on *Salvatore Giuliano* (pages 8-42), a masterpiece which inaugurates the season of Rosi as an internationally acclaimed filmmaker: "something changed in the history of cinema with *Salvatore Giuliano*".[4] Rosi's film shows that the rigorously documented study of an historical and social phenomenon, such as the post-Second World War Sicilian independentist movement and its relation to the Mafia, can overcome the traditional distinction between fiction and documentary, and create a gripping style that is both individually tragic and historically persuasive, both methodologically accurate and psychologically refined.

Manuela Gieri's contribution (pages 43-59) highlights the political and social aspects of Rosi's second major work, *Hands Over the City*. Gieri reconstructs the film's socio-historical framework: real estate speculation during the Italian *miracolo economico*, corruption in the civil service, and links between the Neapolitan (and national) political world and that of the *camorra*. She shows that the film, over and above its documentary value, also has a symbolic value as an illustration of "the morality of power": in Italy, among the long-ruling Democrazia Cristiana (Christian Democrat Party – DC), but also in the universal sphere of politics.

The meteoric rise and mysterious death of Enrico Mattei are the subject-matter of *Il caso Mattei* (*The Mattei Affair*, 1972), which is explored in Harry Lawton's essay (pages 60-86). In the 1950s Mattei was head of ENI, the Italian nationally owned oil company, on behalf of which he aggressively moved to challenge the major cartels' control over world oil production. Far from concerning itself with the mere praise of a hardly idealistic personality, the film peers into supra-personal issues that, because of the interests they threatened, had been hushed up by the status quo, both in Italy and internationally. Harry Lawton inscribes Mattei's name among the many that dot Rosi's artistically and historically engaged filmmaking, as, over decades, he bears witness to the evolution of the young Italian republic.

Claudio Mazzola's essay on *Lucky Luciano* (1973) (pages 87-100) illustrates the difference between Italian cinema and American cinema in dealing with the theme of the Mafia, and in order to do so it focuses on certain traits that are unique to Rosi's work. The interconnection between the historical and political levels, on the one hand, and Luciano's figure as an individual, on the other, forms the core of Rosi's inquiry. Mazzola explores this link as he comments on Rosi's highly personal technique and as he highlights the director's originality in dealing with a genre whose canon systematically tends to downplay many of the positive qualities for which Rosi is best known – a real-life narrative style, multifaceted inquisitiveness, historical factuality and open-endedness.

The essay by Salvatore Bizzarro on *Cadaveri eccellenti* (*Illustrious Corpses*, 1975) (pages 101-115) pursues the political implications of an arch-political (yet entirely metaphorical) film in Rosi's œuvre. Inspired by Leonardo Sciascia's book, *Il contesto* (*Equal Danger*), the film combines the devices of the detective story, skilfully adapted by Sciascia to the Italian (and particularly Sicilian) situation, in order to make statements about a society in which political criminality strikes while vested interests conspire to hide the truth, and – in the words of Tomasi di Lampedusa's Leopard – "everything changes so that everything can remain the same".[5]

Millicent Marcus's contribution on *Three Brothers* (pages 116-137) – a free adaptation of a novella by Andrei Platonov – examines the complex texture of Rosi's three-plus-one analysis of Italy at the end of the conflictual 1970s. Raffaele, the oldest son, is a judge in Rome, exposed to retaliation from terrorist groups; Rocco, the youngest, works in Naples in a community for the reform of juvenile delinquents; Nicola, the middle one, is a disgruntled car worker in Turin. When the fourth major character in the film – Donato, the father – calls upon his sons to join him for their mother's funeral, they all meet in the ancestral village they have long ago abandoned to pursue careers in faraway corners of Italy. Marcus shows how different regions, political views and personalities "hold together" in *Three Brothers*, and how different generations "close the circle" in Rosi's memory and in the identity of his country.

Our critical selection closes with Marcus's essay on the film inspired by Platonov's novella, less because no more remains that should be written about Rosi's cinema than out of sheer necessity. Constraints of space and time, in addition to the limited availability of certain material in North America, prevented the inclusion in this book of essays on, for example, *Just Another War*, *Carmen*, *Chronicle of a Death Foretold*, *Cristo si è fermato a Eboli* (*Christ Stopped at Eboli*, 1979), *Dimenticare Palermo* (*The Palermo Connection/To Forget*

Palermo, 1990) and *Diario napoletano* (*Neapolitan Diary*, 1992). Rosi is now filming Primo Levi's *La tregua* (*The Truce*). It is planned that these films will be the subject of a complementary volume.

The last contribution in this volume is written by Rosi himself (pages 155-158), having originally appeared in the cultural pages of the daily *la Repubblica* on the occasion of the 49th anniversary of Italy's liberation from Nazism (April 1945-April 1994). Rosi's article, here translated into English for the first time, is an impassioned appeal, stressing that the most urgent task for the current and future generations of Italian filmmakers is to foreground again the strong, vital link between the history of their country and the stories they wish to narrate.

The crucial issue as to how Rosi himself theorizes about his own artistic production is one of the many themes broached in the interview with him (pages 138-154). The topics covered range from the technical (how Rosi relates to free trade issues raised by the 1994 GATT negotiations on cultural products; how he views directors' rapport with their literary sources, for example) to philosophical ones – what is the ultimate purpose of filmmaking?; what is the purpose of narrating through images?

Rosi's overarching principle is that a dialectical approach to the osmosis between individual stories and communal history must prevail, if Italian cinema is to renew its vital contribution to the intellectual life of the country. Rosi's cinema stands apart from that of, for example, otherwise deserving filmmakers who contributed to the *commedia all'italiana* during the same period: for Rosi, the episodic *must* just add up to a whole, to the recognisable visage of a country in evolution (in some extreme cases, arguably, in *in*volution). The poet of civic courage cannot be such unless he has a large and detailed social canvas on which to paint.

It thus comes as no surprise to learn from Rosi how painful an experience for him were the years of Italian terrorism – the *anni di piombo*, straddling the 1970s and 1980s: the pursuit of History, and particularly of recent and contemporary History, was almost a taboo subject at that time, since historical inquiry stood accused (however improbably) of having mechanically fostered a subversive mentality, ultimately leading to cruelty and mindless bloodshed. As this phase has passed for the time being, Rosi is now optimistic; or rather, he pursues the "pessimism of Reason and the optimism of Will"[6] so strong-mindedly suggested by Gramsci as an appropriate maxim of world-immanent morality.

It will be noticed, however, that the interview with Rosi is devoid of any sense of exuberant triumphalism on his part. To explain the reason for this, it should suffice to remember that the encounter with

Rosi took place at a time which not only was marked by the recrudescence of war in ex-Yugoslavia and the resurgence of heinous racist acts in Germany, but also represented a particularly sensitive moment in Rosi's own country. In the midst of European and North American celebrations for the 50th anniversary of the Allied landing in Normandy, Italy was then in the immediate aftermath of the rise to power of the media tycoon, Silvio Berlusconi, the leader of a one-man party which, in an ad hoc bond against the immortal Red Threat, had allied itself with the federalist Lega Nord (Northern League) – *and* the neo-Fascists. In those weeks Europe and the world witnessed a convulsive, but entirely straight-faced, Italian debate as to whether Mussolini had in fact *always* been wrong in his policies. "New" opinions were then voiced to the effect that the *Duce* had simply started straying from the desirable path after certain regrettable junctures in history. As the world was trying to fathom the mysteries of Italian identities, so were many Italians themselves.

Rosi's current project is the filming of Primo Levi's *La tregua* (*The Truce*): a work about the difficulty, and the exciting novelty, of coming out of the concentration camps and back to life after long years spent enduring the horrors of war.[7] May his metaphor for Italy's recent past be fulfilled; may his contention that the "hostilities" are now over – that the world (or, more modestly, Europe) could, if it seriously wanted to, head for a period of increased peace, tolerance and appreciation for art and beauty – prove to last for longer than just the time of a "truce".

May Rosi's intuition be true, and the overcoming of past sufferings soon to be evoked in *The Truce* by our poet of civic courage prove prophetic.

Notes

[1]   Roland Barthes, *The Pleasure of the Text*, translated from the French by Richard Miller (Oxford, UK; Cambridge, USA: Blackwell, 1990): 22-23. Emphases in original.

[2]   I am aware that some (possibly ranging from Camus to Brecht) would disagree on this point; they would presumably argue that they had other, different types of beauty in mind. My point is precisely that their beauty was of a nature specifically *different* from that of Western aesthetic tradition.

[3]   This is not to say that there were not excellent reasons to think so at the time. The dreadful First World War-Nazism/Fascism-Second World War sequence had been a particularly powerful disincentive from indulging in the aestheticism and relativism that had originated during the *fin de siècle* period; and the complaint that aestheticism shared great responsibilities for the rise of Nazism/Fascism is a frequent one in the social and political

literature of the interwar years. For an outstanding specimen of the genre, see Johan Huizinga's contemporaneous *In the Shadow of Tomorrow* (London and Toronto: William Heinemann, 1936). To very few artists – the young Visconti, for example – did the dualism between beauty and seriousness appear to be beside the point. Rosi continued the artistic legacy he received from the master of *La terra trema* (*The Earth Trembles*, 1948).

[4] Translated from the French: "Quelque chose a changé dans le cinéma avec *Salvatore Giuliano*". Roger Boussinot (ed), *L'encyclopédie du cinéma par l'image* (Paris: Bordas, 1970): 651.

[5] The words are actually those of his nephew, Tancredi: "Se vogliamo che tutto rimanga come è, bisogna che tutto cambi". Giuseppe Tomasi di Lampedusa, *Il gattopardo* (Milan: Feltrinelli, 1985): 24.

[6] See Antonio Gramsci, *Quaderni del carcere*, edited by Valentino Gerratana (Turin: Einaudi Editore, 1975): (volume 2) 762, 1131 and (volume 3): 2332.

[7] See the interview with Rosi in this volume, pages 138-154.

Salvatore Giuliano: Francesco Rosi's revolutionary postmodernism

Ben Lawton

This film was shot in Sicily, in Montelepre, where Salvatore Giuliano was born. In the houses, in streets, on the mountains where he reigned for seven years. At Castelvetrano, in the house where the bandit passed the last months of his existence, and in the courtyard where one morning his lifeless body was seen.[1]

As Francesco Rosi's *Salvatore Giuliano* (1961) opens, these words scroll up the screen. Slowly they disappear, the screen goes black for a couple of seconds, and then, from above, there is a long shot of what appears to be a dead man's prone body sprawled in a courtyard. As the film closes, another man collapses to the ground, dead, in virtually the same position, he too killed by unseen assassins. Two deaths, separated by a decade but connected by a mysterious force; a black hole around which the events in the film rotate, tethered by this invisible gravity which keeps order, but which also gradually but ineluctably sucks everything into its maw.

As a child growing up in Italy, I can vaguely remember older children talking about Giuliano's adventures, as they had heard about them from their parents. For disaffected, working-class children in an economically depressed country which had just lost a war, he was a very real hero, a Robin Hood of sorts, because – at least according to the generally accepted legend – "he took from the rich and gave to the poor". Later, I remember people talking about his death and about the mysterious death by poisoning of his "cousin", Gaspare Pisciotta.[2] Oddly, even the children did not believe the official story of either death – perhaps because all my friends were children of partisans who had fought against the Fascist government during the war. It was a mystery which fascinated us, which obsessed the media throughout the world, and which inspired two films (Rosi's *Salvatore Giuliano* and Michael Cimino's *The Sicilian*), a novel (Mario Puzo's *The Sicilian*), an opera (Di Leva and Ferrero's *Salvatore Giuliano*), several biographies, and countless newspaper and magazine articles.[3]

I was absolutely unprepared for Rosi's masterpiece.[4] Here was a film which, at a first viewing, appeared to achieve Bazin's description of *Ladri di biciclette* (*Bicycle Thieves*, 1948): "No more actors, no more story, no more sets, which is to say that in the perfect aesthetic illusion of reality there is no more cinema".[5] Certainly, more than any neo-realist film it satisfied – or gave the impression that it satisfied – the call for real locations, real people and real events. The landscape and the people had to be Sicilian, and, even if they were not, they appeared to fulfil the neoplatonic ideal of what Sicilian landscape and people of that time should have looked like. As for the events, again at first blush they conveyed all the irresistible and inevitable improbability, absurdity and mystery of reality. More than any of the great neo-realist classics (*Roma, città aperta* [*Rome, Open City*, 1945], *Paisà* [*Paisan*, 1946], *Bicycle Thieves*, *Umberto D*), *Salvatore Giuliano* appeared to eschew all the categories of conventional Hollywood films.[6]

The importance of the film was acknowledged immediately, both in Italy, where it also generated political controversy,[7] and abroad.[8] The film was financially successful in Italy where, notwithstanding the absence of "stars" and its complexity, it was the tenth most profitable film of the year.[9] Since then, its reputation has, if anything, grown;[10] and while there are only three books dedicated to Rosi's films in general,[11] there are three books dedicated entirely to *Salvatore Giuliano*.[12]

The more perceptive critics and reviewers since 1961 have generally praised the film in similar terms. The film, they all agree, is not about Salvatore Giuliano;[13] while he may have been something of a media star, he was little more than a puppet dancing to the tune of hidden masters.[14] The real protagonist of the film, according to Rosi, is revealed by its original title, *Sicily 1943-60*.[15] Thus, it is entirely appropriate that throughout the film we see Giuliano rarely, and that the film focuses instead on the half-perceived forces which controlled him and the island of Sicily. In answer to those who objected that the film is too much of a chronicle,[16] Rosi repeatedly asserted that his film is not a documentary, but a document based on a careful, detailed study of the events surrounding the life and death of Salvatore Giuliano.[17]

Interestingly, most reviewers and critics of the time appear to understand and admire the mixed photographic style employed by Rosi. "I want", Rosi said during the shooting, "the photography to have three different tones: an evocative tone for past events, a photojournalistic tone for the events of Castelvetrano, and...a television tone for the scenes of the trial".[18] And while some did not immediately appreciate the editing, with its leaps in time and space, its flashbacks and flashforwards,[19] others writing when the film first appeared cited this as precisely one of the most significant aspects of the film.[20] More recently, Gary Crowdus, in a very perceptive essay, has suggested that the "alternations between historical periods function not merely as conventional temporal flashbacks or flashforwards, but express more of an ideological movement within the film designed to connect a particular fact or event with its causes or consequences".[21]

In short, one might argue that with *Salvatore Giuliano* Rosi did for the "political" film what Fellini did for the "personal" film with *Otto e mezzo* (*8½*, 1963). The latter, with his *construction en abyme*, destroyed the traditional temporal divisions between past, present and future, and replaced them with memory (clearly understood to be of a subjective nature), confusion, doubt and possibility, and transformed the alienation of one man into a universal experience which ends with the search for the actors who are to appear in the film we have just finished seeing. Rosi, on the other hand, took facts, documented historically as much as anything can be,[22] and presented them in such a manner as to deliberately generate confusion, raise questions and engage the audience in a dialogue: Who killed Giuliano? Why? Who killed Pisciotta? Why? Why did Giuliano continue to fight, even after the amnesty? Why did Giuliano become involved in the massacre of Portella della Ginestra? What happened to Giuliano's diary? Jean Gili has astutely observed that the shifts in time – from the death of Giuliano, back to earlier events, forward to the trial at Viterbo, back to Giuliano's death, forward again to the trial and to the death of Pisciotta, and finally to yet another Mafia murder in 1960, the year in which the film was made – project the film "without cease into the [their] present".[23] By extension, they project it into our own present, when the collusion between the Mafia and the powers that be still continues unabated, and when the hand of unseen killers still strikes down anyone in Sicily or in Italy who dares raise a voice against the "honoured society".[24]

Thus, it is odd and regrettable that, outside the better film schools, the film appears to be virtually unknown, particularly in the United States. Even more astonishing is the fact that, with the exception of books dedicated to Italian cinema,[25] there exist few references to Rosi and virtually none to *Salvatore Giuliano* in works published in the English language.[26] Moreover, even in European publications, references to Rosi are rare.[27] In many works in which one might expect to find mention of this work because of their subject-matter, references are non-existent.[28] One exception is James Monaco, who describes *Salvatore Giuliano* as an example of "muckraking" films, together with Costa-Gavras's *Z* (1969) and *État de siège* (*State of Siege*, 1973), and *The China Syndrome* (1979).[29] He also describes Rosi as the "most underrated of contemporary Italian directors".[30] In fact, after the first flurry of reviews in 1962, in the 34 years since the film was made, I have been able to find approximately only a dozen essays worldwide which deal significantly with *Salvatore Giuliano*.

Why this descent into oblivion? Given the almost obsessive attention the media paid to the putative subject of the film, Salvatore Giuliano (the "hip-firing Robin Hood", as he was described in one article in *Newsweek*),[31] and the continuing relevance and quasi-prophetic nature of the film as confirmed by the ongoing revelations of Mafia involvement in the highest levels of Italian government,[32] I would suggest that a number of factors conspired to this end.

Firstly, while *Variety* gave the film a glowing review ("An outstanding film, sure to rank among the best of the season, has been fashioned by Francesco Rosi using the story of Sicilian bandit Giuliano as a pretext for a historical, political, and social document of its times...and of the island setting...which made it possible"),[33] when it was first screened in Italy, I could find no other references to it in US media until its 1966 screening at the Los Feliz Theater, Los Angeles, as part of a "Cinema Italiano" series. Since that time, to my knowledge the film has never been in general release in this country, nor has it been available on 16mm or on video. Apparently, 16mm prints, described as "less than useless", were available in Great Britain in 1966.[34] By 1988, there too the film was "available only in a dubbed TV print".[35]

Secondly, in 1966, the general distrust of the United States government – that was later to flourish in the aftermath of Vietnam, Watergate, Waco and other assorted scandals – had yet fully to develop. Viewers in the United States had not yet become sufficiently cynical to accept without question the assumption of governmental criminality which underlies *Salvatore Giuliano*. Because of these factors, and perhaps also because it is more complex and more pessimistic, *Salvatore Giuliano* did not acquire the cult following that *La battaglia di Algeri* (*The Battle of Algiers*, 1966) had among college students a few years later, when it became generally accepted that colonialists were *a priori* criminal.[36]

While Rosi is deservedly respected and admired for his entire opus, the consensus would seem to be that *Salvatore Giuliano* is his masterpiece.[37] When the film first appeared, it was so novel, different and revolutionary that not everyone was able to appreciate it. Thus, while most critics admired Rosi's courage and Gianni Di Venanzo's photography, some faulted precisely those aspects of his film which more recently have been identified as postmodern: his syncopated editing and the pastiche of different styles.[38]

Lastly, the film did not satisfy certain leftist critics who, in the best tradition of Socialist Realism, wanted their enemies clearly labelled and properly dispatched. For example, Pio Baldelli, writing in *Mondo*

11

Operaio, acknowledges the courage of the film when it shows shocking events, but adds that "the director limits himself to observing, without digging into the interpretation that ties the facts together", and criticises him for his "lack of interpretation concerning the essential knot between the dominant forces, banditry, and the subordinate classes".[39]

Nevertheless, even if *Salvatore Giuliano* had been Rosi's only film, his reputation as filmmaker would have been secure. Better than any film before or since, it conveys the elusive mystery concealed in the fog of Sicilian *omertà*, the code of silence which is both the premise for the existence of the Mafia, and a result of its presence. Moreover, while the film does not intend to be a documentary, as Rosi has stated repeatedly in various interviews, it is, with the exception of minor details, an absolutely faithful "document" of the confusing events which swirled around the legendary Sicilian bandit/freedom-fighter.[40] Under its seemingly straightforward documentary appearance, however, the film is deliberately as elusive as truth in Sicily. The narrative moves erratically and spasmodically; at several instances it shifts back and forth in time, while at others the episodes are connected by subject-matter. A narrative voice, identified in the Italian-language script as the "Speaker", appears from time to time.[41] Occasionally, this "Speaker" serves as a bridge between episodes; at other times it comments on events as they transpire. Shots, both cinematographic and from various weapons, are frequently unmotivated and just as frequently unexplained. No one can be trusted. Death lurks everywhere, strikes unexpectedly and then smiles ironically on the foolishness of human pretensions. The lies begin before the first character, a policeman, opens his mouth. While Giuliano's body was indeed "officially" discovered in the position in which we see it in the opening shot, he was in fact not killed in that location, wearing those clothes and with those weapons near at hand.

While the film does not tell a story in any conventional sense, every image of *Salvatore Giuliano* is pregnant with meaning. Virtually all critics agree that every shot warrants a detailed analysis. The first person to attempt to unravel the Gordian knot of *Salvatore Giuliano*'s plot is Jean Gili.[42] He states that "*Salvatore Giuliano* is composed of fifteen principal sequences which are edited according a non-chronological principle: the film alternates sequences situated in different moments of the history of Sicily between the end of the war and the death of a 'Mafioso' in 1960".[43] He then adds that the first nine sequences "are distributed according to a to-and-fro movement in time which always has as point of reference the death of Giuliano, [perceived] as the present in relation to [other] past [events]",[44] while the last six sequences which begin with the trial at Viterbo for the massacre at Portella della Ginestra, include flashbacks to past events, such as the killing of Giuliano, and end with the assassination of the "Mafioso".[45] In broad, general terms, Gili's outline is useful, at least as a point of departure, even though it is incomplete and fails to document many persons, events, dates and locations.

More recently, P Adams Sitney, who divides the film into eleven episodes, furnishes what to my knowledge is the only attempt to correlate the film's ever-changing style with its content.[46] He points out how the somewhat "static montage" of the opening episode,[47] establishes a contrast for the second, in which "the camera moves or pans in almost every shot".[48] In the third, he notes how "the now fluid camera follows the reporters as they probe contradictions in the official report".[49] He continues in this manner, analyzing the visual style throughout the film. On occasion he also comments on the use of sound. For example, he writes that in the fifth episode "sound plays a distinctive role in counterpoint to the shifts between static and moving shots".[50] Occasionally, notwithstanding his generally perceptive and useful analysis, he is frustrated by the fact that, because the film rarely mentions names, dates or locations, the "sequences...are so elliptical, with unmarked leaps in time describing the trajectory of the conspiracy, that it is difficult to follow the narrative without outside information on the case".[51]

Through a comparison of the several biographies of Giuliano's life now available,[52] the script,[53] and the film, I have been able to identify virtually every individual and date virtually every event in the film.[54] I have therefore prepared an alternative outline, which from time to time diverges from those of Gili and Sitney. I have somewhat arbitrarily divided the film into numbered sequences whenever there is a significant shift in time. When there are subject-matter changes within the same time period, I have added an alphabetical indicator. I have italicised every scene in which Giuliano appears, and indicated whether he is living (L) or dead (D).

1   *5 July 1950. Alleged discovery of the body of Giuliano (D).*

2   1945, Palermo. Separatist demonstrations; meetings.

2a   October 1945. Separatist leaders visit Giuliano.

2b   *December 1945/January 1946. Guerrilla action (L).*

3   *5 July 1950. Police transport Giuliano in hearse; media questions; the official story; the Sicilian version (D).*

4   *1946. Guerrilla action; curfew at Montelepre (L).*

4a   1946. Amnesty; *picciotti* hide weapons in the mountains; cynical lawyer predicts death of Giuliano.

4b   *1946. Police harass peasants; search for Giuliano; arrest townspeople (L).*

13

5   *July 1950. Cemetery: distraught mother identifies Giuliano (D).*
6   *30 April 1947. A goatherd is drafted by bandits (L).*
6a   1 May 1947. Massacre at Portella della Ginestra.
7   Date uncertain (1947-50). Policeman questions Giovanni.
8   *19 July 1950. Giuliano's mother caresses his photograph (D).*
9   4 December 1950. Policemen burst into Pisciotta's home.
10   11 April 1951. Pisciotta states that he has important news.
10a Summer/autumn 1951. The judge questions the *picciotti*.
10b Summer/autumn 1951. Pisciotta is sick, and absent from court.
10c Summer/autumn 1951. Pisciotta is back with revelations.
10d Summer/autumn 1951. Judge questions chief of police.
10e Summer/autumn 1951. The judge questions the intermediary.
10f Summer/autumn 1951. The judge questions General Luca.
11   Spring 1950. Meeting of Mafia boss and General Luca.
11a Spring 1950. *Carabiniere* threatens Mafioso.
12   Summer 1950. The Mafia betrays Giuliano's men.
12a *Summer 1950. Giuliano and Pisciotta capture Minasola (L).*
12b Summer 1950. Pisciotta guards Mafioso alone.
13   *4 July 1950. Pisciotta leads the* carabinieri *to Giuliano (L).*
13a 5 July 1950, after midnight; *carabinieri* wait and worry.
13b *5 July 1950. Three shots are heard. The* carabinieri *rush in (D).*
13c 5 July 1950. Pisciotta escapes.
13d *5 July 1950.* Carabinieri *position the corpse; shoot it (D).*
14   Summer/autumn 1951. Judge questions De Maria, Pisciotta and
     Perenze.
15   May 1952. The judge reads the sentences.
16   10 February 1954. Pisciotta dies, poisoned in prison.
17   20 September 1960. Minasola killed by persons unknown.[55]

This abbreviated outline of the film is intended to show the shifts in time and subject-matter. It may also help to explain why critics have had such difficulty in trying to analyze the film. The constant shifts in time generate an almost dreamlike effect. The mind attempts to recreate some form of logical order, putting together similar events. The major confusion in this sense occurs in the first eight sequences. The film actually progresses fairly programmatically from the separatist parades in Palermo (2), to the scene in which his mother caresses his photograph at the cemetery (8). However, the constant flashforwards to the discovery of his corpse (1), its transportation to the cemetery (3) and his mother's identification of the body (5), disorient the viewer.

The central part of the film, the trial at Viterbo, which advances chronologically, at first appears to give the mind a chance to reorient itself (10-10f). But, as the judge states quite explicitly, the trial does not concern the murder of Giuliano, but the massacre at Portella della

14

Ginestra. In other words, the trial in a sense begins a second story and thus creates disorientation on another level.

Just when the viewer's mind has adapted to this more linear progression and to this new story, the film shifts back in time to the betrayal and murder of Giuliano (11-13d). Given the title of the film, this sequence might seem like a fitting closure. As repeatedly noted, however, Giuliano is not the real protagonist of the film; rather, it is Sicily, that mysterious island incomprehensible to mainland Italians. Furthermore, there is also the story of the trial to be resolved. And thus we return to the courtroom where we see the interrogation and conviction of the *picciotti*, and more evidence of the reciprocal incomprehension and of the absolute impossibility of communication between islanders and mainlanders (14, 15). The Italian viewer in 1962 knew that the film could not end at this point. Pisciotta had betrayed Giuliano, and thus everyone expected him to be killed somehow. When he was poisoned in jail, there was much speculation as to how it had been done, by whom and at whose orders, but no one was surprised (16). Nor should anyone be surprised when the film leaps forward to 1960 and the murder of Minasola (17) – or that even now, in any given week, if you scan Italian newspapers you will read about further mysterious assassinations in Sicily.

An expanded version of the plot of the entire film follows. In order to give some sense of the richness and complexity of each sequence, I have analyzed the first few scenes in some detail. The entire film deserves to be analyzed in a similar manner. Regrettably, limitations of space precluded studying each scene in this manner. However, I have commented where I felt clarification is necessary and, to the extent possible, I have identified persons, events and locations.

1 5 July 1950. "Official" discovery by the police of the body of Giuliano at Castelvetrano. Arrival of reporters who are immediately sceptical of the official story, and of Colonel Luca and Captain Perenze.[56]

The film opens with an almost vertical long shot of what appears to be a dead man's prone body sprawled in a courtyard. Sitting in the shade at the edge of the courtyard are several unidentified men. The camera moves to what could be the point of view of one of the bystanders. A man is taking photographs. Another man in civilian clothes is dictating a police report: "July 5, 1950. In Castelvetrano, in the De Maria courtyard, in Via Fra Serafino Mannone, there is a male body of approximately 30 years of age." As the policeman drones on, we observe a machine-gun just beyond one of Giuliano's outstretched hands. A semi-automatic pistol lies between his hand and his head. To the left of his body is a pouch. A stream of blood runs at a diagonal

15

angle from his head to the pistol and beyond. As the description continues, the camera approaches the body and shows in close-up what is being described: the back of the man's T-shirt, covered with blood; his buckled sandals of a type worn only by children or poor people in the south. The policeman states that he is wearing a ring of white metal with one stone, and that in his pockets are a ten-lire note and an unidentified photograph. A person in authority dictates a correction. All is calm, almost lethargic under the bright, hot Sicilian sun.

This is the official story,[57] a story which was to be reported with minor variations by the all the major news media. In *Time* magazine we read:

> Last year, Rome sent to Sicily hard-eyed Colonel Ugo Luca, a World War II Italian intelligence officer. With a special task force of 2,000 picked men, mostly bachelors, Luca set about combing Sicily for his prey... [Luca] baited a trap for Giuliano's vanity. He sent a troop of *carabinieri* [the Italian national paramilitary police] into the wine district camouflaged as a moving picture unit. They were ordered to spread the word that they were making a picture about bandits. The unit was told to drop strong hints that a leading role might be available for Giuliano. With no names mentioned, a series of return hints from Giuliano soon led the 'moviemakers' into the town of Castelvetrano. There one night last week they found their man. The *carabinieri* opened fire. Giuliano fled, firing over his shoulder as he went. For 15 minutes the chase led on through labyrinths of twisted alleys and courtyards. Captain Antonio Perenze, leader of the *carabinieri*, hid in a doorway. A stalking figure crept up, machine gun set. Perenze blasted point-blank. The figure whirled, tottered and fell face down, a dark red splotch welling up under his white shirt. A few minutes later Salvatore Giuliano lay dead, his upper body shattered by bullets. In his pocket was a package of mentholated cigarettes, a small flashlight and a photograph of himself.[58]

The report in *Newsweek* is shorter but just as melodramatic and incorrect:

> As Giuliano left a brothel on the morning of July 5 [1950], carabinieri caught him in a courtyard. He fired wildly. After 52 rounds his submachine gun jammed. He emptied his Lüger. Then police rifle bullets smashed into his head and shoulders.

The faint dawn light was just enough for officers to identify his body sprawled on the bloody cobblestones. His pockets were empty.[59]

But the "official story", as we have come to realise increasingly over the past decades, is almost invariably a lie reported with embellishments by the media.[60] In reality, as Rosi's film shows and as all the major biographies tell us, the story began to unravel almost immediately. As soon as the news leaked out that Giuliano had been killed, reporters from around the world rushed to Castelvetrano. In the film, we see them as they arrive. There is chaos outside Cortile De Maria. A car full of reporters arrives. The police in civilian clothes and in uniform at first keep them from the courtyard. The camera cuts rapidly up to the adjacent rooftops, to windows, back to the rooftops, where lines of Sicilians are looking down on the dead body. Eventually the authorities allow the reporters to take a few photographs and then order them from the scene. However, in the brief time in which the newsmen are exposed to the corpse, they begin to ask each other questions which at the time had no answers. Why, if Giuliano is lying in the position in which he fell, is the back of the prone bandit's T-shirt sodden with blood? Why is there no blood under his body?[61] As the sequence ends, an official orders unseen observers to close their windows and get off the rooftops.

In this very brief sequence, Rosi establishes many of his central concerns. Salvatore Giuliano is not to be the star of the eponymous film; this will not be a Hollywood hagiography of the outlaw. He will remain a mystery whose character will be as hidden from us throughout the film as his face is in this opening sequence. His death will not be the romantic, heroic event concocted by the police, which Giuliano himself might have desired. Rather, it is both ironic and pathetic. The man lying with his face in the dust is Salvatore Giuliano, the outlaw/freedom fighter and media star, who came to be known as "king of Montelepre" and who in his day was more famous than Che Guevara. News briefs and articles about him appeared regularly in newspapers and magazines, including *Time* and *Newsweek*. His picture graced the pages of three issues of *Life* magazine.[62] He was the subject of at least two lengthy articles in *The New Yorker*.[63] His death was reported by virtually all the major newspapers, including *The New York Times* on 6 July 1950. During his seven years as an outlaw, he was said to have killed more than 100 policemen and *carabinieri*, and to have collected more than US$2 million in ransom from victims of kidnapping and extortion. Women from around the world allegedly swooned over him, and men were said to fear, admire and respect him. How did this man come to die alone, with the equivalent of two 1950 US cents and a photograph of himself in his pockets? Equally to the point, Rosi begins to ask "the question[s] to be pursued throughout the text":[64] why, how and by whom was Giuliano killed?

In this first sequence, Rosi also begins to establish the chasm that separates Sicilian peasants from "continental" Italians and from all authorities. As they stand on the rooftops, watching the police and the press, the Sicilians are reminiscent of the natives in American westerns, as they stood on high bluffs looking down on the intruding wagon trains. Like the native Americans, to the invaders they appear stoic, laconic and vaguely threatening, and are quite inscrutable. For the outsider, the film suggests, it is impossible to tell a "good" Sicilian from a "bad" one. Thus, all are presumed to be bad and somehow subhuman. This confrontational relationship is underlined by the policeman's arrogant order to the unseen men on the rooftops and at the windows to go away and close the windows. However, this very brief scene also serves, in conjunction with the opening scene, to establish the presence of something which the viewer may or may not have seen, but which can be felt. As in some westerns, here too someone, something, is watching. Who or what it is remains to be determined.

2   1945, Palermo. Parades and demonstrations in favour of Sicilian independence.[65] (The Speaker tells about the birth of the Movimento per l'Indipendenza della Sicilia [MIS – Movement for the Independence of Sicily] and of the Esercito Volontario per l'Indipendenza della Sicilia [EVIS – Voluntary Army for Sicilian Independence].) The separatist leaders discuss the arrest of Varvaro and Finocchiaro Aprile, the failure to achieve a political solution, and the need for an armed insurrection.[66] They decide to recruit outlaws[67] to fight for them, and first among them is Giuliano.

As the second sequence opens, there are crowds agitating for the independence of Sicily, and we hear a voice-over which explains that in 1945, encouraged by the United States, Great Britain, the great landowners and the Mafia, Sicilians began a struggle for the independence of their island. The narrator explains that rebellious elements formed a political party, the MIS, buttressed behind the scenes by its military arm, the EVIS. The struggle for independence became violent, and resulted in deaths on both sides. On 30 September 1947 the first government of national unification, the Comitato di Liberazione Nazionale (Committee for National Liberation – CLN), ordered the arrest of the leaders of the MIS, Aprile and Varvaro. In those turbulent times, the leaders of the MIS decided to offer the position of Colonel in the EVIS to the 23-year-old Giuliano.

In exchange, when Sicily is freed, he would receive an amnesty for his crimes.

The documentary-like footage, usually of crowd scenes, is generally reminiscent of both newsreels and classical neo-realist films such as *Paisan* and *Bicycle Thieves*, and anticipates some of the street scenes in *The Battle of Algiers*. Together with the voice-over narration, it serves to lend verisimilitude to the reconstructed events. Scenes of crowds clashing with the police in the streets are underscored by the voice-over narration describing the birth of the Sicilian independence movement, its repression by the Italian government, and the arrest of specific individuals. The film then cuts to a meeting of unidentified politicians who discuss how best to achieve their ends through violent means, while keeping their party free of blame. The viewer is told in general terms who these people are: the voice-over narration states that they are the leaders of the MIS. It specifically mentions the names of Aprile and Varvaro.[68] We know that the MIS existed and that it strove to achieve Sicilian independence. And yet, as we listen to them talk, they remain unidentified: no names are spoken by them or by the voice-over narration.

2a October 1945. The mountains near Ponte Sàgana. Separatist leaders visit Giuliano. (The Speaker: "October 1945. Representatives of the EVIS visit Giuliano and offer him the rank of colonel in the EVIS and rehabilitation when the separatist victory will have been achieved. Giuliano was then 23 years old. He had become a bandit at 21 when he killed a *carabiniere* while trying to avoid being arrested for carrying two sacks of black market grain".)[69] One separatist leader enters the house where Giuliano is staying. The others talk with the bandits. An elderly separatist tells them that they will fight to be free from Italian domination.[70]

In this sequence, the representatives of the EVIS who visit Giuliano in his lair remain unidentified. Furthermore, we do not see Giuliano, nor do we know what he and the separatists said to each other. All we know is what other members of EVIS tell Giuliano's followers, and what the bandits tell each other: if they fight for the independence of Sicily, they will go home as free men. Rosi here continues his practice of mixing documentary-like footage and reconstructed events, both of which are limited to what might have been known as the events shown were taking place, and a voice-over narration of facts which, by the time the film was made, had become part of the historical record. The voice-over narration has various fairly conventional functions: it serves to introduce scenes; it explicates and expands on events which occur on the visual image track; and it lends a sense of realism to the film by its references to historical events and persons.

Somewhat less conventional, particularly when the film was made, are the multiple diegeses established when the voice-over narration and the visual image track exist independently of each other.[71] For example, as the EVIS representatives are going to visit Giuliano to invite him to become a colonel in their ranks, the voice-over narration tells us how he became a bandit.

2b December 1945/January 1946. On the wall of a Sicilian village we see Giuliano's famous poster calling for the separation of Sicily from Italy, and its union with the United States,[72] followed by a relatively rapid montage of bandit attacks on the *carabinieri*.

This sequence might be described as an example of what Christian Metz calls a "bracket syntagma...a series of very brief scenes representing occurrences that the film gives as typical samples of a same order of reality, without in any way chronologically locating them in relation to each other".[73] It is comprised of three relatively brief scenes which appear to be related to each other only as somewhat generic examples of guerrilla activity.[74] A brief description will give some idea of the manner in which this series of seemingly unmotivated, random events becomes an integral part of the narrative.

Day. Pisciotta and others wander through a sleepy Sicilian town. We see a *carabinieri* station. Night. They hear the sound of a jew's harp. Someone comes out of the police station. A shrill whistle shatters the silence. Shots ring out in the night. Day. Men are running, partially concealed by a herd of cows in a mountain field. For the first, time we see in the distance a figure wearing a white raincoat who, we intuit immediately, is Giuliano because he is clearly the leader of the band. They attack an isolated police station with machine-guns and hand-grenades. It catches fire. Day. A jeep with three *carabinieri* is advancing along a deserted mountain road. We hear someone whistle. A man waves his hand. Shots ring out. A *carabiniere* falls from the jeep. The jeep goes off the road. The other *carabinieri* hit the ground and begin shooting.

This process of taking events, which by all accounts occurred, and presenting them as concealed, confused, fragmented and incomplete as they might have been while Giuliano was alive, continues throughout the film and becomes progressively more intense. While in the first three sequences the Speaker explains at least in part what is happening, in the fourth sequence no one is identified, nor are any explanations given for the actions which occur. And yet, although nothing is explained, the viewer cannot but make a series of conceptual leaps. Because Giuliano was forced into banditry by poverty and injustice, he will join the separatists. Because he has joined the separatists, he will attack the police and the Army.

However, just as we are beginning to be comfortable with these leaps of faith, suddenly Rosi pulls the carpet out from under us once again. We see a long shot of rebels shooting at the three *carabinieri* in the jeep. We see one *carabiniere* fall from the jeep; presumably he is dead. Without pause and without any cinematic punctuation, we see a medium shot of men carrying a casket between two lines of soldiers. Inevitably, we assume that it contains one of the dead soldiers. In fact, it does not, and we have suddenly leaped five years into the future and into the next sequence.

3   5 July 1950, Castelvetrano. The police are transporting Giuliano to the cemetery morgue in a horse-drawn hearse. The media question the police who tell the official story. Giuliano, they say, died after a intense, protracted shootout. The media question the inhabitants of Castelvetrano who deny every aspect of the official story. The government officials and the *carabinieri* celebrate the death of Giuliano in a restaurant. A reporter calls in his story: "The only certain thing is that he is dead".[75]

This sequence, which opens with the passage of the hearse carrying Giuliano's body, is comprised of four short scenes. In the first half of the sequence we observe the police as they try to foist the official story on the numerous reporters, among whom, presumably as witness to the international interest in the story, is one American. Whenever any reporter asks for any clarification or points out a seeming contradiction, the police either refuse to answer entirely or cut short the conversation, promising more details at some future time.

In the second part of the sequence, the reporters speak to local townspeople. The latter clearly are not actors. Because they are not, they appear to be as real as the stones of Castelvetrano.[76] Their roughness, unkempt appearance, laconic directness and intensity contrast sharply with the glibness and evasiveness of the more cosmopolitan police. The traces of 2000 years of foreign domination, absentee landlords and callous exploitation can be read on their faces. Rosi captures the essence of their suffering in this sequence when he shows a reporter approaching a man and asking him for something to drink. What may not be clear to those who do not know Sicily is that this man is selling water by the glass. The reporter asks him: "What do you know about Giuliano?". He answers: "He took from the rich and gave to the poor". When the reporter asks if that is all he knows about Giuliano, the man replies by asking him where he comes from. When the reporter answers, "From Rome", the water-seller rebuts: "What can you understand about Sicily?". By having the water-seller make this statement, Rosi adds a visual exclamation point to the question. What can the reporter, a man who lives in a world where when you are thirsty you turn a tap, understand about a world where in the middle of a city you have to buy water by the glass?

The film cuts abruptly to a shot of what appear to be high-ranking policemen and civilians celebrating the death of Giuliano.[77] We see them from the perspective of a reporter through tall French windows whose bar-like frames separate them absolutely from the reporter. As the sequence ends, the reporter is filing his story from a busy, noisy press room: "The only sure thing is that Giuliano is dead. The witnesses sharply contradict the official version. This notwithstanding, it is thanks to the *carabinieri* that the bandit has been killed. There is more to the story...".

Once again, we have a very short scene, replete with irony. If there is one thing which was not sure at that time, it was who killed Giuliano. Beyond this, as the reporter observed, there is definitely more to the story of Giuliano's death. Its genesis may be said to be buried in Sicilian antiquity, while its impact continues to be felt through various assassinations until the 1960s, as the film implies, or to the present, as Gili suggests.[78]

4   January 1946. The plain of Montelepre, dusty roads, Montelepre itself. (The Speaker: "Giuliano reigns in the Montelepre region where he is protected by omertà, terror and passion. The town is full of *carabinieri*, but Giuliano cannot be captured. Conversely, he keeps the town under his gaze. In the east of Sicily, the Army has defeated the separatist forces".) A column of military vehicles arrives. The people of Montelepre run and hide. Police complain that they are the last to hear of the arrival of the soldiers ("Giuliano has a radio, we don't even have a telephone"). The military commander, a major, orders the police to find accommodation for 300 soldiers.[79] The police advise against it. A soldier and a policeman go to look at a warehouse. The soldier is shot and killed. The Army retaliates: a town crier announces a curfew; soldiers climb the mountain towards Giuliano. Giuliano, Pisciotta and his men look down on them, hide among the boulders, and then open fire with a heavy machine-gun. The soldiers retreat, then counter-attack with heavy mortar. The bandits flee. A town crier announces that the curfew is suspended for an hour. The townspeople and animals crowd around the public water-trough. Heavy machine-gun fire is heard. The townspeople run and hide.

While in earlier sequences we heard separatist leaders talk about their desire to be free of the Italian yoke, it is in this sequence that Rosi suddenly confronts us most explicitly with what has been described as the Italian colonialist attitudes towards southern Italy in general and Sicily in particular. The Italian Army major has the same tranquil arrogance that Colonel Mathieu will manifest in *The Battle of Algiers*. What he does not show, at least at first, is the same respect for his opponents. He simply cannot take Giuliano – or Sicilians in general – seriously. When he is immediately disabused of his patronizing attitude, he retaliates in a manner reminiscent of all anti-guerrilla efforts: he strikes directly at the bandits by sending over 1000 soldiers against Giuliano's small band of no more than 50 outlaws. When this fails, on 13 January he attacks Giuliano indirectly by imposing martial law on the town of Montelepre. The curfew was to remain in effect for 126 days. During this period, elements of four divisions, the police and the *carabinieri* all occupied Montelepre. They searched for Giuliano to no avail, questioning, arresting and mistreating the populace.[80] While some might argue that these tactics are reprehensible, in conjunction with a promised amnesty, they began to have the desired effect of isolating Giuliano from both his sponsors and his friends.

In the two sequences which follow, we see the results of further government attempts to co-opt the separatist cause and to isolate Giuliano.

4a May 1946. *Picciotti* hide weapons in the mountains. (The Speaker: "May 1946: Sicily obtains administrative autonomy; the separatist effort has not been useless. In June the King leaves government. Amnesty is proclaimed for rebels, including those who served in EVIS.") *Picciotti* go to see a lawyer. They claim they are "political" and thus fall within the parameters of the amnesty. The lawyer is sceptical and sarcastic. He says that now Giuliano will have to become a common criminal and predicts that he will be killed when he is no longer useful. Cut to kidnapping of a businessman. (The Speaker: "With the dissolution of EVIS, Giuliano engages in kidnappings and thefts worth hundreds of millions of lire. But, what is his take, and how much must he give the Mafia? The protection of the honoured society is expensive.") Car on a country road. It stops near a house. Once again, we hear the whistle that we have come to recognise as the all-purpose signal of Giuliano's band.

In sequence 4a, the *picciotti* respond to the carrot, the Italian government's statute of Sicilian autonomy; in 4b, the government forces continue to wield a big stick. The principal target, as the middle scene of sequence 4b makes clear, is still Giuliano. It is sandwiched between oppression which ranges from police harassment of the peasants on their way to work in the fields in the opening scene, to the arrest and deportation of anyone in any way connected with Giuliano.

4b 1946. Cut. The police stop peasants. (The Speaker: "A wall of silence protects Giuliano".) The police take bread and water from the peasants and dump them on the ground. They accuse the peasants of selling food to Giuliano. Cut. Convoy of trucks at night. Montelepre at night. Someone warns Giuliano's mother that soldiers are coming. Giuliano escapes. Soldiers burst into Giuliano's home and find his sister in his bed. Cut. Montelepre, day. Soldiers take over the town, ransack houses, and gather all the men in the main square; some will be taken to Palermo. Screaming women try to stop the abduction of their men, to no avail.

In these brief scenes, we can observe the contradictions which characterise life in Sicily as depicted in Rosi's film. Each scene has at least two possible interpretations. From one perspective, the police action in the first scene is justified, given that many inhabitants of Montelepre and the surrounding area sold food and water to Giuliano. And yet, when the police deprive of food and water men who have to travel many miles to work in an arid country, they are causing them hardship and suffering, and generating more hatred for the authorities. In the second scene, when the soldiers burst in and find Giuliano's sister in his bed, they are breaking a taboo which requires that women be respected. And yet, we know that she is using precisely this taboo to give her brother more time to escape. In the third scene, the Army is once again seemingly randomly brutalizing the population; they are depriving poor families of their men, of their major source of sustenance. Yet, we know that among them are those who are hiding Giuliano and his *picciotti*.[81]

5   July 1950. Castelvetrano cemetery: Giuliano's distraught mother is brought to identify her son, but at first is not allowed to see him. Attorney General Pili arrives and authorises her to see "Turiddu". She recognises him and erupts in keening, kissing his face, wounds, hands and feet.[82]

While in sequence 5 Giuliano is seen, at least aesthetically, as a Christ figure of sorts, his demystification begins in the two sequences which follow. In the first sequence, a young man is drafted into Giuliano's band and put through a very rudimentary basic training, much as he might have been with the Italian Army. Giuliano, in other words, has become very much like the forces against which he is fighting.

6   30 April 1947. A goatherd, Giovanni, is walking with his goats. (The Speaker: "In 1947 the Popular Bloc[83] wins the elections. Sharecroppers want to implement legally authorised land redistribution.") He is compelled to join Giuliano's band on the spot.

He is taught how to use a rifle.

6a 1 May 1947. Giuliano and his band leave. When the goatherd asks what they are doing, he is told that they are going to shoot the Communists at Portella della Ginestra, and that Giuliano has said that the hour of their liberation has come. Cut. Flag-waving columns, reminiscent of Eisenstein's *Alexander Nevsky* (1938),[84] come to Portella della Ginestra. Eventually, a man rises and addresses the crowd at some length.[85] We hear machine-gun fire. At first it is ignored; then bullets strike people and animals. Suddenly, everyone is running desperately. Many bodies lie scattered on the field.[86]

Sequence 6a depicts the most important and most controversial event in Giuliano's life. Why did this Robin Hood, this popular hero, lead an attack on members of his own social class – on farmers, shepherds and labourers, on women and children? Theories abound in every book on Giuliano, and most authors offer several possible reasons. Giuliano attacked the Communist Mayday celebration at least in part because of his anti-Communist convictions; he engaged in this action in exchange for a promise of a pardon by a highly placed politician; he intended only to scare the crowd; he was betrayed by one of his men.[87] In the film, we see the happy, life-affirming Mayday crowd; we see many women and children; we see horses followed by their foals, and then suddenly we hear shots. We see the effect of bullets hitting people and animals. People and animals run in terror, but we never see Giuliano. This, however, does not absolve him. The film has already told us that he planned to attack those gathered at Portella. Rather, by not showing him, Rosi is stating that he has become one of those who kill from hiding; he has become a tool of the state and of the Mafia; he has become like the very forces against which he had fought for so long. The coalition of state and Mafia has coerced even him into joining in the oppression of the Sicilian peasant.

7 Date uncertain. A policeman shows Giovanni photographs of Giuliano's men, and then asks him if they too were present at Portella della Ginestra. He claims that he did nothing and cries that he wants to go home. He is returned to the cell where the bandits involved in the massacre at Portella della Ginestra are held.

8 19 July 1950. Maria Lombardo Giuliano caresses a photograph of her son. (The Speaker: "July 1950. Years have passed since the massacre of Portella della Ginestra. Giuliano has continued his many criminal activities. He has killed more than 100 policemen.[88] The authorities responsible for apprehending him have been changed

repeatedly, but he cannot be found, except by a few reporters.")[89]

9   4 December 1950. Vehicles on road. Policemen burst into the house of Pisciotta's mother. They question her. She refuses to speak. (The Speaker: "Giuliano ambushes the police at Bellolampo. Six policemen die.[90] The government establishes the Comando Forze Repressione Banditismo (Command of the Forces for the Repression of Banditry – CFRB) and puts Colonel Luca in charge. After eleven months of activities, the majority of the gang, including Giuliano, were dead or captured. Only Gaspare Pisciotta could not be found.") The police decide to wait until Pisciotta appears. Eventually, he comes out of hiding and is arrested.

The ensuing scenes of the trial at Viterbo suggest that there is a conflict between the modern Italian state and the Sicilian peasants that is even more intense than the clash of armed forces. This is a conflict between torrents of words and volumes upon volumes of laws, all frequently signifying very little, and profoundly meaningful glances and grunts, and "Xs" in the place of signatures. In reality, both lie to protect their own interests, and both are quite willing and able to be extremely violent when they feel it is necessary.

10   11 April 1951. Pisciotta states that he has news that will interest the public opinion of Italy and of the world.[91] The judge at first refuses to let him speak because he contends that what he has to say is irrelevant to the Portella della Ginestra case. After a heated debate with several lawyers, the judge reads a letter written by Pisciotta in which he states that "having made a personal agreement with the higher authorities, I killed Giuliano".[92] The judge still maintains that this information is irrelevant to the case at hand. Chaos breaks out in the court.

10a   Summer/autumn 1951. The judge questions the *picciotti*. They all deny that they were present. They also state that they do not know anything, nor each other, and that their confessions were extracted by torture.[93] Pisciotta appears to be very much in control of the *picciotti*.

10b   Summer/autumn 1951. Pisciotta is sick and therefore absent from court. A *picciotto*, Giovanni, breaks the wall of silence and identifies the participants in the massacre.[94] When the judge sends him back to the cage in which the defendants are held, he is attacked.

10c   Summer/autumn 1951. Back in court, Pisciotta states that Giuliano had prepared a diary in which he identified not only the participants in the massacre, but also the person who had ordered the attack. He adds that he had given the diary to "the *carabinieri* colonel" with whom he had collaborated, and that he had also worked with the police: "Bandits, police and Mafia were all one 'trinity'".

10d Summer/autumn 1951. As a result of Pisciotta's revelations, the judge questions Inspector Ciro Verdiani, head of the Ispettorato di Pubblica Sicurezza (General Inspectorate of Public Security) in Sicily from February to August 1949. Verdiani denies having received the diary, but admits having had dealings with Pisciotta through intermediaries. The judge asks for the names of the intermediaries. Verdiani reveals the name of one intermediary.

10e Summer/autumn 1951. The judge questions Domenico Albano, the Mafioso who served as intermediary between Verdiani and Pisciotta.[95] He states that he observed Verdiani, Giuliano and Pisciotta embrace like real friends.[96]

10f Summer/autumn 1951. The judge questions General Luca.[97] He states that when he took over the hunt for Giuliano, Verdiani refused to give him the names of his stool-pigeons, and that, contrary to what Pisciotta stated, he did not obtain the diary.

Just when the viewer's mind has adapted to this more linear progression and to this new story, the film shifts back in time to the betrayal and murder of Giuliano (11-13d).

11 Spring 1950. Cut to the corridors of the Palermo *carabinieri* headquarters where two representatives of the Mafia meet with Colonel Luca, the commander of the CFRB (who is not shown onscreen).

11a Spring 1950. Cut to a warehouse where a *carabinieri* warrant officer, Giovanni Lo Bianco, meets with a Mafioso, Benedetto Minasola.[98] When Minasola refuses to hand over Giuliano, Lo Bianco threatens to begin arresting Mafiosi. Intimidated, Minasola offers to give him Giuliano's last remaining followers.

12 Summer 1950. The Mafia betrays Giuliano's men, Frank Mannino, Nunzio Badalamenti and Castrense Madonia, to the *carabinieri*.[99]

12a Summer 1950. Giuliano and Pisciotta capture Minasola. Giuliano asks him where his men are.

12b Summer 1950. Giuliano leaves Pisciotta to guard the tied-up Minasola. However, no sooner has Giuliano left to attempt to capture the Micelis, than Minasola, playing on Pisciotta's fears, convinces him to betray his friend and leader to Luca.[100]

13   4 July 1950. Pisciotta leads the *carabinieri* to the house of law school graduate, Gregorio De Maria, where Giuliano is hidden.[101] Around midnight, while the *carabinieri* wait outside, Pisciotta goes to Giuliano. Giuliano shows Pisciotta a letter which accuses him of having betrayed him to the *carabinieri*.[102] Pisciotta laughs and allays Giuliano's fears.[103]

13a   5 July 1950, after midnight. The *carabinieri* wait. A *carabiniere* orders bakery employees back into their store. Captain Perenze worries about having allowed to Pisciotta to go to Giuliano alone.[104]

13b   5 July 1950. Suddenly we hear three shots. The *carabinieri* rush towards the house. Giuliano is on the bed, dead. Perenze orders De Maria to get Giuliano's clothes and dress him.

13c   5 July 1950. Pisciotta disarms the *carabiniere* who was taking him to Palermo and escapes.

13d   5 July 1950. The *carabinieri* place the body of the bandit in the courtyard in the position we saw in the opening shots. They spray the body with machine-gun bullets.

14   Summer/autumn 1951.[105] The judge questions De Maria, Marotta,[106] Pisciotta and Perenze about Giuliano's diary. Everyone denies having it.

15   May 1952.[107] The judge reads the sentences; many of the accused, among them Pisciotta, are condemned to life imprisonment. Pisciotta is outraged and promises to tell all at the right moment.

16   10 February 1954.[108] Pisciotta is poisoned and dies in the Palermo prison.[109]

17   20 September 1960. Minasola collapses in Monreale's horse market, killed by an unseen shooter.

* * *

As noted earlier, in *Salvatore Giuliano*, Rosi asks many difficult, disturbing questions. Who killed Giuliano? Why? Who killed Pisciotta? Why? Why did Giuliano continue to fight, even after the amnesty? Why did Giuliano become involved in the massacre of Portella della Ginestra? What happened to Giuliano's diary? To what extent was the Italian government involved in all these events? To what extent was the Mafia involved? On the one hand, Rosi does not explicitly answer any of these questions, nor does he even imply that there are answers for some of the questions. No one seems to know what happened to Giuliano's diary. It still is not clear why Giuliano became involved in the massacre at Portella della Ginestra. On the other hand, notwithstanding the deliberately difficult style, and the constant shifts in time and subject-matter, the viewer who becomes engaged in a dialogue with the film cannot help drawing certain inevitable conclusions. Giuliano continued to fight because the politicians and the Mafiosi who had used him to advance their interests wanted him dead. It does not matter who pulled the trigger on Giuliano, or who actually poisoned Gaspare Pisciotta – both were killed by the collusion between certain elements of the Italian government and of the Mafia because they knew too much. Crowdus observes:

> Perhaps Rosi's most significant artistic contribution has been in his development of what is most appropriately called – please excuse the trendy expression – a *postmodern* esthetic which audaciously combines disparate formal elements and styles – fiction, documentary, historical re-creation, archival materials, and so on – *so that his films are finally as much political for the way they are structured as for the choice of subject matter.*[110]

Crowdus's perception is confirmed *ante litteram* by Rosi himself in an interview with Ciment: "The way in which *Giuliano* was edited responded to a narrative necessity which was to narrate the facts in such a manner as to give the public that impression of confusion, of absence of clarity with which the events occurred in reality".[111] The result was a film which "completely burst the bounds of conventional neorealism, replacing its romanticized social portrayal of the working poor and dispossessed with a desentimentalized, in-depth social analysis. This landmark film is widely recognised as marking a distinct departure in both form and content not only for Rosi but also for Italian cinema and even European cinema in general of that era, advancing the mode of consciously political cinema to more formally complex and politically sophisticated levels".[112]

One might add that Rosi not only is postmodern in an aesthetic sense, but also contributed significantly to that particularly Italian form of constructive revolutionary postmodernism elaborated in innumerable films and theorized by Pier Paolo Pasolini.[113] While acknowledging that there are no more grand, totalizing narratives, they would appear to argue that there is an infinity of small narratives that, while all texts are at best asymptotes of reality, we should heed the advice of Machiavelli and join him in the search of the *verità effettuale*, the "effectual truth" of things as they really are, rather than fanciful imaginings.[114] In this case, the inescapable conclusion is that the Italian government and the Mafia were responsible not only for the deaths of Giuliano and Pisciotta, but also for creating the conditions which generated Salvatore Giuliano, and which continue the oppression of the south in general, and of Sicily in particular.

Notes

[1]   Translated from the Italian: "Questo film è stato girato in Sicilia. A Montelepre, dove Salvatore Giuliano è nato. Nella casa, nelle strade, sulle montagne dove regnò per sette anni. A Castelvetrano, nella casa dove il bandito trascorse gli ultimi mesi della sua esistenza e nel cortile dove una mattina fu visto il suo corpo senza vita."

[2]   "Contrary to an oft-repeated error, they were not cousins" (Billy Jaynes Chandler, *King of the Mountain: The Life and Death of Giuliano the Bandit* [DeKalb, IL: Northern Illinois University Press, 1988]: 190). Pisciotta's role was played by Frank Wolff, an American actor who resembled the bandit to an astonishing degree.

[3]   I must thank Roger Simon for sharing the wealth of information he has collected on Salvatore Giuliano, and on the film of the same name. Particularly useful were the photocopies of contemporary articles and reviews. I also wish to thank him for bringing to my attention William Asher's *Johnny Cool* (1963), the highly fictionalised adventures of a Giuliano gang member who had, allegedly, escaped to the United States.

[4]   "Ce livre est né d'un choc: la vision, en février 1963, de *Salvatore Giuliano* et le sentiment qu'un nouveau cinéma politique 'de gauche' venait de naître". ("This book was born of a shock: the vision, in February of 1963, of *Salvatore Giuliano* and the feeling that a new leftist political cinema was being born".) Michel Ciment, *Le dossier Rosi* (Paris: Editions Stock, 1976): 11.

[5]   André Bazin, *What Is Cinema?*, volume II, essays selected and translated by Hugh Gray (Berkeley; Los Angeles; London: University of California Press, 1971): 60.

[6]   Peter Wollen, "Godard and Counter-Cinema: *Vent d'Est*", *Afterimage* 4 (autumn 1972): 6-16 (reprinted in Philip Rosen [ed], *Narrative, Apparatus, Ideology: A Film Theory Reader* [New York: Columbia University Press, 1986]: 120-129). Robert Stam, Robert Burgoyne and Sandy Flitterman-Lewis, *New Vocabularies in Film Semiotics: Structuralism, Post-Structuralism and Beyond* (London; New York: Routledge, 1992): 214-215.

[7]   Gary Crowdus, "Francesco Rosi. Italy's Postmodern Neorealist", *Cineaste*

20: 4 (1994): 21.

[8] For a representative sampling, see Tullio Kezich and Sebastiano Gesù (eds), *Salvatore Giuliano* (Acicatena: Incontri con il cinema, 1991): 24-37, who provide excerpts of the major Italian, French and British reviews published when the film first appeared. Among the authors and critics cited are Robin Bean, Bernard Cohn, Adelio Ferrero, Giovanni Grazzini, Morando Morandini, Alberto Moravia, Pierre Philippe, Georges Sadoul, Leonardo Sciascia, Mario Soldati and Sandro Zambetti.

[9] Sandro Zambetti, *Francesco Rosi* (Florence: La Nuova Italia, 1976): 50.

[10] Geoffrey Nowell-Smith, "Salvatore Giuliano", *Sight and Sound* 32: 3 (summer 1963): 142-143. Dale Munroe, "*Salvatore Giuliano* Complex Crime Pic", *City News* 8 April 1966. John Thomas, "Salvatore Giuliano", *Film Society Review* (September 1966): 18-21. Kevin Thomas, "*Giuliano* Unveils World of Crime", *The Los Angeles Times* 6 April 1966. Gene Youngblood, "Rosi's *Giuliano* Starkly Modern", *Los Angeles Herald Examiner* 10 April 1966: K4. Marcel Martin, "Salvatore Giuliano", *Revue du Cinema* 435 (February 1988): 48. Maria-Teresa Ravage, "The Mafia on Film: *Salvatore Giuliano*", *Film Society Review* (October 1971): 33-39. Crowdus. Stuart Klawans, "Illustrious Rosi", *Film Comment* 31: 1 (January/February 1995): 60.

[11] Michel Ciment, "Rosi in a new key", *American Film* 9: 10 (September 1984): 36-42. Jean A Gili, *Francesco Rosi: Cinéma et pouvoir* (Paris: Éditions du Cerf, 1976). Ciment (1976). Zambetti.

[12] Tullio Kezich, *Salvatore Giuliano* (Rome: Edizioni FM, 1961). Francesco Bolzoni, *Salvatore Giuliano* (Rome: Gremese Editore, 1986). Kezich and Gesù.

[13] Ferrero in Kezich and Gesù; Crowdus: 21.

[14] Gesù in Kezich and Gesù: 17.

[15] Gili: 37; Zambetti: 38; Gesù in Kezich and Gesù: 17.

[16] Grazzini in Kezich and Gesù: 27.

[17] Ciment (1976): 90; Gili: 37; Klawans.

[18] Translated from the Italian: "Io voglio...che la fotografia abbia tre toni diversi: un tono evocativo per le vicende del passato, un tono da servizio fotografico per Castelvetrano, un tono...televisivo, per le scene del processo." Quoted in Zambetti: 48.

[19] Patti in Kezich and Gesù: 30.

[20] Gallo in ibid: 26; Soldati in ibid: 28; Cohn in ibid: 33.

[21] Crowdus: 21.

[22] While virtually every study of *Salvatore Giuliano* (Ciment [1976], Crowdus, Gili, Sitney, Zambetti) mentions the intensity of Rosi's research in

Sicily and elsewhere, Kezich's diary of the shooting of the film offers the best actual description of Rosi at work in Sicily (43-83). *Salvatore Giuliano* was not Rosi's first filmmaking experience in Sicily. He served as Luchino Visconti's assistant director on *La terra trema* (*The Earth Trembles*, 1948).

[23] Translated from the French: "sans cesse à un temps actuel". Gili: 47.

[24] The Mafia's war against the state and among and between the various "families" reached something of a peak in March 1995. The leading article in the 7 March 1995 *Corriere della Sera* reports the following information. The chief of *carabinieri* (maresciallo) of the city of Terrasini (near Palermo), Antonino Lombardi, committed suicide after being accused of being connected with the Cosa Nostra. Domenico Buscetta, nephew of famous Mafia boss, Tommaso Buscetta, who "repented" in 1982, was killed on 7 March. The father and the brother of Domenico Buscetta were killed in 1982, soon after "Don Masino" turned state's evidence. In the first week of March 1995, eight other people were killed in Palermo. Three people were killed in Catania.

[25] Peter Bondanella, *Italian Cinema: From Neorealism to the Present* (New York: Continuum, 1991): 167-170. Robin Buss, *Italian Films* (London: Batsford, 1989): 42-44. Pierre Leprohon, *The Italian Cinema*, translated by Roger Greaves and Oliver Stallybrass (London: Secker & Warburg, 1972): 190. John J Michalczyk, *The Italian Political Filmmakers* (London; Toronto: Associated University Presses, 1986): 19-63. P Adams Sitney, *Vital Crises in Italian Cinema: Iconography, Stylistics, Politics* (Austin: University of Texas Press, 1995): 199-206.

[26] Pierre Sorlin, *European Cinemas, European Societies 1939-1990* (London; New York: Routledge, 1991): 214.

[27] Pierre Sorlin, *Sociologie du cinéma: ouverture pour l'histoire de demain* (Paris: Aubier Montaigne, 1977): 251-257. Gian Piero Brunetta, *Cent'anni di cinema italiano* (Bari: Editore Laterza, 1991): 517-518.

[28] Mas'ud Zavarzadeh, *Seeing Films Politically* (Albany: State University of New York Press, 1991). Christopher Williams (ed), *Realism and the Cinema: A Reader* (London; Henley: Routledge & Kegan Paul, 1980). Bill Nichols, *Ideology and the Image: Social Representation in the Cinema and Other Media* (Bloomington: Indiana University Press, 1981). James Roy MacBean, *Film and Revolution* (Bloomington; London: Indiana University Press, 1975).

[29] James Monaco, *How To Read a Film: The Art, Technology, Language, History, and Theory of Film and Media* (New York; Oxford: Oxford University Press, 1981): 233.

[30] Ibid: 273.

[31] *Newsweek* 19 September 1949: 36.

[32] Giuseppe Fava, *Mafia da Giuliano a Dalla Chiesa* (Rome: Riuniti, 1984). Pino Arlacchi, *Mafia Business: The Mafia Ethic and the Spirit of Capitalism*, translated by Martin Ryle (New York: Verso, 1986). Pino Arlacchi, *Addio*

Cosa Nostra: La vita di Tommaso Buscetta (Milan: Rizzoli, 1994). Michele Pantaleone, *Omertà di Stato: da Salvatore Giuliano a Totò Riina* (Naples: Pironti, 1993). The links between the Mafia, the Italian Secret Service, neo-Fascist extremists, the leaders of the failed attempt to overthrow the Italian government in 1970, and Christian Democrat politicians, both in the Sicily and in national government, have been the object of an ongoing investigation in Italy which has been reported widely in all the major newspapers. The most prominent politician to have been accused of being a tool of the Mafia is Senator for Life and seven-times Prime Minister of Italy, Giulio Andreotti. The Mafia does not appreciate these investigations. Fava was assassinated by unknown killers one year after his book was originally published under the same title by Siciliani Editori in 1982.

[33] Hawk, *Variety* 27 December 1961: 6.

[34] John Thomas: 21.

[35] Ravage: 38.

[36] Ironically, Alberto Moravia foreshadows, at least in part, both the production and the legal problems of *The Battle of Algiers* when, in his review of *Salvatore Giuliano*, he writes: "Non conosco alcun paese oggi nel quale una realtà analoga, altrettanto attuale e altrettanto scottante, potrebbe essere affrontata con così intrepido scrupolo della verità. Immaginiamo un simile film in Francia sulla guerra d'Algeria o negli Stati Uniti sull'impresa di Cuba" ("I don't know any country today in which an analogous reality, so contemporary and stinging, could be faced with such a daring attention to truth. Let us imagine a similar film in France on the war in Algiers, or in the United States on the Cuban operation") (Kezich and Gesù: 25). Pontecorvo's debt to Rosi would appear to range from the Army's door-to-door searches to the seemingly irresistible torrent of black-clad women, to the keening of the women, to the seeming confusion of flashforwards and flashbacks. This should not be particularly surprising given that Franco Solinas was involved in the scripts of both films.

[37] Gianni Rondolino (ed), *Catalogo Bolaffi del cinema italiano 1956/1965*, third edition (Turin: Giulio Bolaffi Editore, 1979): 222. Ciment (1976): 11; Gili: 36; Crowdus: 21; Klawans.

[38] Grazzini in Kezich and Gesù: 27; Patti in Kezich and Gesù: 30; Youngblood: K4, Crowdus: 20.

[39] Translated from the Italian: "si limita all'osservazione, senza scavare nella interpretazione che lega i fatti...carenza d'interpretazione attorno al nodo essenziale di forze dominanti, banditismo e classi subalterne" (Zambetti: 50). For analogous opinions, see also Patti in Kezich and Gesù: 30.

[40] Ciment (1976): 90. Klawans.

[41] In my extended outline of the film's plot, I will paraphrase and condense the "Speaker"'s commentary.

[42] Gili: 44-48. Actually, according to Rosi, in an interview in Bolzoni (26-

27): "[I]la distributrice americana Columbia tentò più tardi, a mia insaputa, di rimontare il film collegando secondo un ordine cronologico i diversi episodi. Non ce l'hanno fatta. Si sono trovati con delle sequenze che non sapevano dove mettere. E hanno concluso: 'Deve restare così com'è'. Lo presentarono in edizione originale, senza pubblicità, in qualche cinemino degli Stati Uniti." ("The American distribution company, Columbia, tried later, unknown to me, to re-edit the film, organising the various episodes according to a chronological order. They failed. They ended up with sequences that they didn't know where to put. They concluded: 'It has to remain as it is.' They presented it in its original version, without publicity, in a few small theatres in the United States.") However, the very complexity which caused the film to disappear rapidly from the commercial circuit ensured its survival in film schools: "Se ne accorsero dei giovani. Lo ripresentarono, nel circuito universitario, adesso lo proiettano di continuo: è un classico. Francis Ford Coppola, Martin Scorzese [sic] lo hanno studiato, come del resto tutti i giovani registi americani hanno fatto per il cinema italiano." ("Some young people noticed it. They re-presented it on the university circuit, and now they show it constantly: it is a classic. Francis Ford Coppola, Martin Scorzese [sic] have studied it, as all young American directors have studied the Italian cinema.")

[43] Translated from the French: "*Salvatore Giuliano* se compose de quinze séquences principales qui sont montées selon un principe non chronologique: le film fait alterner des séquences situées à divers moments de l'histoire de la Sicile entre la fin de la guerre en 1945 et la mort d'un 'mafioso' en 1960." (Gili: 44).

[44] Translated from the French: "Les neuf premières séquences du film se distribuent selon un mouvement de va-et-vient dans le temps qui prend toujours la mort de Giuliano comme point de référence, comme moment présent par rapport au passé." (Ibid: 45).

[45] Ibid: 46-47. The general assumption of all biographies of Giuliano is that he was not a Mafioso. On the contrary, he not only killed Mafia "chief among chiefs", Santo Fleres (Chandler: 135), he also covered the face of one of his Mafioso victims with cow dung, and placed a placard with the following words around his neck: "This is how Giuliano treats Mafiosi!" (Pantaleone: 30). The consensus is that the Mafia, having used Giuliano until he became a liability, cooperated with the government in his assassination (Chandler: 188-194). The only exception to this chorus is the notorious "repented" Mafioso, Tommaso Buscetta, who, in his self-serving autobiography, states that Giuliano had always been a "man of honor" and that the Mafia had nothing to do with his death (Arlacchi: 39-43).

[46] Sitney: 201-204.

[47] Ibid: 201.

[48] Ibid.

[49] Ibid.

[50] Ibid: 202.

[51] Ibid: 204. Sitney points out that, among others, there is no mention of Mario Scelba, Italian Minister of the Interior, who was widely suspected of having ordered the massacre of Portella della Ginestra. Scelba had held that ministry at the time of the massacre, during the search for Giuliano, and also when Pisciotta was poisoned. Sitney (206) adds that Rosi "astutely avoided censorship by quoting court documents whenever the corruption of the state was in question". One might also suggest that Rosi astutely avoided Mafia retaliation by not mentioning Mafiosi by name.

[52] Sandro Attanasio and Pasquale "Pino" Sciortino, *Storia di Salvatore Giuliano di Montelepre* (Palermo: Edikronos, 1985). Chandler. Lucio Galluzzo, *Meglio morto: storia di Salvatore Giuliano* (Palermo: Flaccovio, 1985). Gavin Maxwell, *God Protect Me From My Friends* (London: Readers Union, 1957). Enzo Magri, *Salvatore Giuliano* (Milan: Mondadori, 1987).

[53] My primary sources are the film itself and *Salvatore Giuliano* by Kezich and Gesù, unquestionably the single most important volume for pursuing the study of the film. The book contains not only the script of *Salvatore Giuliano*, but also Gesù's introduction; excerpts from all the major Italian and French reviews of the film; Kezich's personal impressions of the shooting of the film, compiled as he wrote the lengthy production diary; a history of Sicilian banditry and of the Sicilian separatist movement; excerpts from the Italian newspaper articles that broke the news that the "official story" was, in fact, a lie; and prints of the negatives found on Giuliano's corpse.

[54] The various biographies of Giuliano have been particularly useful, and in particular Chandler's and, once again, *Salvatore Giuliano* by Kezich and Gesù. Where events are confirmed by more than one biography, I will only cite Chandler, given that it is the most recent, the most historically objective, and in English. Chandler conveys better than most how effective Giuliano was as a guerrilla leader. Attanasio and Sciortino's *Storia di Salvatore Giuliano di Montelepre*, which was written with the cooperation of Giuliano's brother-in-law, tells the story from a Sicilian perspective. In this book, Giuliano does not become a bandit and a secessionist by accident. Here, he is a Sicilian everyman of sorts who becomes a bandit and a secessionist as a result of specific socio-political conditions caused by foreign (i.e. Italian) oppression. According to the authors, he was never just a bandit; he was always a revolutionary partisan. This book deals less with the military conflict than with the background, and with the fact that the entire Sicilian society backed him. It also details the way in which the representatives of all political parties, the Church, the police and the *carabinieri* all tried to deal with him and use him to their own advantage. Then, when he was no longer necessary, they all wanted him dead because he was an embarrassment alive. The book also presents in detail the absolute corruption of the postwar Italian government, its shocking, brutal treatment of the people of Sicily, its employment of torture and murder squads, its secret prisons, and so on. It also accuses the government of accepting obviously false information concerning the murder of Giuliano and others, of destroying documents, and of collusion with the Mafia which eventually resulted in its return to power in Sicily. Maxwell includes a very interesting first chapter on Sicily, its history and its many invasions, and the

particular character of its inhabitants. The rest of the book presents an Englishman's well-researched but very subjective encounter with Giuliano's Sicily. The other biographies cited are just as fascinating in different ways.

[55] It is immediately obvious that even this breakdown of the film is less than completely satisfactory. For example, it is my assumption that "Giovanni" was questioned not long before the trial at Viterbo, and therefore I assigned number 7 to this sequence. However, if he was questioned immediately after the events of Portella della Ginestra, sequence 7 should have been sequence 6b. We know that some of Giuliano's men were captured soon after the massacre, while others were not. Unfortunately, here as elsewhere the film furnishes us with virtually no frame of reference. Although we see the same young man in several scenes (6, 7, 10), his name is never mentioned. I have used the name "Giovanni", because in the script he is called "Giovanni Provenza". However, the script, here as elsewhere, appears to be incorrect or misleading. No person by this name is mentioned in any of Giuliano's biographies. One might also argue that sequences 11-13 all take place in the same general time period, or that I might have subdivided them differently.

[56] Colonel Ugo Luca, commander of the *carabinieri* in Lazio and an expert in antiguerrilla warfare, was given over 2000 men to find Giuliano. His plan was to "isolate and neutralize the bandits". He replaced Chief Inspector Ciro Verdiani, who had headed the General Inspectorate of Public Security in Sicily. Verdiani was so incensed by his relief that, when he left Sicily, he took all his files with him, thus forcing Luca to start from scratch (Chandler: 165-168). The script incorrectly identifies Luca as a general in the opening scene (Kezich and Gesù: 95). An exception to policy was made to promote him to the rank of general after his successful elimination of Giuliano (Chandler: 195). Captain Antonio Perenze was Luca's second in command. He had "fought brigands in Labia and Ethiopia when they were Italian colonies" (168). He and his assistants dressed Giuliano's body, and moved it from De Maria's bedroom to the courtyard. He shot it with his machine-gun, and initially took credit for killing Giuliano (196-199).

[57] Galluzzo (178-183) reproduces the official after-action report prepared for the Minister of the Interior by Colonel Luca, commander of the police forces arrayed against Giuliano. Galluzzo (183) comments that this is "un documento eccezionale. Non perchè quasi interamente falso; ma per il gusto del particolare, per la fantasia descrittiva" ("a remarkable document...not because it is almost entirely false, but because of the wealth of details and the descriptive fantasy").

[58] "Bandit's End", *Time* 17 July 1950: 33-34.

[59] "Death at Dawn", *Newsweek* 17 July 1950: 37.

[60] Maxwell reports in some detail all the lies told by the police and the *carabinieri* to explain how they trapped Giuliano. In particular, he debunks the notion that Giuliano was hoodwinked by the van which, in different police versions, carried a motion-picture crew or was decorated with the names of prominent newspapers. Maxwell also rejects out of hand the story

that he was caught leaving a prostitute. Giuliano distrusted women in general; he was not known to frequent prostitutes; he understood the security risk involved in such activities in small towns; he was known to have punished his men for associating with prostitutes (161-163).

[61]   Chandler: 197-198; Galluzzo: 186; Attanasio and Sciortino: 250; Maxwell: 170.

[62]   23 February 1948; 16 January 1950; 4 February 1950.

[63]   8 October 1949; 4 February 1950.

[64]   Stam, Burgoyne and Flitterman-Lewis: 192.

[65]   Many Sicilians resented what they considered their occupation by Italy, and in particular their treatment by the Fascists. The Allies, and the British in particular, allegedly encouraged the Sicilians' separatist aspirations, at least until the fall of Mussolini. The Soviet Union was very opposed to an independent Sicily under British hegemony (Chandler: 23-30).

[66]   This scene would appear to conflate meetings which took place over a period of several months. Among the separatists who were frequently present at these meetings were Lucio Tasca Bordanaro, a large landholding rightist and former Mayor of Palermo; Mafia boss, Calogero Vizzini; leftist radical, Antonio Canepa; Andrea Finocchiaro Aprile, public leader of the Committee for Sicilian Independence; leftist lawyer, Antonino Varvaro; Concetto Gallo, son of the former Mayor of Catania; and a smattering of unnamed dukes and barons (Chandler: 25-51).

[67]   In the discussion of whether to use outlaws, one separatist leader calls them "*picciotti*", and then describes them as young men forced into the hills by injustice – the same kind of people, he says, whom Garibaldi used to free Sicily. When referring to Giuliano's men, I will use the terms *picciotti*, bandits and outlaws somewhat interchangeably.

[68]   Andrea Finocchiaro Aprile was a public leader of the Committee for Sicilian Independence, an organisation which evolved into the MIS; Antonino Varvaro, also active in the separatist movement, was a leftist lawyer.

[69]   Giuliano, like many young Sicilians during the harsh war years, sought to survive by smuggling goods from one village to the next. He became a bandit on 2 September 1943 (Chandler: 8).

[70]   The old man, Pietro Franzone, is a separatist who spent time in jail because of his political convictions. Rosi chose him for the role because he accompanied the EVIS representatives when they visited Giuliano. Rosi tells him that the shot will end on him, and asks him to "Dovrebbe dirmi qualcosa sulla Sicilia: una frase che le piace, una poesia, una dichiarazione d'amore" ("say something about Sicily, a sentence, a poem, a declaration of love") (Kezich and Gesù: 46-47). Franzone begins to recite the Sicilian hymn of independence, "Sicily Awaken!", but he begins to cry and cannot continue. He tries repeatedly. The words he speaks eventually are: "Sicilia

37

svegliati! Troppo è durato questo sonno vergognoso e in questo triste sonno tutto hai perso anche l'onore! Or son suonate forte le trombe e tu non devi più dormire, perchè dormir sarebbe morte. Rose, rose, rose bianche di Sicilia, diventerete rosse col nostro rosso sangue. Ma i figli, i figli dei figli vivranno liberi in terra libera e potranno alzar la fronte al cielo e sorriderci nell'avvenire" ("Sicily awaken! This shameful sleep has lasted too long, and in this sorrowful slumber you have lost everything, including your honour! Now the trumpets have sounded and you must no longer sleep, because to sleep would be to die. White, white, white roses of Sicily, you will become red with our blood. But our sons, the sons of our sons, will live free in a free land and will be able to raise their faces to the sky and smile at us in the future") (Kezich and Gesù: 97).

[71] Wollen: 124-125.

[72] Sicily is connected by chains to both Italy and the United States. A man, presumably Giuliano, cuts the chain with a sword. Another man, presumably President Truman, pulls Sicily towards the United States. The clear, but grammatically incorrect text on the poster reads: "A morte i sbirri succhiatori del popolo siciliano e perche sono i principali radici fascisti. Viva il separatismo della libertà. Giuliano." ("Death to the pigs, because they exploit the Sicilian people and because they are the principal roots of Fascism. Long live the separatist freedom. Giuliano.")

[73] Christian Metz, *Film Language: A Semiotics of the Cinema*, translated by Michael Taylor (New York: Oxford University Press, 1974): 126.

[74] In reality, I propose that they refer specifically to the 27 December 1945 attack on the *carabinieri* post at Bellolampo (Chandler: 57-58), the attack two days later on the isolated *carabinieri* station at Grisi, near Partinico (58), and the ambush at the Belvedere Curve on 7 January 1946 (60).

[75] This is clearly an allusion to the article written by Tommaso Besozzi, *L'Europeo*'s special correspondent in Castelvetrano. The article's banner headline reads: "Di sicuro c'è solo che è morto" ("The only certain thing is that he is dead"). The article, which occupied the entire front page of the 16 July 1950 issue, is continued on page 2. The complete text is reproduced in Kezich and Gesù (169-173).

[76] Kezich and Gesù describe at some length the working-class Sicilians selected to act in the film and their identification with their roles (43-83).

[77] "...nella sala da pranzo dell'Albergo Selinus gremita di commensali, autorità, funzionari e giornalisti festeggiavano l'evento. Perenze...invitò i presenti a brindare 'alla fine del banditismo in Sicilia'" ("The dining hall of the Selinus hotel was crowded with diners, authorities, functionaries and newspapermen who were celebrating the event. Perenze...invited those present to toast 'the end of banditry in Sicily'" (Attanasio and Sciortino: 251).

[78] Gili: 47-48.

[79] The major is played by one of the few recognisable actors in the film: Francesco Grandjaquet, the actor who portrayed Francesco, Pina's lover, in

[80] Chandler: 61.

[81] At least two of these scenes will find specific analogues in Pontecorvo's *The Battle of Algiers*. In particular, see the black-clad women confronting the soldiers as the film ends, and the young bride pretending to sleep in front of the hiding place of the rebels. In more general terms, Pontecorvo adopts Rosi's technique of presenting a seemingly balanced picture. In both films, however, the underlying social injustices clearly tilt the viewer's sympathy towards the underdog.

[82] As Sitney points out, the figure of Giuliano on the oval slab is reminiscent of "Mantegna's and Annibale Caracci's dead Christs" (202). This is not the only parallel between the two "saviours" ("Salvatore" in Italian means "saviour"). Giuliano's mother's dirge is reminiscent of Jacopone da Todi's "Lament of the Madonna", written c.1300 and expressing a very similar obsessive, all-consuming sorrow. Maria Giuliano: "Figghiu miu madri, Turiddu. Figghiu miu, Turiddu. Tradituri. Figghiu miu beddu ti tradiru e t'ammazzaro. Sangue, du mio cori, Turiddu." ("My son, oh mother, Turiddu. My son, Turiddu, Turiddu. My beautiful son they betrayed you and they killed you. Blood of my heart, Turiddu.") Jacopone da Todi: "O figlio bianco e biondo, figlio, volto giocondo! Figlio, perchè t'ha il mondo, figlio, così disprezzato? Figlio dolce e piacente, figlio de la dolente! Figlio, atti la gente malamente trattato." ("O white and blond son; son, cheerful face! Son, why has the world, son, so despised you? Sweet and pleasing son, son of the sorrowful one! Son, people have ill-treated you.")

[83] The Communists and Socialists won 30% of the vote; the Christian Democrats won 20% (Chandler: 85).

[84] Sitney also perceives the allusion to Eisenstein, but for him the scene of the massacre at Portella della Ginestra contains "fleeting allusions to the Odessa Steps scene from Eisenstein's *Battleship Potemkin*" (202).

[85] Originally, Girolamo Li Causi, a prominent Sicilian Communist, was supposed to be the featured speaker. He did not appear for reasons which were never satisfactorily explained, nor did his replacement, a young labour leader from Palermo. Eventually a cobbler, Giacomo Schirò, who was the secretary of the Socialist Party of the nearby town of Piana degli Albanesi, began to introduce a far less famous substitute orator: "He had scarcely said 'Comrades' when a burst of explosions shook the air" (Chandler: 93). In this scene, Rosi takes considerable liberties with history. Schirò's words in the film might be summarized as follows: "Comrades, friends, workers. Today is the first of May. We have won a great first victory. But having won the land is not enough. We need tools, we need ploughs, roads, light and water. Comrades, we need to bring civilisation into the countryside. We want our children to learn how to read and write. We want to avoid the shame of illiteracy."

[86] "...lasciano sul terreno 11 morti e 56 feriti, oltre a 29 quadrupedi uccisi e feriti" ("There were 11 dead and 56 wounded, in addition to 29 dead or wounded four-legged animals"). Pantaleone: 31.

[87] Attanasio and Sciortino: 120-121; Giuseppe Montalbano, *Giuliano e la strage di Portella della Ginestra: 10 maggio 1947* (Caltanissetta: Krinon, 1988): 10; Chandler: 83-98.

[88] The numbers given vary. Chandler (166) puts the figure at 120, of whom 87 were *carabinieri*.

[89] Three reporters succeed in interviewing Giuliano. In 1947, Michael Stern was assigned to interview Giuliano by *True* magazine. Because Stern wore the Army uniform he had worn as a Second World War correspondent, Giuliano thought he was a representative of the United States government, as did other media in Italy and the United States. Giuliano gave Stern a letter for President Truman (reprinted in Attanasio and Sciortino: 279-281). When Stern heard that other American reporters were trying to visit Giuliano, he sent him a telegram informing him that they were Italian secret police agents (Chandler: 87-89). In 1948, Maria Cyliakus, a 32-year-old Swede separated from her Greek industrialist husband, succeeded in remaining with Giuliano and his band for over 24 hours. Her article, which depicted the police as persecuting a Robin Hood, angered the police. Eventually, she was expelled from Italy (Chandler: 150-153). In 1949, soon after Colonel Luca took over the hunt for Giuliano, Jacopo Rizza, an Italian reporter for *Oggi*, visited the bandit and interviewed him for six hours. Giuliano told him that he wanted to make a movie and sell it to Americans (Chandler: 171-173).

[90] The ambush took place on 19 August 1949. According to Chandler (163-165), there were two dozen casualties, of whom eight were killed.

[91] The Viterbo trial of the *picciotti* accused of having committed the massacre of Portella della Ginestra opened on 12 June 1950.

[92] According to Maxwell (185), the text of Pisciotta's confession reads: "I, Gaspare Pisciotta, assassinated Giuliano. This was done by personal arrangement with Signor Scelba, Minister of the Interior". This version is confirmed by Chandler (203), and by Attanasio and Sciortino (242). Maxwell writes that he was told that Pisciotta had not killed Giuliano; one man implied he knew who had done it, but was not willing to tell him the name (223-229). Attanasio and Sciortino state that, while Pisciotta had conspired in the killing, Nunzio Badalamenti actually pulled the trigger (247-255).

[93] While the judge condemns "[u]sare violenza contro chi si trova a disposizione delle forze dell'ordine è cosa che ripugna a ogni coscienza" ("the use of violence against those who are at the disposal of the forces of order") (Kezich and Gesù: 110), to the best of my knowledge no one was punished or even reprimanded for actions which included twisting of a testicle of Francesco Gaglio to such an extent that it atrophied (Attanasio and Sciortino: 276), the deliberate murder of Rosario Candela (Chandler: 182), and keeping Frank Mannino tied hand and foot in an underground location for over three months (Chandler: 183). In the film, one of the accused, Pietro Monreale, assures the judge that he was not mistreated, and that he was only shackled hand and foot for 110 days.

[94] As I have noted above, no person named Giovanni Provenza appears in any biography of Giuliano. However, Francesco Gaglio, a shepherd who

had never belonged to EVIS or to Giuliano's band, was arrested and tortured. Under police pressure, at first he accused many people of participating in the massacre. He then retracted his accusations. Later still, he once again denounced several persons, and then retracted his accusations one final time. He was eventually condemned to life in prison. He was released after 30 years and six months in jail (Attanasio and Sciortino: 276).

[95] Chandler: 176. While the intermediary's name is given as Albanese in Kezich and Gesù (113), it is given as Domenico Albano in Chandler (176) and in Attanasio and Sciortino (15).

[96] This story is confirmed by Attanasio and Sciortino (218-219).

[97] By the time of the trial, Ugo Luca, who had replaced Verdiani in August 1949 after the disastrous attack at Bellolampo, had been promoted to the rank of general for his part in elimination of Giuliano (Chandler: 165-168).

[98] Chandler: 181. Attanasio and Sciortino identify the Mafioso as Minasola, but do not mention the *carabiniere* (222-224). Also involved in the betrayal is Antonino Miceli, nephew of Mafia boss, Don Ignazio Miceli (Chandler: 181-182; Attanasio and Sciortino: 224). Kezich and Gesù incorrectly identify the *carabiniere* as Rossi and the Mafioso as Mirafiore (114). In Sicily, even 40 years after the fact, it is apparently not safe to name names.

[99] Chandler: 182-184. Both Chandler (182) and Attanasio and Sciortino (223) add Rosario Candela to the betrayed bandits. Attanasio and Sciortino also describe the capture, interrogation and summary execution of Salvatore Pecoraro. The official *carabinieri* report will describe his death as having occurred as a result of a gun battle (222-223).

[100] Chandler: 189-190; Attanasio and Sciortino: 225-226.

[101] According to Chandler (174), De Maria is not a Mafioso; according to Attanasio and Sciortino (216), he is somehow connected with the Mafia.

[102] Humiliated and resentful because he had been replaced by Luca, Verdiani wanted to redeem himself by bringing the dead body of the bandit to the authorities. As a result, when he discovered Luca's plan to trap the bandit, he sent two messages to warn Giuliano. Luca intercepted one message, but the other reached Giuliano. It read: "Dearest friend, be warned that Pisciotta has passed to Luca's side. Protect yourself immediately" (Chandler: 193).

[103] According to the most reliable sources (Chandler: 194; Attanasio and Sciortino: 246), Giuliano had been warned in writing that Pisciotta would betray him. This notwithstanding, the bandit who had ruthlessly killed several persons whom he merely suspected of treason, accepted Pisciotta's protestations of innocence and promptly went to sleep. Giuseppe Di Leva, librettist of the opera, *Salvatore Giuliano*, argues that "Giuliano muore perchè *vuole* [sic] morire, ucciso dal suo migliore amico e 'discepolo', cosí come avviene in molte saghe, in molte mitologie religiose e laiche" ("Giuliano dies because he *wants to* be killed by his best friend and 'disciple', as occurs in many tales, in many religious and lay mythologies")

(Giuseppe Di Leva, "Tradimenti", in Giuseppe Di Leva (libretto) and Lorenzo Ferrero (music), *Nascita di un'opera: Salvatore Giuliano* [Bologna: Nuova Alfa Editoriale, 1987]: 29-31; emphasis in original), thus making explicit the parallels with the willing martyrdom of Jesus.

[104] Chandler: 195-199; Attanasio and Sciortino: 237-241.

[105] Chandler: 203-206.

[106] Giuliano had originally planned to hide at the farm of Giuseppe Marotta, a Mafioso. However, the latter did not want to host the bandit, and therefore asked De Maria to shelter Giuliano (Chandler: 173-175).

[107] Chandler: 207. According to Maxwell (199), Pisciotta was sentenced on 4 May 1951.

[108] Chandler: 208.

[109] How he was poisoned remains something of a mystery to this day (ibid). Attanasio and Sciortino (260) offer the most concrete theory. Pisciotta, who had stated that he expected to be killed, was under guard 24 hours a day. He shared his cell with his father and prepared all his own food. On the morning of 9 February 1954, he prepared coffee for himself and his father. Both added sugar to it and drank it. Almost immediately Aspanu began to feel ill and yelled, "They poisoned me". Eventually, he died in intense pain. He had been killed by a dose of strychnine allegedly sufficiently strong to kill 40 dogs. Since strychnine was later found in the sugar, no one could understand why his father did not also die. Attanasio and Sciortino's answer is that the poison was in pills Pisciotta took for his tuberculosis, pills that were furnished to him by the prison administration. They contend that the strychnine was added to the sugar after the fact to deflect attention from the real killers.

[110] Crowdus: 20. Emphasis in original (first instance); emphasis added (second instance).

[111] Translated from the French: "La manière de monter *Giuliano* répondait à une exigence narrative qui était de raconter les faits en donnant au public cette impression de confusion, d'absence de clarté avec laquelle ces faits sont advenus dans la réalité" (Ciment: 89).

[112] Crowdus: 21. See also Umberto Eco, as quoted in Sitney: 200.

[113] See Pier Paolo Pasolini, "Il cinema impopolare", *Nuovi Argomenti* 20 (October/December 1970): 166-176 (reprinted in Pier Paolo Pasolini, *Empirismo eretico* [Milan: Aldo Garzanti Editore, 1972: 273-280]. Pier Paolo Pasolini, *Heretical Empiricism*, edited by Louise K Barnett, translated by Ben Lawton and Louise K Barnett (Bloomington; Indianapolis: Indiana University Press, 1988): 267-275.

[114] Niccolò Machiavelli, *"Il Principe" e "Discorsi"* (Milan: Feltrinelli, 1971): 65. Peter Bondanella and Mark Musa (eds), *The Portable Machiavelli* (Harmondsworth; New York: Penguin Books, 1979): 126.

Hands Over the City: cinema as political indictment and social commitment

Manuela Gieri

The year of the release of Francesco Rosi's *Le mani sulla città* (*Hands Over the City*) is 1963, a date which constitutes an important step in the history of Italian postwar cinema. It was the year of Federico Fellini's *Otto e mezzo* (*8½*), Marco Ferreri's *L'ape regina* (*The Queen Bee*), Lina Wertmüller's *I basilischi* (*The Lizards*), but also of Dino Risi's *I mostri* (*The Monsters*), which came just one year after his *Il sorpasso* (*The Easy Life*), a film with which Risi definitively transformed the *commedia all'italiana* by employing the *grotesque* in his powerful and devastating indictment of contemporary Italian society. In *The Monsters*, Risi again offered a grotesque gallery of monstrous portraits drawn by Italian contemporary society, a society that had been affected by the rapid growth experienced in the aftermath of the Second World War and had been the breeding ground for monstrosities of different kinds. The *grotesque* is also the mode of discourse chosen by Ferreri in *The Queen Bee*, and by Wertmüller in *The Lizards*. In her directorial debut, Wertmüller constructs a political satire of Italian provincial life which displays only a superficial similarity with Fellini's *I vitelloni* (*The Young and the Passionate*, 1953), a film with which it has often unfairly been compared. In this film Wertmüller describes "the reactionary apathy of some zones of southern Italy in analogy with the typical immobility of lizards in the sun".[1]

The theme of the apathy of the south is instead historically explicated in another 1963 film, Luchino Visconti's astonishing cinematic tour de force, *Il gattopardo* (*The Leopard*), an adaptation of Giuseppe Tomasi di Lampedusa's 1958 novel. Visconti's film finds in the melodramatic imagination its privileged territory as it exposes the historical and political contradictions of Italian 19th century Risorgimento. By 1963, Fellini, on the other hand, had already provided us with his own uncompromising portrayal of contemporary Italian society amidst the general crumbling of Western civilisation in his cinematic allegory, *La dolce vita* (1959), and with *8½* he seemed to withdraw into the more private territories of creative imagination and artistic freedom.

Within this extremely composite panorama, *Hands Over the City*,

43

Rosi's fourth feature film, was a surprise winner of the Golden Lion at the 24th Venice Film Festival. The film provoked a wealth of conflicting and even violent reviews from both the Right and the Left. In general, critics reacted to its content and form alike, since the former was clearly undermining the collective attempt to build a Centre-Left government, and the latter was fast moving away from the heritage of neo-realism as Rosi elaborated his own personal and provoking interpretation of "realism". From the right wing, who saw themselves directly attacked onscreen, the protest was fierce, as one reads in *Il Secolo d'Italia*, the daily newspaper of the Fascist party: "Since *Hands Over the City* is not art but politics, let's talk politics...it's not cinema but factious political speech...Francesco Rosi has given a defamatory and partisan speech, he has made a marxist film".[2] In another right-wing newspaper, the *Corriere Lombardo*, one reads of "the worst film ever seen at the Venice Film Festival. And there will be no smart ass or menacing letter that will make me change my mind".[3] In the Centre-Right, the reactions were equally – if not more – outraged, as exemplified by Gian Luigi Rondi's review in the daily *Il tempo*:

> No, no and no. Don't come and tell us that this is how one should make movies...This is neither cinema or healthy polemic: it is a political speech, an electoral harangue transformed into cinematographic spectacle merely with political intentions, and with very limited cultural and artistic preoccupation.[4]

Equally extreme but positive were the reactions of the Left, as exemplified in the review by Ugo Casiraghi in *L'Unità*, the daily newspaper of the Italian Communist Party:

> A wonderful film...Rosi has authored his most mature work. Even more mature than *Salvatore Giuliano*, it equals the former in dramatic effect but surpasses it in coherence and clarity. *Hands Over the City* addresses the audience with increased lucidity...It is a film-essay with the clarity of a limpid and documented sociological study...The only weakness on the artistic level seems to be the internal and dialectic relationship between 'public' and 'private' character.[5]

One of the most frequently recurring accusations in the many critiques the film received was exactly the lack of depth of the characters – i.e. the scarce psychological delving which would have supposedly given the story scope and profundity. Rosi has repeatedly commented on this aspect of his filmmaking in general, and on one occasion specifically stated:

I think that the psychology of a film springs from the editing since it is not so much *the psychology of the individual characters but it is that of the narrative structure, of the relationships the director, the author, weaves with the subject-matter and with the characters; it is not the psychology of the various characters taken and developed one by one,* but it is that of the general picture given by the narrative structure from which there emerges the general psychology of the characters together with that of their individual behaviour...The true psychology is in the editing. *I am the psychologist when I make the film.*[6]

In Rosi's filmmaking, editing is therefore of utmost importance. So too are casting and shooting insofar as he often re-creates events in actual places and with "real" people. For instance, in *Salvatore Giuliano* one finds the *real* Portella delle Ginestre and some of the people who witnessed Giuliano's story; in *Hands Over the City*, Naples and its people provide the perfect setting for the film, in addition to two of the protagonists in its story. Such a casting and shooting strategy is meant to obtain a particular dramatic atmosphere which Rosi has defined as "psicodramma" ("psychodrama").[7]

The critical response in Italian film journals was also lively and controversial. Here Rosi was generally praised for the ethical substance of his work, mostly recognised as inherited from neo-realism, but was often criticised for his aesthetic choices, considered a step backwards when compared to his previous film, *Salvatore Giuliano.* Such a perspective is exemplified by the words of Lorenzo Quaglietti:

The distance that separates *Hands Over the City* and *Salvatore Giuliano* is substantial...Often Rosi has deviated from that rational line of ideal debate that he intended to follow: the subsequent unbalances greatly undermine the stylistic unity of the film, and make it difficult to accept it on an artistic level. This is not to say that the film has no relevance, since its importance lies mostly in two undeniable qualities: the choice of the theme and the intentional rejection of the canons of spectacle.[8]

Stefano Roncoroni's assessment of the film in his article on Rosi's cinematic evolution answers Quaglietti, when he states that "[f]or Rosi *Hands Over the City* represents a move forward in relation to

45

Salvatore Giuliano because of its better defined ideological commitment and its stronger moral attitude".[9] Yet, the critic continues by stating that Rosi's cinema is still unclear as to which direction to take, caught between two fundamental tendencies, one leaning towards description and the other towards narration.[10]

To conclude, therefore, one has to acknowledge the fundamental controversy created by the releasing of *Hands Over the City* in a critical entourage which reflected the political and ideological debate in Italian society as a whole. Outside Italy, on the contrary, the film received a generally positive and enthusiastic response, especially in France where, since neo-realism, critics have proved to be constantly receptive and attentive to Italian cinema. One example is Amédée Ayfre's review in *Téléciné*, where she underlines the rigorous political indictment and the powerful stylistic innovations which the film displays:

> This film, because of its ardent style, its polemic efficiency and its unquestionable generosity, gives the patent of cinematographic nobility to an aesthetics of the *logos*, grounded on the word, on language, that is, the kind of eloquence thought to be proper of other means of expression.[11]

* * *

Hands Over the City, although moving from a case of real estate speculation, is unquestionably a film about the morality of power, and as such is an abstract work organised as a debate on ideas. The filmic tale is episodic and constructed with essentially verbal means. The action springs not from the characters, as they are essentially "non-characters", true abstractions, but from language in its dialectic and creative function. Every narrative sequence contains an introduction as well as an initial and a conclusive debate. With the exception of the opening sequence – where, in a piece of cinematic bravura, Rosi films the tumbling down of a building, juxtaposed with the silent close-up of developer Edoardo Nottola's face – in general the camera neutrally records the verbal activity of the various participants in this inclement trial to an entire collectivity.

The plot of the film develops around a case of real estate speculation, within the larger context of the corrupt political situation in a huge Italian city of the south, Naples. The demolition of a building in a street within one of the oldest sectors of the city provokes the denunciation of developer Nottola, City Councillor of the Right. The investigation, enacted by a multi-partisan committee nominated by the city council, sheds no light on the events, thanks to the connivance of the city council, where the Right has the majority, and to Nottola's intervention. The name of the developer, however, is so thoroughly compromised that his party asks him to withdraw from the electoral list; after all, the gain they have been planning from the real estate speculation is more important than his victory in the elections. Yet, Nottola knows that if he is not elected he will soon have to beg for permission to build, and pay his way. He knows that his failure to be elected will make him a slave of the politicians.

Thus, on the eve of the elections, Nottola offers his votes and those of four friends involved in the speculation to the party of the Centre. This move provokes the reversal of the political arrangement in the city council, as the Centre wins the elections. Later, even the powerful ill feelings between the Right and the five turncoats are recomposed because of their common interest in exercising power over the city. Nottola is nominated City Councillor for Real Estate Development and will continue building in the designated area, even gaining the benediction of the Church, an institution that does not find a concrete embodiment in any of the characters of the film, but is ever-present. At one point in the film, for instance, as he is deciding to switch sides, Nottola goes to church and prays. Later, when Balsamo, a representative of the Left within the Democrazia Cristiana (Christian Democratic Party), visits their leader, Professor De Angeli, the latter shows him with pride an altar he has in the house, and this event prefaces one of the most poignant moments of the story. In the closing sequence of the film, the bishop of the city of Naples gives his blessing to the laying of the first stone in the new construction site, sanctioning the ultimate corruption of men and their environment.

The characters are split between the dominators and the dominated. The latter are most often physically absent from the diegesis of the film, yet they are constantly present insofar as they are the significant "Other", the "absent Other" in everyone's discourse. Over the years, Naples has provided Italian cinema with a large metaphor for the country, as Italy was moving out of the immediate postwar years, through the *miracolo economico* and an all-too-fast growing society into the present. From Roberto Rossellini's *Paisà* (*Paisan*, 1946) – where, in the Naples episode, the director gave a portrayal of corruption and deterioration – to Vittorio De Sica's *L'oro di Napoli* (*The Gold of Naples*, 1954), gold was to be found in Naples in the ability of Neapolitans to regenerate themselves through their relentless creativity and joy of life. Yet, necessarily prefaced by Nanni Loy's *Le quattro giornate di Napoli* (*The Four Days of Naples*, 1962), *Hands Over the City* finally shatters that fertile image of the city and presents an unquestionably gloomier situation. In the opening segment of the film, as the camera pans over a labyrinthine landscape of cement, a voice-over informs us: "There it is...This is the gold of today". Clearly referring to De Sica's film, in which Naples still belonged to its people, and which documented its rich and colourful popular culture – its "gold" – Rosi's work from its very beginning elucidates the cynical philosophy of the dominators which necessarily prevails over that of the dominated, whose position is instead as labyrinthine and confused as their landscape:

> The beginning immediately takes the spectator within the polemical, crude and violent reality by showing the city from above, grasping the chilling significance of a disproportioned growth, one enacted without thought and without clear choices in the programming...It is the radiograph of a disordered city, a photo-document able to capture in reality the truth that is identified with dialectic clarity.[12]

The end-titles running over the same panning shot of the city inform the audience that, while the characters and events we have just viewed are imaginary, the reality that produces them is authentic. Rosi is obviously commenting on the critical realism that informs his cinema and is the result of the choices imposed upon him by a rigorous ideological critique of the social and environmental reality which produces inequalities and injustices. In this sense his cinema removes itself from Italian neo-realism and displays the powerful influence of the great American social realists such as Elia Kazan and Jules Dassin.

Edoardo Nottola, masterfully played by Rod Steiger, is only apparently the evil character, the corrupted developer who patiently weaves the complicated plot which will lead him to make the 5000% profit he talks about in the opening of the film. Yet, Rosi himself once stated that evil is not Nottola, but the social condition which produces him, paralleling Orson Welles's statement that evil is not Othello, but jealousy.[13] Another tempting parallel here is between Welles's Citizen Kane and Rosi's Nottola, as both characters are driven by thirst for power. Yet, the two directors' approach to characterisation is fundamentally different. Welles pointedly delves into and patiently draws Kane's psychology through a remapping of his memories. Rosi, on the other hand, consistently avoids psychological investigation of the character. In this respect, Quaglietti seems partially correct and partly confused when he states that

> The characters of the film, especially because they are non-characters, in the common definition of the term...with only

few exceptions (Salvo Randone, for instance),[14] are drawn geometrically, they lack the flexibility necessary to express fully and dialectically...the social group they symbolize.[15]

In an interview given during a recent visit to Toronto on occasion of the presentation of the complete retrospective of his works, Rosi commented on the positions taken by some Italian critics on his method of characterisation:

When the films were first released in Italian movie theatres specific sectors of aesthetic criticism scolded me since they saw in this kind of procedure not a novelty, but a poverty of artistic representation. But I wondered how it was possible not to see that the characters were treated in such a fashion as to emphasise the context, to underline what happens collectively in society. The developer Nottola in *Hands Over the City*, who, in order to achieve his own goals, involves the general political entourage of the city and creates the premises for the corruption of the various powers -- political power, economic power with the complicity of organised crime -- seemed more interesting to me than Nottola's psychology, if he had a wife, two lovers, three children.[16]

It is true that the characters escape traditional definitions inasmuch as Rosi is trying here to perfect a new mode of filmmaking, his own personal interpretation of *cinema vérité* which forces the spectator to participate in the action as the documentation of truth progresses, and certainly not to identify with the characters and their dramas.

It is accurate to say that the characters are designed geometrically. They are just one element of a film as perfect as a theorem, a geometric work which proceeds with the lucidity of an investigation into a crime, however, that is in the making as the film unfolds. That is, the significant "crime" is not the tearing down of a building; rather, this is just an effect, a symptom of the crime that is truly perpetrated, which is the ultimate corruption of political power, the interruption and severance of the relationship of trust between the people and those they elect. Rosi's film expresses the indictment of an entire political class, and in this sense the work is an arraignment of the entire collectivity. With its trial-like atmosphere, the film becomes increasingly claustrophobic as Rosi's camera consistently avoids openings and digressions, and impassively records the facts. Our gaze is encaged within the frame of the screen. Panning shots are relegated to the beginning and the closing of the film, but they merely record the labyrinthine landscape of cement, thus conveying an effect of closure. Nothing can be seen beyond the labyrinth, and nothing else exists but a muddle of cement born out of corruption and degradation.

The discursive strategy of the film is the *ars oratoria*, the public speech filled with social commitment:

> *Hands Over the City* is indeed a work with an oratory style, as it aims at overcoming the didactic coldness and unavowed artifice of a certain *cinéma vérité* with the warmth and candour of a discourse that openly declares its nature, that wants to be *discourse* and thus employs situations, feelings and characters as subject matters, without getting to abstract symbols or arbitrary superimpositions.[17]

It is certain that the *ars oratoria* flourished in times of civil passion and has always reflected a collective tension to redefine issues such as the morality of power in periods of social and political turmoil. Italy in the early 1960s was undoubtedly a tormented battlefield of opposing ideologies concerning the proper direction the country ought to take. Such a situation was paralleled by a movement aimed at overcoming instances of neo-realism in the cinema, and acquiring new discursive strategies for cinematic realism in general. Rosi plays a central role in the definition of a new mode of filmmaking which is political, engaged in social critique, and committed to realism.[18]

Hands Over the City relies abundantly on words, as they proliferate in a text which is internally episodic. In each episode there is an introduction, an opening speech and a closing speech. The first sequence is exemplary insofar as the panning shot over the city constitutes the introduction. This is followed by Nottola's speech where he lays bare his plot involving a global transformation of the land just outside the city to his own gain, in addition to that of his accomplices. The "closing speech" of this episode is given by the panning shot over the labyrinthine city as his last words are heard over the image: "There it is...This is the gold of today". We are then taken inside the municipal council of the city of Naples, where Nottola's plan to change the original city planning is presented by the Mayor not only as an economic, but also as a moral commitment. These words evoke the next sequence as a helicopter pans over the planned construction site where men in black are gathered to foreshadow the future alliance between Right and Centre which at the end of the film will be sanctioning the fully accomplished "crime", the real estate speculation and the remapping of power. With the reorganisation of city planning comes the reshaping of power.

After this prologue, in which we have been shown the three *loci* of the action – the city of Naples, the municipal council, and the site of the crime, the land of the speculative development – the opening credits run over a screen fully occupied by images of a crowded and chaotic urban situation. Rosi's camera then leads us to a construction site in an old downtown neighbourhood, as the workers are perforating the soil to set the foundations for a new building. While it is normally impassive, the camera in this sequence becomes powerfully present and sympathetic as it records the daily activities in Vicolo Sant'Andrea, a poor, lower-class district in Naples. Rosi then proceeds to show the tumbling down of a building next to the construction site in a spectacular piece of cinematic bravura. This is the only instance in the entire film where the director makes his presence clearly felt in both the visual and the sound track. Here he adopts subjective techniques, such as accompanying a deafening roar in the diegesis with a non-diegetic, thoroughly unrealistic silence broken by the diegetic sound of the siren of the ambulance as a wounded child is taken to the hospital. After this emotional moment, the camera will relocate itself in an impassive position and will neutrally record the development of Rosi's investigation.

Yet, although the plot is a case of real estate speculation, the filmic investigation will not aim at uncovering the responsibilities behind the crash. That particular inquiry is developed within the diegesis of the film by a special committee nominated by the city council following a fiery meeting the day after the events in Vicolo Sant'Andrea. On the contrary, Rosi's own investigation begins with the opening of the film, is in the making throughout it, and coincides with the film's progression. It is not the plot, but the story of the tale told. The true story of *Hands Over the City* deals with the morality of power and its ethics, or lack thereof. The real estate speculation is a pretext; on the contrary, the true subject-matter is the inner logic of power. The film is a dispassionate investigation of the morality of power through the progressive unmasking of the lie behind a façade of social harmony and political consensus.

Within this fluid work, where the coordinates change but the form constantly aims at reaccessing the originary geometry, the catalyser is Nottola. He is the owner of the construction company, Bellavista (ironically, "beautiful view"), which is responsible for the destruction of the building; he is a municipal councillor representative of the Right who will later join the Centre, specifically the Christian Democratic Party. He will offer them his votes, acquired with money and favours, but especially with the backing of Neapolitan organised crime, the *camorra*, in exchange for the position of City Councillor for Real Estate Development. He is also the perfect embodiment of the ideology of power, and, like those who dominate, he moves in an eccentric and disconnected way aiming at returning everything to that apparent harmony which will allow him to dominate. Being moved and defined only and exclusively by his greed for power, Nottola moves within the political entourage and remaps the power structure to his advantage. If the rules do not work, they must be altered, and will be; consequently, nothing really changes. Impressive parallelisms can be established with Visconti's *The Leopard*,[19] insofar as both films address this very issue, albeit from different visual angles. Contrary to other works in his filmography, such as *Salvatore Giuliano* or *Il caso Mattei* (*The Mattei Affair*, 1972), which investigate past events, *Hands Over the City* deals with the present and prefigures the future. Such a discursive strategy bears powerful similarities with Visconti's film, despite the fact that *The Leopard* is set in the 19th century.

The opponent to Nottola is Councillor De Vita, a vocal representative of the Left. They face each other directly only once in Vicolo Sant'Andrea, when the police force the inhabitants to leave their homes after Nottola has managed to convince the majority party in the city council (i.e. his party, the Right) that the only solution is to declare all the buildings in the street uninhabitable. The sequence is reminiscent of the first meeting between Romolo Catenacci (Aldo Fabrizi), a corrupt real estate developer, and Gianni Pelago (Vittorio Gassman), a former Resistance fighter who becomes a young and ambitious lawyer, in Ettore Scola's 1974 film, *C'eravamo tanto amati* (*We All Loved Each Other So Much*). Yet, ten years and major social and political transformation – or rather deterioration – separate the two films. In Rosi's work, the young leftist councillor De Vita is not lured by Nottola's manipulative speech about his fundamentally good intentions as he shows De Vita the interior of one of his new buildings. During the film De Vita is one of the few who mentions and brings forth issues of morality and remains unchanged as the story unfolds, since he is the mouthpiece of an awakened yet now silenced "Other". There is no agreement here with those who maintained at the time of the release of the film that De Vita's character is unconvincing due to the fundamental artificiality and schematism with which he originates discourse in opposition to the logic of power. The repetitiveness of his discourse is the product of his only motivating tension, that of denouncing social conflict and political injustice: he stays clearly on the side of those who lose, those who are dominated, and, insofar as he is their agent and their mouthpiece, he has no reason to bring everything back to an artificial harmony.

There is no consonance in the chilling universe Rosi depicts in *Hands Over the City*, and thus one finds there a young and ardent Jiminy Cricket that reminds the viewer of this disharmony. A decade later, the situation would evolve (or deteriorate) to a point that Scola will no longer be able to afford a fully positive character such as De Vita. His embodiment in *We All Loved Each Other So Much* is Gianni Pelago, who after the war sells out to the corrupt developer, Romolo Catenacci. Having lost sight of the ideals that animated his actions during the civil war, he espouses the logic of the dominators to a point where, later in the film, he changes so profoundly as to become even worse than Catenacci himself. Scola's statement, although within the boundaries of comedy, expresses in the best spirit of a national comedic tradition a thorough indictment of postwar Italy. The fundamental difference between the two films is not the diverse stylistic choices but the target: in Rosi's work the accused is the Italian political class, while in Scola's film it is the entire society in its various class articulations. The only class that is partially "saved" in Scola's film is the working class as embodied by Antonio (Nino Manfredi). This fact ultimately reconnects Scola's film with the ideology of Rosi's discourse, as De Vita essentially speaks for the working class.

The core and true motor of Rosi's discursive strategy, however, is neither Nottola nor De Vita. On the contrary, it is Professor De Angeli, the representative of the Centre, of the Christian Democratic Party, who will eventually become the new Mayor of Naples. He is the mastermind behind the film's elliptic and abstract structure. The core of the story is provided by his meeting with Balsamo, a young representative of his own party, who is in dissent with the party line that wants Nottola to join their group. As a doctor and as the director of the city hospital, Balsamo sympathizes with those who suffer and are expropriated by heartless political rulers. This is exemplified when, at the end of a meeting of the special committee that has to investigate the crushing of the building in Vicolo Sant'Andrea, he asks De Vita to join him for lunch, but first shows him the true victims, the children who live in those asphyxiating neighbourhoods with no air or sun, and especially the boy who has lost his legs during the accident. As Nottola is about to enter the list of candidates to office for the Christian Democratic Party in local elections, Balsamo visits Professor Angeli at his home. The masterfully planned sequence opens with tracking close-ups of paintings as a voice-over asks, "Do you like painting?". As the camera unveils the source of the questions, Professor De Angeli, he is smiling and leading Balsamo (and us) to uncover another beauty hidden in his house, an altar surrounded by walls filled with *ex votos*. After all, quite ironically, his surname means "of the angels" – he is the messenger of Christian planning, since he is the leader of the Christian Democratic Party, a political organisation officially backed by the Catholic Church. When Balsamo questions the appropriateness of being in politics side by side with Nottola, De Angeli begins his long harangue, which constitutes the ideological justification of the crime perpetrated in front of our eyes within and without the film – the speculation that corrupts our environmental, social and political reality:

> Dear Balsamo, we are the ones who make public opinion. A big party such as ours can digest people such as Nottola at any time. Think instead of the responsibility taken on by a politician in face of such dilemma. You can alter the situation drastically, and you don't do it because of a question of moral incompatibility. And the beauty of this is that by doing so you don't destroy the Nottolas, you merely pretend they don't exist.[20]

To this Balsamo answers in outrage: "You seem to imply that power is everything" ("Lei parla così come se il potere fosse tutto"). And promptly and unequivocally comes De Angeli's reply: "Dear Balsamo, in politics moral indignation is of no use. Do you know what is the only mortal sin? To be defeated." ("Caro Balsamo, in politica l'indignazione morale non serve a niente. L'unico grave peccato sa qual è? Quello di essere sconfitti.")

Unquestionably, this is the ideological fulcrum, the chilling philosophy that guides the actions leading to the "crime". The climax will be reached in the sequence where De Angeli manages to lead the exponents of the Right to make peace with the "traitors", Nottola and his accomplices. The atmosphere is that of a black mass, an eerie ceremonial that introduces an element of the uncanny and of surrealism in an otherwise "realistic" story. The ending of *Hands Over the City* serves as a necessary preface to *Cadaveri eccellenti* (*Illustrious Corpses*, 1975), a baroque tale of eminent deaths amongst magistrates and judges in an unnamed southern Italian city. Reality no longer needs to be investigated, as it surpasses imagination in this Kafkaesque tale with Buñuelian tinges, where the trial is over and executions must be performed.

If, prior to *Hands Over the City*, Rosi had any hesitation over the path that had to be taken to overcome neo-realism, with this film his message was loud and clear, and he thereafter continued his work towards the creation and development of his own personal interpretation of realism by focusing quite openly on narration, rather than description. In this he followed the suggestions offered in an Italian context by Visconti, and in the United States by the powerful tradition of cinematic social realism. In opposition to the regressive line followed by other masters of neo-realism, such as Roberto Rossellini and Vittorio De Sica, in the mid-1950s Visconti committed himself to a type of cinematic narration no longer revolving around immediacy and chronicle, but focusing on both documentation of facts and interpretation of reality. It is in this period that the crisis of neo-realistic certitudes occurs, both in the cinema and in literature; this crisis will eventually lead to the innovative trends in both fields expressed in the early 1960s. In 1963, the world of letters recorded the birth of the so-called "Gruppo '63", that is the Italian *neoavanguardia* whose action was entirely ideological in form and content. In the cinema, although never formalised officially, one records a similar innovative and almost revolutionary tension as Italian directors moved definitively away from neo-realism, although choosing diverse discursive strategies. For Rosi and others, such as Gillo Pontecorvo and Elio Petri, the goal was to develop a form of *critical realism* aimed at unmasking the lie behind the surface of things, to make cinema an instrument for knowledge. As Rosi himself once stated:

I strongly believe in cinema as an instrument for a knowledge of things. For instance, let's consider these famous 'Italian mysteries' people talk about...I have investigated these mysteries...worrying not so much about giving answers, since to give answers is the main preoccupation of the traditional mode of filmmaking. I concerned myself more with asking questions, with raising questions to the audience so that the spectator would become a protagonist of the stories, not remaining a passive viewer.[21]

Asking questions instead of giving answers is ultimately a strategy aimed at building within the audience not only the capacity to interpret reality, but also the ability to foresee the effects of present actions on the future. Such an ability is intrinsically significant to the possibility for a radical transformation of society. Ultimately and paradoxically, some of the questions posed by Rosi in many of his films were to be matched by history itself. The recent earthquake in Italian politics enacted by the pool of magistrates called "mani pulite" ("clean hands") finds an anticipation in Rosi's work with such films as *The Mattei Affair*, but most importantly, *Hands Over the City*. Ironically, there is an important moment in the film when, immediately after the falling of the building and during an animated session of the city council, representatives of the majority party, the Right, raise their hands screaming that they are clean. The 1978 murder of Aldo Moro, former Prime Minister of Italy and leader of the Christian Democratic Party, was lucidly foreseen by Rosi's *Illustrious Corpses*, as history is proving that, while the killing was physically enacted by the Brigate Rosse (Red Brigades), mystery surrounds the instigators of Moro's death.

Powerfully grounded in historical materialism, Rosi's method of cinematic investigation of reality declares the deceit concealed behind social harmony, and the contradictions lying behind a political consensus built on lies and false promises. This is his most valuable legacy to the young generation of Italian directors as they are trying to rejuvenate a tradition of critical realism that seemed to have been eclipsed.[22] One ought to distance oneself from the reality and find the necessary detachment to make cinematic works valid in time and for eternity, such as *Hands Over the City*, since, in Rosi's words, "a film when it is successful is valid for eternity and for universality".[23]

Notes

[1] Quoted in Ernest Ferlita and John R May, *The Parables of Lina Wertmüller* (New York: Paulist Press, 1977): 10.

[2] Translated from the Italian: "Poichè *Le mani sulla città* non è arte, ma è politica, ebbene bisogna buttarla in politica...più che cinema è fazioso comizio politico...Francesco Rosi ha fatto un discorso diffamatorio e partigiano, ha realizzato un film marxista". Marco Monti, *Il Secolo d'Italia* 8 January 1964.

[3] Translated from the Italian: "Il peggior film visto...a tutte le mostre di Venezia. E non ci sarà barba di santo, né lettere minatorie che mi potranno far cambiare idea". F M Pranzo, *Corriere Lombardo* 12/13 October 1963.

[4] Translated from the Italian: "No, no e no. Non ci si venga a raccontare che è così che si fa del cinema...Questo non è cinema e non è neanche sana polemica: è comizio, è fazione, è discorso elettorale, trasformato in spettacolo cinematografico solo a scopi politici, con pochissime preoccupazioni culturali ed artistiche." Gian Luigi Rondi, *Il tempo* 6 September 1963.

[5] Translated from the Italian: "Un film splendido...Rosi ha firmato la sua opera più matura. Più matura anche nei confronti di *Salvatore Giuliano*, che eguaglia in drammaticità, ma sopravanza in coerenza e in chiarezza. *Le mani sulla città* parla ancora più lucidamente al pubblico...E' un film-saggio, con l'evidenza di un limpido e documentato studio sociologico...l'unico punto sostanzialmente debole, sul piano dell'arte, ci sembra quello del rapporto interno, dialettico, tra personaggio 'pubblico' e 'privato'." Ugo Casiraghi, *L'unità* 6 September 1963.

[6] Translated from the Italian: "Io penso che la psicologia di un film viene fuori dal montaggio perché *la psicologia di un film non è tanto la psicologia dei personaggi quanto quella della struttura narrativa, delle relazioni del regista, dell'autore con la materia e con i personaggi; non è la psicologia dei vari personaggi intesa e sviluppata una per una*, è il quadro generale della struttura narrativa dalla quale viene fuori una psicologia generale dei personaggi insieme con quella del loro comportamento singolo...Quindi la

vera psicologia è nel montaggio. *Lo psicologo sono io quando faccio il film.*" Quoted in Franca Durazzo Baker (ed), "Sono lo psicologo del film e non del personaggio. Colloquio con Francesco Rosi", *Cinema nuovo* 28: 261 (October 1979): 21. Emphasis in original.

[7] Ibid: 20.

[8] Translated from the Italian: "La distanza che separa *Le mani sulla città* da *Salvatore Giuliano* è notevole...spesso Rosi ha deviato da quella linea razionale di dibattito ideale, che ha dichiarato di aver voluto seguire: i conseguenti scompensi minano fortemente l'unità stilistica del film, ne rendono piuttosto difficile l'accettazione sul piano dell'arte. Ciò non vuol dire che il film non abbia una sua...non trascurabile importanza, che risiede, soprattutto, in due sue innegabili qualità: la scelta del tema e l'intenzionale ripudio dei canoni dello spettacolo." Lorenzo Quaglietti, "Fermenti anticonformistici nei film italiani e inglesi", *Cinema 60* 4: 39 (November 1963): 62-63. See also Stefano Roncoroni, "Evoluzione filmica di Francesco Rosi", in *Filmcritica* 14: 137 (September 1963): 520-528.

[9] Translated from the Italian: "*Le mani sulla città* costituisce per Rosi rispetto a *Salvatore Giuliano* un passo avanti per il più preciso impegno ideologico e per il più forte atteggiamento morale". Roncoroni: 525.

[10] Ibid.

[11] Translated from the Italian: "Questo film, per il suo stile acceso, la sua efficacia polemica e la sua incontestabile generosità, dà la sua patente di nobiltà cinematografica a una estetica del *logos*, fondata sulla parola, cioè l'eloquenza che si poteva credere riservata ad altri mezzi di espressione". Amédée Ayfre in *Télécinè* 113-114 (1963), as quoted in Francesco Bolzoni, *I film di Francesco Rosi* (Rome: Gremese Editore, 1986): 73. More recently, foreign critics have payed homage to Rosi's cinema as testified by the numerous articles appeared in internationally renowned film journals. For example, see Gary Crowdus, "Francesco Rosi. Italy's Postmodern Neorealist", in *Cineaste* 20: 4 (1994): 19-25.

[12] Translated from the Italian: "L'inizio immette subito lo spettatore nella realtà polemica, cruda, violenta, mostrando la città dall'alto, cogliendo il senso agghiacciante di una crescita sproporzionata, fatta senza mediazioni, senza scelta di programmazione. È la radiografia di una città disordinata, una fotografia-documento che coglie, nella realtà, quella verità che si individua con chiarezza dialettica." Edoardo Bruno, "Poesia e impegno civile", *Filmcritica* 14: 139-140 (November-December 1963): 652.

[13] See Michel Ciment, *Le dossier Rosi* (Paris: Editions Ramsay, 1987): 28.

[14] Randone plays Professor De Angeli, the leader of the Centre, which will eventually become the new Mayor of the city of Naples.

[15] Translated from the Italian: "I personaggi del film, anche e proprio in quanto non-personaggi nella comune accezione del termine...sono, ad eccezione di alcuni (Salvo Randone, ad esempio) delineati geometricamente, mancano di quella duttilità indispensabile proprio per esprimere

compiutamente, dialetticamente...la categoria sociale di cui sono il simbolo".
Quaglietti: 62-63.

[16] Translated from the Italian: "Quando i film sono usciti per la prima volta nelle sale italiane mi fu anche rimproverato da una certa critica estetica che vedeva in questo procedimento non tanto una novità ma una povertà di rappresentazione artistica. Ma io mi chiedevo com'è possibile non vedere che questi personaggi sono trattati così per dare più evidenza a un contesto, per dare più evidenza a quello che accade collettivamente nella società perchè il costruttore Nottola in *Mani sulla città* che per raggiungere i suoi interessi coinvolge la politica generale della città e crea il presupposto della corruzione dei vari poteri, del potere politico, del potere economico con la complicità anche della criminalità organizzata, ai miei occhi sembrava estremamente più interessante che occuparmi della psicologia del costruttore Nottola, se avesse avuto una moglie, due amanti, tre figli". Rosi, quoted in Manuela Gieri, "*Le mani sulla città*. Il cinema di Francesco Rosi a Toronto", *Corriere Canadese* 3 November 1994: 7.

[17] Translated from the Italian: "*Le mani sulla città* è, effettivamente, un'opera di carattere oratorio, tende cioè a superare la freddezza didascalica e l'artificio inconfessato di certo cinema-verità con il calore e la sincerità di un discorso che si dichiara apertamente tale, che vuole essere *discorso* e impiega perciò situazioni, sentimenti e personaggi come argomenti, senza finire nell'astrattezza dei simboli o nelle forzature arbitrarie". *Cineforum* 3: 30 (December 1963): 966-967. Zambetti retrieved the analogy for his discussion of *Hands Over the City* included in his volume on Francesco Rosi for Il Castoro Cinema published by La Nuova Italia in 1976. The chapter is indeed entitled "L'oratoria come stile (*Le mani sulla città*)" ("The ars oratoria as style [*Hands Over the City*])": 51-71. Emphasis in original.

[18] His lesson was to be followed by many in Italy, as testified by Gillo Pontecorvo, overwhelmingly in his *La battaglia di Algeri* (*The Battle of Algiers*, 1966) and by Elio Petri, especially with *Indagine su un cittadino al di sopra di ogni sospetto* (*Investigation of a Citizen Above Suspicion*, 1969), but also abroad and even in the United States, as testified by the homage to Rosi at the 1994 presentation of a retrospective of his works at the Lincoln Center in New York paid by US directors such as Oliver Stone, Francis Coppola, Stanley Kubrick, Steven Spielberg and Sidney Lumet.

[19] It is sufficient here to remind one of the conversation between Don Fabrizio, the Prince of Salina, played by Burt Lancaster, and his nephew, Tancredi, played by Alain Delon. To the young man's worry over the events that could change their situation dramatically and take away their power, Fabrizio Salina answers: "If we want everything to stay the same, then everything must change. Did I make myself clear?" ("Se vogliamo che tutto rimanga come è, bisogna che tutto cambi. Mi sono spiegato?"). See Giuseppe Tomasi di Lampedusa, *Il gattopardo* (Milan: Feltrinelli, 1985): 21.

[20] "Caro Balsamo, l'opinione pubblica la facciamo noi. Un grande partito come il nostro, i Nottola li può digerire quando vuole. Ma pensi piuttosto alla responsabilità che si assume un uomo politico di fronte a questo dilemma. Lei può cambiare la situazione da così a così e non lo fa per una

questione di incompatibilità morale. E il bello è che facendo così lei non distrugge i Nottola, fa solo finta che non esistano."

[21] Translated from the Italian: "Credo molto nella funzione di partecipazione del cinema al processo di conoscenza delle cose. Per esempio, prendiamo la questione di questi famosi 'misteri italiani' di cui si parla tanto...questi misteri io li ho indagati". Quoted in Gieri: 7.

[22] Such a tension is powerfully testified by the films of Gianni Amelio, Silvio Soldini, Carlo Mazzacurati, but also of Gabriele Salvatores who, even though moving within the tradition of Italian cinematic comedy at its best, nevertheless makes a cinema aimed at questioning the foundations of Italian contemporary historical, social and thus political discourse in the name of "realism".

[23] Translated from the Italian: "Un film quando riesce è un film che è valido per l'eternità e per l'universalità". Quoted in Gieri: 7.

Enrico Mattei: the man who fell to earth

Harry Lawton

The freebooter, or swashbuckler, has made regular appearances in Italian history, in the guise of a free-ranging gun (or sword) for hire, hiding out in the mountains at the head of an armed band, swooping down into the valleys to plunder in the name of some rapacious patron or now-forgotten cause. Occasionally he dons the mantle of Robin Hood to be embraced by a stoic population of peasants labouring under the yoke of an immemorial poverty, who detect in his vigour and defiance an enactment of their desperate battle with authority. The tradition stretches back through a lineage of anonymous banditry to medieval and Renaissance *condottieri* such as the Englishman Sir John Hawkwood (known to Italians as Giovanni Acuto)[1] and the Medici, Giovanni delle Bande Nere.[2] In more modern times it has extended to those who began on the outside and ended up in service to, or in charge of, a centralised authority. Examples include Giuseppe Garibaldi, the embodiment of the altruistic guerrilla, and even Benito Mussolini, whose *squadre* certainly made him an outlaw until he was invited to assume supreme power. From an historical point of view, this figure of roving gadfly, who can appear simultaneously as hero and menace, is a sign of the traditional fragmentation of the peninsula and the corresponding distrust felt by most citizens towards central authority.

Given that tradition, it is only logical that at least three key films of Francesco Rosi, a director with a sharp eye for history, are studies of recent examples of the political and industrial maverick: *Salvatore Giuliano* (1961), *Il caso Mattei* (*The Mattei Affair*, 1972) and *Lucky Luciano* (1973). None of these films is remotely similar to certain Hollywood biographies (or "bio-pics"), a popular genre of the 1930s and beyond, which were in fact hagiographies sanctifying the life and achievements of a world-famous personality, and serving as a backdrop to the performance of a star. Rosi's focus on personality is purely political. His characters are chosen because they embody an identifiable crisis at a precise moment in the life of the republic, whether banditry, government monopoly or criminality. The lives of the men he has chosen to represent on screen were intimately and often agonisingly intertwined with the workings of the state. Such intimacy ranges from acute antagonism to an alliance of convenience. Each case nevertheless underlines a constant feature of Rosi's cinema, linking almost all his films (certainly the major ones) in a coherent discourse. The theme that fascinates the director is the handling of power in Italy in the contexts of governance, economic control and political influence. The probing and analysis extend to the lives of ordinary people ignorant of how they are ruled or whom they serve. Excluded, therefore, from Rosi's screenplays are distracting forms of melodrama and the details of private lives, including the theme of love (note the minimal appearances of the wife in *The Mattei Affair*). It is evident that the arena of power, whether relating to Sicilian separatism, the Mafia or the politics of oil, is an exclusively male preserve, and the feminine presence is reduced to a minimum.

The very title of *The Mattei Affair* reminds us that each of these characters has been chosen because each is, in fact, a *caso*, a case-study of the ways in which power is used, dispensed and abused in Italy. These studies are of recent figures, each film being made within ten years of the protagonist's death. Rosi is part-artist, part-investigative journalist. His work has always had a contemporary impact on the viewer, as he keeps the public mind riveted on issues which simply will not go away, and to which the citizen must remain alert as a matter of civic duty. This consistent form of enquiry underlines a basic irony in postwar Italian history (one that may well be applied to other politically advanced Western States): in a republic born out of the collapse of a totalitarian regime, with constitutionally established institutions the guarantors of a functioning parliamentary democracy, there remains a curious residue of monopolistic groups, together with traditional habits of mind, that not only place democracy in jeopardy, but also underline its fragility. In fixing our gaze not on the personalities of his protagonists, but on the issues which their lives and deaths raise, Rosi remains faithful to his own beginnings in Italian neo-realism, and specifically to his apprenticeship to Visconti on *La terra trema* (*The Earth Trembles*, 1948). That film too was one of enquiry, an historical study, and a work which emphasised the economic and political dimensions of the central characters.

The thread linking the bandit (Giuliano), the oilman (Mattei) and the gangster (Luciano) is their maverick status. The fact that two of them are Sicilians established their credentials as outsiders from birth, and the condition of Sicily is a factor binding together all three careers. Mattei himself was a northerner who came to Sicily with ambitious plans for industrial expansion in an attempt to bring prosperity and opportunity to the land and its people. There he ran into opposition both open and covert, and Rosi's film adds to the speculation that some of the forces opposed to Mattei conspired in his

61

death.

Giuliano and Luciano, as native Sicilians, take a more predictable road out of the wretchedness of the island's condition – that of violence – but with quite different purposes. Giuliano dramatises his civic alienation as a Sicilian in extreme political form, by challenging the state head-on and becoming a bandit. Adopting the dubious cause of separatism, he convinces himself that he is doing something for his fellow islanders. Certainly in their eyes he is a saviour and martyr. In the end, we must acknowledge his naïvety in not recognising that he serves as a pawn for powerful paymasters, major landowners and important Mafia leaders, who, once they see him as a liability, have him shot and hand his corpse over to the military police. Giuliano is the first of many corpses in Rosi's œuvre whose death would be the subject of lengthy enquiry ultimately resisting complete explanation.

The story of Lucky Luciano is that of the emigrant's dream of riches in the United States. His way to that goal is through criminal violence, not honest endeavour. As depicted by Rosi, the American mob is an extension of the Sicilian Mafia, whose methods are adapted to the demands of the modern metropolis. The mob operates as an underground version of a capitalist enterprise run on corporate lines. The state, represented by its ambitious Attorney General, Thomas Dewey, jailed Giuliano for 30 years on prostitution charges, but released him only a few years later (the same Thomas Dewey now being Governor of New York) for his contribution to the war effort.[3] While granted pardon for his patriotic contribution, he was also deported (to save the state's face) as an undesirable, and immediately went into the international drug business. In the case of Luciano, Rosi established with lucid irony the close and contradictory relationship between the activities of the criminal outsider and established central power – a recurrent theme in his work.

Mattei's relationship with state power is at once more complex and intimate. His position initially is not that of an antagonist. He is both a creature of the power structure, while also, from the start of his career, at odds with his masters. As a member of the Democrazia Cristiana (Christian Democratic Party), with a distinguished resistance record, Mattei was the ideal choice to run Italy's energy industry after the Second World War. From the start it was clear that he would run his agency as a virtually autonomous empire, but always (as he proclaimed) with the national interest at heart. His policies and administrative methods created formidable enemies for him as he pursued his initiatives. In dealing with the Soviet Union and Eastern bloc nations, he angered the Western powers and the forces of NATO. In moving into the Middle East, he antagonised the major international oil companies. His move into Tunisia was seen as a threat to French interests in Algeria. Later we can examine the hostility that faced him in Sicily. Sicily marks Mattei's last public appearance. It is linked to his death by the fact that his private planes took off from the airport at Catania. Surrounding circumstances suggest that this is more than a matter of coincidence. Mattei's violent death is a further example of the risks attendant on the career of the maverick. Such a death should not surprise us in the case of a bandit or gangster, who chooses violence as a means of survival or conquest. But a public servant should not have to assume that his efforts in the public interest, even when they break the mould of established protocol, would result in the same risks. That this is indeed the case turns Mattei's career and demise into a legitimate object of public scrutiny, adding a chapter to Rosi's consistent enquiry into the conduct of Italian public life.

In *The Mattei Affair* the protagonist dominates the action; his charismatic presence controls the narrative flow. His is a complex and contradictory figure who inspires mixed emotions. He rejoices in what he believes is his mandate to apply power for the public and national good. Listening to Mattei's arguments justifying his means feels like observing in practice what can be read in theory in the pages of Machiavelli's *Il principe* (*The Prince*), which is itself a primer for the buccaneering tradition in Italian politics, and in which decidedly unorthodox action is justified in the name of the broader public interest. *Corsaro* ("pirate" or buccaneer"), therefore, is an apt word to describe the man and his career, a man who demolishes the received image of the Italian as the passive recipient of fate. Notwithstanding the dynamic examples of Agnelli and Olivetti in the annals of Italian capitalism, Mattei might have modelled himself on American captains of industry (Ford, Carnegie or Rockefeller, for example). Naturally, in his aggressive challenge to entrenched power at home and abroad, Mattei made many enemies. His death (the point of departure of Rosi's film) needed investigating, and the subsequent legal enquiry revealed only that it could have come from a variety of sources.

Rosi chose Mattei's life and career not as an example of personal success resulting from of natural talent and inexhaustible energy, but as an historical event that illuminates a very particular Italian crisis at a delicate moment in the country's development. Notoriously, Italy is a country blessed in its geographical position more than in its geological resources. It arrived late at industrialisation, deprived of almost any coal reserves and (as would be verified later) natural oil supplies. Since the Risorgimento, the country has had to depend on foreign sources of fuel for its industrial development and defence needs. Among the notable failures of Fascism was not developing a national energy policy. An immediate challenge facing the first postwar Italian administration was to fill the gap left by the Fascists and establish a coherent energy plan – one that would ensure the country's industrial viability, guarantee access to expanding international markets, and prove Italy's reliable membership in the Western Alliance.

Enrico Mattei was the ideal candidate to head this effort and thus restore a heavily damaged industrial base. From his mid-twenties he had managed his own chemical manufacturing plant in Milan. He had a distinguished record in the Resistance, and was a loyal member of the Christian Democratic Party. Thus, the Christian Democrats had no need to worry about a man with a tainted past, and could look approvingly towards his previous experience as a manager.

Mattei's first assignment was to liquidate Agenzia Generale Italiana Petroli (AGIP), of which he had been put in charge, partly because it was a virtually comatose public agency, and partly because it was a relic from the Fascist era. What the government had in mind was for Mattei to negotiate reliable energy supplies from existing foreign distributors, rather than concentrate on national exploration and production. Mattei had other ideas, and AGIP was to serve as the basis of his plan. He had heard reports of vast methane gas fields in the Po Valley. He resisted government directives to liquidate his agency, while publishing tempting and deceptive announcements about untapped petroleum reserves, together with methane, in the same area. In the event, major deposits of methane were discovered at Cortemaggiore in 1949, but no oil. The episode is indicative of Mattei's methods. He was prepared to deceive on a large issue (in this case, mythical oil supplies), while delivering on at least 50% of the gamble. Certainly the discovery of the vast deposits of methane did much to improve living standards in northern Italy, and made Mattei a popular national figure. The next stage was to establish a national distribution system through the construction of a pipeline network, and then to create a related web of industrial enterprises dependent on the production and refinement of gas and oil. The initiatives taken by Mattei in the early 1950s announced a clear intention to free Italy from dependence on the major oil companies (the majority of which were American, known at the time as "the Seven Sisters") which effectively controlled every stage of the production of oil and, of course, its price on the world market. Mattei's policies thereafter placed the Italian government in a dilemma. While the standard of living rose and industry (at least in the north) expanded, Mattei's direct challenge to the oil giants angered powerful interests, and through them Italy's major sponsor and guarantor (the United States) in the Cold War era.

In 1953 Ente Nazionale Idrocarburi (ENI) was formed. This was an enormous national holding company with overall responsibility for the financing and supervision of all government agencies involved with energy exploration and distribution. As head of ENI, Mattei became Italy's energy tsar, directing the production and distribution of national gas at home and leading the continuous search for oil abroad. Officially a branch of a nationalized industry, ENI under Mattei acted autonomously and frequently in defiance of government directives. Mattei envisaged an expansion eastwards, planning a pipeline through Eastern Europe into the Soviet Union, and the construction of oil platforms in the Persian Gulf. The battle was also fought on the political front, with ENI money channelled towards those political parties and individual politicians who supported Mattei in his aggressive search for energy sources, which was seen as a series of steps towards full employment. Understanding the power of the press and the need for a high profile in order to have an impact on public opinion, Mattei even founded and financed (with ENI funds) the Milanese daily newspaper, *Il Giorno*, to air his views and respond to his critics. Rosi's film shows Mattei alert to the expanding medium of television and the role it would play in national life and in shaping people's political beliefs. It shows him cultivating journalists (a staff writer for *Time*, William McHale, died with him on his plane). We also see how his whole career suddenly comes into being, the segmented parts being arranged into a comprehensive whole by way of a television documentary put together immediately after his death, in the form of a transcendental tribute. Television raises Mattei's life to a mythic status (in a process similar to the mythical elevation of the life of President Kennedy following his assassination).

Certainly the most controversial aspects of Mattei's career concern his foreign interests. In striking deals directly with oil-producing countries in the Middle East and North Africa, Mattei tore up the established "50-50" arrangement whereby the host government and the foreign oil company equally split all profits on sales. Mattei offered a 75%-25% arrangement to the advantage of the host country, provoking outcries in international oil circles. When he signed the agreement with the Soviet Union in 1960, guaranteeing a market for much cheaper Russian oil in exchange for Italian industrial goods and technology, it was a breach of the barriers between Eastern and Western Europe, established by the Cold War since 1945. Such an initiative received rapturous applause from Italy's Communist Party, but provoked downright anger at the State Department in the White House in Washington, and in NATO circles in Europe. For some, Mattei was Public Enemy Number 1.

Further interference in foreign affairs was evident in the expansion into North Africa. Not only was Mattei active in Tunisia, but also, most disturbingly from the French point of view, he made approaches to the leaders of the National Liberation Front in Algeria even before it had won independence. Incurring the open wrath of the diehard Organisation de l'Armée Secrète (OAS),[4] formed of ex-paratroopers and military men implacably opposed to Algerian independence, Mattei met with Ben Bella, the new head of the Algerian government, shortly after the signing of the Peace Treaty at Evian. Mattei's policy on this front had always been consistent. Cheap crude for Italy could offer a steady stream of foreign currency to the governments of Third World countries that desperately needed to build up their economies and raise the living standards of their impoverished populations. The same impulse prompted ENI's policy in southern Italy, where only an infusion of money and industrial expansion could reduce unemployment, poverty and the mass annual emigration of southerners seeking jobs abroad. It is true that ENI moved rather late into the south, and in Sicily it found itself in competition with Gulf Oil, who had begun to develop a promising field at Ragusa, leaving Gela to the Italian conglomerate where the discovery of crude was far less than expected, and of low quality. Nevertheless, Mattei's last recorded public appearance was in the Sicilian village of Gagliano Castelferrato, during which he hammered home his theme that the reason for ENI's expansion on the island was to produce jobs for the local population. It was on the return flight to Milan, on his private plane, that Mattei died in the crash recorded at the start of Rosi's film.

* * *

For Rosi, the end is the beginning. Like *Salvatore Giuliano*, *The Mattei Affair* starts with the death of the protagonist. The opening images of the film, in sound and vision, thrust us with shattering immediacy into the midst of crisis. The roar of an engine intensifies over the credits, then stops. Anxious looks in the Milan airport control tower confirm our fears. Flashing lights from the emergency vehicles announce the doomed search for survivors in a driving rainstorm. Meanwhile, the announcement of the crash, the timing, and the list of those on board are broadcast impassively by the teleprinter at the bottom of the screen. The first moments of the film establish a set of principles that the director will faithfully follow throughout. The division of the narrative material into fragments necessitates the disruption of a chronological order, the method favoured in *Salvatore Giuliano*, and here notably refined and extended. The form of the film is dictated by the idea of an inquiry into a mystery that resists easy explanation. The film will, in fact, end on the dual note of denunciation and the question mark. The nature of this inquiry will require the assemblage of a host of scattered pieces of information which will finally assume an almost comprehensive whole, but even that will not yield the definitive answer to the question of who killed Enrico Mattei.

Rosi's method in *The Mattei Affair* is most clearly illustrated by the twin lines of imagery he adopts throughout the film. One is the idea of fragmentation; the other is journalism. Those scattered scraps of wreckage and body parts are to Rosi what they are to the official investigators: the pathetic remnants of a life and its tragic dénouement, and a much more pressing intellectual and moral challenge to all engaged in the enquiry to find meaning in what one American journalist describes as "twenty pounds of flesh and bone". The sight later in the film of the remains of the plane assembled for analysis in an aircraft hangar, and arranged in an impressionistic reminder of the vehicle itself, could serve as an analogy of the task facing the director, engaged in extracting a coherent whole out of an assortment of miscellaneous parts.

Form and content are fused in the idea of the enquiry: one that will go beyond and last longer than the official investigation launched by the government and the courts. It is, in fact, the constant references to investigative journalism, both printed and electronic, which hold the film together. Rosi identifies himself with the figure of the investigative journalist, placing himself at the scene of the crash simultaneously with the police and government officials. His actual intervention in his own scenario is striking. There he is in the field at Bescapé the morning after, questioning a witness. There he is a while later examining slides of political personalities as he starts to assemble the film's material. There he is on the telephone to the Sicilian journalist, Mauro De Mauro. And, of course, towards the end of the film he will conduct a further enquiry into the unexplained disappearance of De Mauro several years later. Not only does Rosi fill his screen with journalistic images (press conferences, newsreels, news broadcasts, headlines superimposed on the screen, and so on), but also he presents his film as a documentary in progress. On the night of Mattei's death he documents the mobilisation of the news department at RAI as it prepares a newsreel tribute to the deceased president of ENI. He then frames this television film with his own work which will take us far beyond that official and selective presentation of Mattei's life designed only for immediate consumption.

The crash occurred at night, but an essential visual pattern established in the first few minutes of the film is that of light from a variety of sources, marking a need to peel away the layers of darkness surrounding the mystery of the accident. Firstly, there are the windows of the ENI skyscraper in Milan lighting up in response to the first announcement of the disaster. Then we note the bombardment of the flash bulbs of the photographers hovering ghoulishly around the widow, requesting one more picture. A third image of light comes from a bank of television monitors in an RAI studio in Rome, where a documentary on Mattei's life is immediately being assembled for tomorrow's news. Rosi has arranged these images in an ascending order of importance, and has associated in our minds the square lit windows of the ENI building with the square shape of the screens in the television studio. It is as if the news emanating from the energy agency's headquarters has been instantly communicated to the government-controlled medium of information, thence to be transmitted to the world. This is Rosi's major point: with remarkable compression he conveys the readiness of television to absorb and collate news and almost instantaneously project it around the world. These images of television's global reach are less "contemporary" (i.e. a rendition of the actual technological state of television in 1962) than prophetic: a statement on the potential power of the medium and how it would reshape political discourse, and the way in which the world public would absorb information in the decades to come. 30 years ago, the print medium was equally instantaneous. Spliced into these sequences are scenes of communication between the *Time* offices in Rome and New York. Obviously, the death of Mattei was of immediate interest in American oil circles. *Time* was involved, given the death of one of their journalists, William McHale, on that last flight. Interestingly, the editors of *Time* find it politic to downplay the Mattei story by requesting only 500 words on his life and death. However, Rosi's point is that, while print journalism had probably reached its apogee in the early 1960s, its dominance of the world of information was already being challenged. Most people around the world now receive (and were then starting to receive) their information from the small screen. And how much more dramatic it was for the public to observe the fragments of Mattei's life, to see him move and hear his voice in their own living-rooms, than to read about him in the cooler, more distanced medium of the newspaper.

The news documentary put together in the RAI studios on the night of Mattei's death excludes a scene in which Mattei tells a story, which it appears he often liked to tell, about a little kitten trying to eat from the food bowl of a large dog. The dog grabbed the kitten by the neck, shook it violently and hurled it to the ground, where it died. For Mattei, this incident became an allegory: the kitten represented Italy looking for its share of oil, and the angry dog stood for the consortium of the major international oil companies, jealously guarding their preserve. When Rosi has his protagonist repeat this anecdote to an American oil executive later in the film, Mattei will add that Italy is tired of playing the role of the kitten. The programme director assembling the film cuts that scene on the grounds that it is too polemical. He works for RAI, a government-controlled medium, and this is not the moment to show anything that American companies or government officials might construe as provocative. Rosi's message could not be more pointed, that all television programmes are subject to political and commercial pressures that directly affect their content. By implication, film (above all, the investigative films that he makes) is far more independent, and this film in particular will move beyond the self-censorship which RAI imposes.

The structure of the film is built on journalistic method. Mattei, the continuous subject of enquiry, was himself a skilled manipulator of the press and of journalists. He knew exactly when to confront them when under fire, when to flatter them with the offer of an exclusive interview or a ride on his plane. He financed *Il Giorno*, designed as the voice of ENI – or rather of its master. Mattei used the media in order to construct his own public personality. Rosi's film consequently offers a fragmented portrait of its subject by way of a collage of film strips, interviews, press conferences, television programmes and news bulletins, swinging back and forth between Mattei's self-defence and hostile inquiries into his policies.

Mattei's close rapport with the political power structure is illustrated by a film strip in which Ferruccio Parri,[5] Italy's first postwar Prime Minister and an old ally in the Resistance, explains why he could not give his approval to his old comrade to drill for methane in the Po Valley, and that Mattei's primary task after the war was the liquidation of the once-Fascist corporation, AGIP. Mattei responds to this (in a scene shot in colour) by reconstructing a direct appeal to a Milanese banker for a loan that would permit drilling to proceed. This illusion of an actual dialogue between the real Parri and the "fictional" (or reconstructed) Mattei dramatises a living tension between Mattei and government, dating from the moment of his appointment. The fact that the following sequences record the great discovery of methane at Cortemaggiore, setting the impact of industrial expansion against the images of a peasant culture, shows how Mattei won the debate by simply going beyond words and following his own instincts. This point in his career is marked by another journalistic marker: his face frozen on a magazine cover with a justifiable smile of triumph, while a diagram resembling cracked glass, representing the extent of AGIP's pipeline, spreads beyond the Po Valley into central Italy.

Portraits of political personalities taken from contemporary newspaper archives are used to summarize Mattei's awkward relationship with the leaders of the Christian Democratic Party. Photographs of Don Sturzo,[6] De Gasperi,[7] Vanoni[8] and Scelba[9] are accompanied by a brief commentary by Rosi himself, by now engaged in assembling material for his film. His intervention at this point is much more than informational. He has chosen to become a participant in his own film, and allies himself with other investigative journalists who have pursued the mystery of Mattei's death independently and at some professional risk. Rosi assumes the voice of an aroused public which (a decade later) seriously doubts the official explanations of the industrialist's death. The alliance with a band of independent journalists is made clear at the end of this sequence, when he places a call to the correspondent Mauro De Mauro, who in 1970 was working on Mattei's last visit to Sicily. Collaboration between Rosi and reporter is thus established, and the director will return to this theme later in the film.

The heart of *The Mattei Affair* occurs over a series of extended sequences, each one tightly linked to the others in a powerfully calculated intellectual flow, that comprise an ongoing debate with a journalist and critic. These sequences are placed at the centre of the film, beginning just before the end of the first half, and continuing into the second. What we witness is a tour conducted by Mattei of ENI's international operations, intended both as a defence of his policies in response to his opponents, and as an informative summary for the bulk of Rosi's viewers. The didactic element dominates; in addition, we are reminded of the fundamental principle to which Rosi has remained faithful since his apprenticeship with Visconti on *The Earth Trembles*: the educational responsibility of cinema.

A frame of reference for the industrial tour is provided by the television discussion programme, *Tribuna Politica* (*Political Forum*), shot in the RAI studios. A bank of reporters pepper the minister with overall responsibility for public agencies (and thus Mattei's immediate superior) with questions on the policies and fiscal responsibility of the president of ENI. These questions amount to an undisguised attack on Mattei and his management style, and on the minister for failing to exercise control over his charge. In vain, the moderator requests that his colleagues simply put questions to the guest, and refrain from *ad hominem* attacks on the absent Mattei. He is accused of creating a state within a state, his own autonomous empire impervious to official enquiry; of funnelling funds into the coffers of parties and individual politicians whom he courts for support; of involvement with the Secret Services; and of financing his own newspaper out of tax revenues. One journalist refers to ENI debits amounting to over half a billion dollars, which remain unaccounted for. Another, quoting his own recently published article, declares that the annual financial records of the agency need to be looked into by the legal branch of the tax collecting services, and by Italy's Ministry of Justice.

In this framing sequence, Rosi focuses on the power of television to shine a spotlight on the workings of government, and on the medium's impact on public opinion (or at least that body of viewers who actually tune into this programme). Rosi must acknowledge the necessity of a free press in a functioning democracy, and its positive investigative role; it is, after all, a role he has chosen for himself. The focus here, nevertheless, is on the object of the enquiry. Fuming at the unaccustomed role of passive spectator in which he has been cast, Mattei goes on the offensive. He first calls the minister who tried to field the questions on the programme, and, speaking in the familiar, denounces him for his ineffective defence. He then concentrates on the conservative journalist who led the verbal assault, and summons him to his office the following day.[10] This character is modelled on Indro Montanelli who, in a series of articles in the *Corriere della Sera* in July 1962, levelled the charges against Mattei's handling of ENI, now summarized and dramatised in Rosi's film in the form of a whirlwind tour of inspection of ENI's holdings.[11]

Mattei's strategy of inviting a leading critic into his camp and providing him with the information that may help modify the accusations, is designed to flatter and cajole through courtesy and hospitality. What journalist, after all, would not be subject to the flattery of a major political figure putting time at his disposal, with the promise of an exclusive that could only be a feather in a writer's cap? This crucial segment of the film, therefore, serves two related functions. It illustrates Mattei's willingness to exploit the media for the defence and promotion of his policies. It further offers the opportunity, in dramatically visual terms, for Mattei in person to explain through the journalist to the public at large the reasoning behind his energy policies and the way in which they serve the national interest. The result is that Mattei emerges from these scenes strengthened and justified, having been photographed at work, on the sites of ENI oil platforms and wells. The journalist, so loquacious on television the previous night, while retaining his scepticism and voicing a series of critical questions, is caught off-balance and forced into the subordinate role of guest and spectator.

Rosi thus offers a dynamic portrait of Mattei at the dead centre of his film, while his defence of his character against charges in the right-wing press comes with attendant ironies. The director must know that he is defending someone who did disguise the way he disbursed huge sums of taxpayers' money, and who regarded himself as beyond the reach of government scrutiny (and parliamentary oversight). Rosi even has Mattei acknowledge that he may have made some payments to some neo-Fascist groups if that might have garnered some political support in areas where he planned to expand. He does so in a cynical image ("I use the Fascists as I would a taxi"), according to which all is justified if the job gets done. There is an air of arrogance about Mattei, born of populism, characteristic of those animated by a vision, and unconcerned with the appearance of illegality and impropriety.

In order to polish an image of financial austerity, before the journalist arrives, Mattei issues an order cancelling company cars for all its top executives, whether or not they have a driver's licence. He then defends the expense of a private plane, which will in fact be justified by the type of journey they are both about to undertake. The jet allows him instant access to ENI sites of exploration; he can be just about anywhere, when summoned by crisis, within hours, while remaining in radio contact with the agency's managers and engineers worldwide. The plane is no executive's toy (says Mattei): it gives substance to the image he wishes to promote of himself as a hands-on manager; it is a badge of ubiquity and command. He resides in a modest suite in a Milan hotel; it is certainly comfortable, but by no means luxurious, the emphasis being on its convenience and central location. This is a man who does not take holidays, and whose only occasional indulgence is a fishing trip in the lakes. As he drives the journalist to his flat, it is emphasised that Mattei does not have a chauffeur. In addition, he stops at one of the famous AGIP service stations, not because he needs the petrol, but to see whether the attendant who wipes his window smiles as he does so. This pause is a form of quality-control.

Only at the last minute does the journalist realise that Mattei plans to take him along on a tour of inspection. Caught without an overnight bag or a toothbrush, he must make a hasty call home to announce an abrupt change of schedule. Mattei may well have planned this from the start. The journalist is caught off-balance and hands the psychological advantage to his generous host. Each place where Mattei takes his companion on their 24-hour tour of ENI holdings in North Africa and the Middle East is an emblem of the extent of an expanding empire (which looks as if it is the creation of a single man). Each is a dot on an advancing map, representing not only Italy's, but also the world's insatiable thirst for oil. Not a word is said about the dangers to the environment, nor about the excess of consumerism.

The first stop is at El Bormia in Tunisia. Here, against the backdrop of a desert sky, huge flames of methane gas testify to ENI's determination to tap the enormous resources beneath these sands. It is an even more dramatic demonstration than that at Cortemaggiore of the intrusion of modern technology into an ancient, even primitive culture. The roar of the flames forces the conversation to be conducted at a shout. Mattei defiantly refers to his continuous battle with American oil interests that are already actively engaged, obviously with French permission and cooperation, on the other side of the border in Algeria. This hints at mounting tension between the French government, at that time engaged in the struggle to contain the demand for Algerian independence, and himself as the head of ENI. Throughout the film, Mattei never disguises his support of what he regards as the legitimate cause of Arab independence, which he also sees as a rich business and industrial opportunity – "If you deal in oil, you are involved in foreign policy", is one of his mottoes.

The great oil port of Abadan in Iran sets the scene for historical reflections. In the early 1950s, the then-Prime Minister, Dr Mossadeq, had attempted to nationalize the Anglo-Iranian Oil Company. In defence of Western investments, the CIA organised a coup against Mossadeq, and his government was overthrown. A much more reliable government was installed under the young Shah to guarantee stability in the area and to protect Western interests. As he now flies over the Iranian oil fields, Mattei has reason for satisfaction regarding Italian activity in the country. In 1954, in the name of ENI, he had applied for a limited partnership in the Anglo-Iranian Oil Company, and had been turned down. His next step was to approach the Iranian government directly for drilling rights and permission to send Italian tankers into Abadan. In exchange, he offered a guaranteed market for Iranian crude to be refined in Italian facilities. By dealing directly with a foreign oil-producing regime, he was thus able to bypass the monopoly of the seven major international oil companies. What he now observes from the air (a tanker steaming into the port of Abadan, for example) represents the fruit of that policy.

The next stop is an oil platform in the Persian Gulf: an example of the sophistication of Italian technology that is making inroads into the Third World. Italy may not have oil, but it has technology in the form of pipelines, platforms, drilling rigs and tankers to offer and export to the Soviet Union, Iran, Tunisia and elsewhere, in exchange for the crude she can then refine in the installations ENI is building along the Adriatic Coast and in the south. While apologising for the relatively modest living conditions of the workers (the canteen, the tiny bedrooms with bunk-beds), Mattei can take pride in the complexities of the whole operation, and in the cleanliness and efficiency with which the drilling and the domestic arrangements are coordinated. The oil platform stands as a symbol that Italy is a fixture in the Persian Gulf, and in any other international oilfield, and that its independent stance has gained it permanent status as a player, a position accepted with whatever reluctance by the oil giants of the rival major powers.

A final shot of Mattei in this series of sequences places him in front of an oil derrick somewhere in the North African desert, contemptuously dismissing those (such as the journalist at this moment) who mock him as a modern Joan of Arc listening to voices no one else hears. The derrick itself illustrates that Mattei has based his calculations on much more than voices. His main claim is that all his actions have been animated by the desire to rev up the dormant economies of emerging nations and that of the Italian south, to allow the world's poor to participate in potential global prosperity. If this also means breaching the barriers established by the Cold War (such as direct trade with the Soviet Union and its satellites), so much the better. Mattei never saw himself as the docile servant of the party in power, itself a silent partner in the Western Alliance. The defiant speech, with its emphatic visual setting, shows how much Mattei always relished the role of buccaneer. Together with the reasoned altruism of his arguments, we note the personal pleasure in the assertion of his own will, his frank desire to leave his signature on this period of history. Rosi brings this chapter of the film to a climax on a both defiant and fatalistic note. Mattei refers to those before him who have defied the oil establishment in the search for energy independence, and to the price they have paid. He will not be intimidated, he says. If necessary, he will go to India, to Australia, in a never-ending fight against "this absurd monopoly". Mattei's intransigence is precisely what put his life in jeopardy; and these are the words with which Rosi chooses to end his film, replaying them over the final images of the scene of the crash at Bescapé.

From this desert sequence, Rosi now cuts to an evening news telecast dated 17 September 1970, announcing the disappearance of the Sicilian journalist, Mauro De Mauro. Thus, this whole range of sequences is set in the framework of journalists at work conducting very different inquiries, and of references to television. De Mauro (a correspondent for the Palermo daily, *L'ora*) is the same journalist whom Rosi telephoned earlier in the film, seeking any pertinent information. De Mauro's disappearance is directly linked to the Mattei affair, since the reporter was working on the story of Mattei's last visit to Sicily. All that is known is that he had arranged an interview with an unknown party, and that he had not returned from that appointment. From a press room in a Palermo hotel, journalists phone home reports to their respective newspapers. All admit that they are working in the dark, and that all they can do is list the more credible hypotheses. There are two repeated themes in these separate reports: that the disappearance of De Mauro is a further chapter in the mystery of Mattei's death; and that in Sicily many are convinced that Mattei did not die accidentally.

Two motifs dominate the last half-hour of the film. One is the meaning of the presence of Mattei in Sicily, and his plans for industrial development on the island; the second is the actual presence of Rosi in his own film. The author of the film is seen conducting his independent inquiry. Connections between the disappearance of De

Mauro and Mattei's death are beyond doubt, and the assumption is that the reporter has been removed for the sin of getting to know too much. In a scene in which the director discusses this story with a group of journalists (who now find themselves investigating the loss of an investigator, and doubtless reflecting over the dangers of their profession), they complain that in Sicily the promise of concrete evidence in a case of this nature has a tendency to vanish into thin air. Proprietors of newspapers also seem to be involved in a conspiracy of silence. Stories worthy of front-page coverage today are buried soon after on the inside pages, only to disappear altogether should the same story prove embarrassing to anyone close to the centres of power. A veteran correspondent sums up by saying that a tradition of cynicism, amounting to a controlled flow of the news, originates in Palermo and is now spreading north.

The scenes involving Rosi with journalists and other experts on the Mafia and this case fracture the chronological unfolding of events. This is characteristic of his narrative method, and he shunts the viewer forward in time so as to cast the light of hindsight onto the circumstances surrounding Mattei's death. We are in the process of watching the director putting his case together, and with him we work at its completion, piece by piece. Rosi's identification with the journalists, whom he now places centre-stage in the drama, is his way of endorsing their role in a fully functioning democracy. The work of the investigative journalist will often run counter to an official government-sponsored report, and it can even put a career or a life in danger. However, it is still necessary if the public is to remain informed. Rosi's film is a work of independent inquiry (likewise the reports of the journalists we see around him). It thus stands in juxtaposition to the bland encomium of Mattei's life broadcast by RAI on the night of his death.

Although Rosi – no more than the judge who conducted the official inquiry – cannot name the actual killers or the group that hired them, he can point to some damaging circumstantial evidence that counters the hypothesis that the crash was an accident caused by bad weather. He conducts interviews with two experts on the affair, one academic, one professional: Michele Pantaleone and Thyraud de Vosjoli. The former is an internationally known scholar of the Mafia;[12] the latter is the retired ex-director of the anti-espionage branch of the French Secret Service. Pantaleone is actually photographed with Rosi as he declares that, on the day of Mattei's departure from Catania, there was no police surveillance on the runway to secure Mattei's plane. He follows this assertion with a series of questions. The very form of the question is significant; for each one is in reality a denunciation, although it cannot yield an answer. In miniature here is the form of Rosi's film. Pantaleone asks: Who gave orders to remove the police or *carabinieri* from the job to which they were assigned? Who replaced them? Where are these men today? And who is protecting them?[13]

Thyraud de Vosjoli offers even more damaging information. One is immediately on the alert, given Mattei's activities in North Africa. De Vosjoli, who is interviewed in New York and replies to the questions in English, has written a book about his old agency, devoting a chapter to Mattei.[14] In his accusations, he is a little more precise than Pantaleone. He refers directly to sabotage, and does name a name. It is, however, an assumed name, a *nom de guerre* – "Laurent", a man of Corsican origin speaking perfect Italian, an agent working for the French Secret Service and an expert in aeronautical engineering. This man had in fact worked for Morane-Saulnier, the manufacturers of Mattei's private plane. He would have been perfectly capable of interfering with the instruments (attention focuses on the altimeter), if he had had access to the cabin. It is de Vosjoli's contention that such interference would have occurred only on a day when bad weather was forecast over Milan. Under this set of hypotheses we have a motive (the anger of the OAS against Mattei), an "instrument" (a possible technical expert for hire) and protection (the Mafia would not have been averse to offering security).

These remain hypotheses, but they are sufficiently weighty, coming from authoritative sources, for Rosi to film what can only be described as a hypothetical sequence of three figures (two in the white uniforms of mechanics, the third dressed as a *carabiniere* officer) advancing towards the plane in question on the tarmac. The brief sequence is filmed with a long lens, and thus in soft focus, while the faces themselves are hidden by a wing of the aircraft. The image represents the credence that Rosi gives to the testimony of his independent experts, while withholding any positive identity of those imagined figures, and even less of those who gave them their orders.

In Sicily, we see Mattei as a man on the run. What adds immeasurably to the drama is the way in which Rosi also casts him in the role of local hero. In the sequence in which Mattei marches into the village of Gagliano Castelferrato at the head of a triumphal procession, surrounded by local politicians and ENI technocrats, we note several iconographic references typical of Rosi's œuvre: the popular enthusiasm of a southern village festival; the central presence of a charismatic figure; the brief surge of hope in a populace which has been disappointed too often. There is also an impending feeling of fate beyond the surface gaiety. Indeed, one Sicilian dignitary, interviewed earlier, says that Mattei's confidence that day was only "official". It is known that he has received threatening telephone calls.

The scene even recalls the Portella della Ginestra sequence in *Salvatore Giuliano* (the difference being that the central figure in this case is at the heart of the sequence and is the bearer of good tidings).

Rosi emphasises primarily the intimate rapport Mattei establishes with ordinary people. It raises the thought that in political circles there was not only opposition to his policies, but also jealousy of his popularity. Pushing through the crowds, he tells one woman to bring her son back from Germany, because from now on there will be work locally. From the balcony of the city hall he reassures a man in the crowd, and everybody listening, that ENI is not taking resources away from Sicily, but reinvesting in the island to guarantee both jobs and a higher standard of living. Seeing him at the centre of public adulation, one might imagine Garibaldi returning a century after the defeat of the Bourbons, with promises of work and a final assault on poverty in which Sicilians had remained trapped since unification. In Sicilian eyes, a true hero is the person who challenges government in the name of the people. It is the promise of worthwhile change brought by the outsider or native son that links the names of Garibaldi, Giuliano and Mattei. What also links them is the ultimate fall from grace: Garibaldi's embittered retirement to Caprera; the shooting of Giuliano; Mattei's crash. In short, the whole sequence is designed to promote the myth of Mattei as the saviour of the Italian economy, the man who would finally bring prosperity to the despised south, and stop the haemorrhage of emigration.

The myth is nevertheless contradicted by a number of uncomfortable facts. It is true, for example, that Mattei was late in expanding ENI activities in Sicily. His claim that, in the future, Sicilians would not have to seek work abroad is somewhat hyperbolical. He faced stiff opposition in Sicily from Gulf Oil, already well-established and working a promising oilfield at Ragusa. Gulf's presence clearly rankled, and was probably the principal motive for Mattei's renewed interest in the island. The field he developed at Gela (once in the hands of British Petroleum, who gave up on it) proved quite disappointing. The oil found there was highly bituminous, very expensive to refine and suitable largely in the manufacture of asphalt. Eventually, Mattei's successors were to develop a facility to refine foreign crude in an attempt to recoup costs. Therefore, Mattei's presence in Sicily is largely symbolic, since he cannot be associated with the later disappointments of the enterprise. It would also have served as a further irritant to those already smarting at his challenge. In 1962 certain elements within the French Armed Services would not forgive him for his intrusion in North Africa. American oil executives (and this is by no means a reference to the managers of Gulf) could still interpret the Tunisian enterprise and his plans in Sicily as an attempt to cut into a potentially profitable market. Furthermore, in Sicily he would have run into the absolutely invisible influence of the Mafia who traditionally controlled, and was determined to control in the future, road and building contracts, the granting of industrial construction projects, and the distribution of labour. Mattei could only have represented a challenge to a previously unquestioned hegemony. While it is impossible for Rosi to point to any one of these groups with certainty and reveal a direct complicity in Mattei's death, his hypotheses are at least grounded in history. Moreover, of one thing he can be sure: that in 1972 public opinion that he had sampled was largely convinced that Mattei had been killed, and the director shares that opinion.

For Rosi to present Mattei in the way he wanted, he required an actor of great force, authority and artistic stamina, both to sustain a comprehensive portrait and to project a coherent ideology throughout. Thus, he turned to Gian Maria Volonté, who had already starred in the director's previous film, *Uomini contro* (*Just Another War*, 1970). After *The Mattei Affair*, Volonté interpreted for Rosi Lucky Luciano and Carlo Levi (in *Cristo si è fermato a Eboli* [*Christ Stopped at Eboli*, 1979]). One might say that he serves as a form of alter ego of the director, rather like Marcello Mastroianni for Fellini. There is, however, a fundamental difference. Whereas Mastroianni has re-enacted his director's private musings, dreams and psychological traumas, Volonté was more of a genuine collaborator, working closely with Rosi on historical interpretation, and clearly sharing the director's political point of view. In *Just Another War*, Volonté plays a commissioned officer, Ottolenghi, who supports a mutiny of his men against the high command in the First World War. It is a powerful story of conscience and a political spirit at war with blind authority. In *Lucky Luciano*, the actor's prime function was not to offer a complex, let alone sympathetic, portrait of a gangster, but rather to expose the symbiotic relationship that can exist between the underworld and established government in the most advanced Western democracies.

This quite unglamorised portrait in *Lucky Luciano* of a criminal international businessman stands in interesting juxtaposition to the softer and more domestic picture of the members of the Corleone family in Francis Coppola's *The Godfather* films, which enjoyed enormous popular success at around the same time. In *Christ Stopped at Eboli*, Volonté came closest to dramatising the social principles that Rosi holds dear. This is a film that quite transcends the Fascist period in which the action takes place. Carlo Levi, in his role as doctor and political prisoner, forms an immediate rapport with a despised and neglected peasantry, whose ill health offers a precise reflection of the state of the body politic of the time. Levi's patient observations draw the spectator's attention to the southern problem that ought to have been the first item on the agenda of a postwar government. At the same time his devotion to his patients, his capacity for popular empathy, and his acceptance of responsibility all define the marks of a modern citizen in a well-run society purged of authoritarianism and endemic corruption.

Volonté was quite frank about his political affiliations.[15] His early work for Sergio Leone gained him fame and success, allowing him the freedom to choose those film projects that corresponded to his notions of seriousness and commitment. He worked with the Taviani brothers, Elio Petri, Jean-Luc Godard and Marco Bellocchio.[16] In the late 1960s and early 1970s, he helped produce militant documentaries on the political views of factory workers, and on the circumstances surrounding the shootings in Piazza Fontana, Milan, and the "accidental" death of the anarchist Pinelli.[17] He also staged street performances, engaging the spectators in dialogue on contemporary issues. He was not an artist who separated his theatre and film work from his political convictions: the latter nourished his performance and interpretation.

When asked whether he had always had Volonté in mind for the role of Mattei, Rosi was quite categorical: "For me he was the only actor who made the production of the film possible".[18] He praises the actor as a person of great intelligence and amazing powers of concentration, who commits himself to the promotion of progressive social ideas, and who obviously shares with Rosi a belief in the educational value of cinema. Intelligence is certainly the central feature of the Mattei portrayed in the film; it is a restless intelligence charged with energy, continuously seeking a resolution to problems in action. Despite Rosi's declaration that he had no intention of creating a hero, his choice of Volonté alerts us to the fact that he wanted his Mattei to be memorable, and that the public would go away with an indelible impression of the man and his ideas. This is a prime example of how the presence of a "star" in a film can work in tandem with the promotion of an ideological point of view. Through Volonté, Rosi grants Mattei far more charisma than he in fact had. He was not in reality a dynamic public speaker, being rather more effective in arguing his case in private behind closed doors. The film offers Mattei plenty of opportunities to press his point in private conversations. However, it also shows him as an effective performer on a balcony, commanding everybody's attention at a dinner table, being the focal point of interest of any room he enters, and winning any face-to-face debate by the sheer weight of statistics and an impressive force of personality. This Mattei would have been a match for any hostile posse of journalists, and his own best defender on television.

While Rosi remains true to his design to have his central character embody the critical tensions in the struggle for public power in Italy, this film goes further than others in utilising a star performer to project the challenging reforms carried forward by the protagonist. One may call this an ideological choice of star, quite different in intent from the Hollywood method of building a film around an actor for the purpose of selling a package or promoting a career. In *The Mattei Affair*, actor and director are close collaborators, even co-conspirators, in presenting an Italian industrial leader who takes on an international consortium, his own government and the very assumptions of Western leadership in a divided postwar world. The portrait is neither unselectively flattering nor blindly uncritical. But when the film has finished, the viewer remembers Mattei as an industrialist of vision and energy, as an enemy of the economic and political status quo, and as a martyr. All this certainly serves Rosi's purpose of keeping alive the issues surrounding the death.

Enrico Mattei's corpse is one of many littering the landscape of Rosi's cinema. These are frequently "illustrious corpses" – the bodies of prominent citizens, judges, top civil servants, those in possession of knowledge which powerful people want suppressed. Following *Lucky Luciano* (1973), in which a less than excellent corpse serves to set in motion a fully documented inquiry, Rosi's next film was *Cadaveri eccellenti* (*Illustrious Corpses*, 1975), based on Leonardo Sciascia's novel, *Il contesto* (*Equal Danger*), a grim fable of state-sponsored terrorism, in which judge after judge is shot while investigating charges of corruption in the judiciary. The novel might have been written with Rosi in mind. Here both writer and director confront one of the most burning issues of the 1970s, that of violence targeting judges looking into acts of terrorism from the Left and the Right, aimed at keeping the country off-balance in a calculated strategy of tension. The theme of judge as target, and with it the sense of the fragility of the justice system, is also central to Rosi's *Tre fratelli* (*Three Brothers*, 1980), in which one of the brothers is a judge living in fear of his life and the security of his family.

The essential unifying factor of Rosi's films, therefore, is their absolute contemporaneity. His preferred method, which seeks to resemble the form of the documentary with the slow accumulation of information and the sense of a continuing inquiry after the official investigation has stopped, emphasises the immediacy of his subject-matter and his desire to keep an issue alive. Informing the public is a moral responsibility for Rosi, for whom film is a medium that asks Italians (and not only Italians) to think seriously about complex facts of a particular episode beyond the banner headlines, and about the broader implications of such an event in the political life of the republic.

The Mattei Affair is sufficiently suggestive that curiosity takes one beyond the possible identity of those who may have engineered the accident. Twenty years after Rosi's film, one inevitably begins to wonder about the history of ENI without Mattei, and about the vicissitudes of other public agencies. Mattei himself paid out money from public funds to ensure political support for his development projects, to purchase land and to bypass local ordinances. It mattered little to him whether he bought votes from Communists, neo-Fascists, Socialists or Christian Democrats, as long as the job got done. In his view, such expenditures were in the public interest, and it is certain that he himself never benefited from the slush funds he kept at his disposal. It is also certain that he kept the records of such payments hidden from official scrutiny. Mattei did not author the habit of political kickbacks to bring an industrial project to fruition, while coming close to advancing the method to a high art. He did leave a culture in which this procedure was accepted without question. Since his death the contribution to a political party by an individual or public agency has become endemic in Italy as the single most effective way of doing serious business in any branch of commerce and industry. The word for "kickback" is *tangente*, and Italians have added a new word to their political vocabulary to describe the national network of bribery and pay-offs that served as the engine and death knell of the first postwar republic: *tangentopoli*, or "kickback city". This "way of doing business" has so ensnared the worlds of finance, industry and politics in meretricious promiscuity that it has led to the indictment and jailing of prominent political leaders, ex-Members of Parliament, heads of public agencies, industrialists, and even some judges. It has led to the demise of political parties (the Socialists no longer exist; the Christian Democrats barely survive as a minority rump, hiding behind the new title of I Popolari [Popular Party]), to a revision of the constitution and major changes in the electoral laws, and to the collapse of the first republic, as stated above, 50 years after its inception. A whole political generation was swept aside in a tidal wave of national revulsion in the General Election in March 1994. The collective outrage which exploded rather late in the day brought into office a government firmly anchored on the Right, including neo-Fascists and the separatist Lega Nord (Northern League), and headed by the television and media tycoon, Silvio Berlusconi, whose appeal to the voters, of course, was that he was not a politician.

All this seems to take us a long way from the case of Enrico Mattei and the cinema of Francesco Rosi. However, hindsight allows us to see Mattei historically placed at the start of a period of spectacular industrial and economic expansion for Italy, which can be attributed to very favourable business conditions in a postwar economic climate, and equally to the ruthless exploitation of those conditions by a brilliant manager who knew how and when to bend the rules. At the end of that period, we see the empire that Mattei created in ruins, having fallen into the hands of men promoted more for loyalty to a particular party than for competence and managerial skills, and the unwieldy and unprofitable branches of ENI being dismantled and sold off piece by piece. It was, of course, the management, or mismanagement, of the public enterprises that lay at the heart of the rot of *tangentopoli*, and the government is deeply involved in the privatisation of enterprises that were started in order to serve the public interest, only to end as the refuge and feather-bed of the party faithful.

The history of these multiple scandals has also claimed its prominent victims and produced moments of high drama and personal tragedy, episodes directly involving Mattei's successors at ENI. In 1989, the then-chairman of ENI, Gabriele Cagliari, entered into what now appears to be a Faustian bargain with the huge chemical monopoly, Montedison, itself the product of an earlier merger between the industrial giants, Montecatini and Edison. Montedison was controlled by the private Ferruzzi chemical group and its chairman, Raul Gardini. The new joint venture, baptised Enimont, linking a public enterprise with private capital, and floated on an ocean of debt, represented 80% of the Italian chemical market and 15% of the European. Naturally, this extravagant purchase of an enormous monopoly by a state agency, with no visible advantage to the public interest, aroused howls of anger from the parties on the Left, but to no avail. The deal went through. It later transpired that Gardini had secretly purchased Enimont shares under the cover of surrogate companies, and had ended up with 51% of control of the chemical colossus. This was in clear violation of the original agreement which limited ENI and Ferruzzi each to a 40% share of the company, the remaining 20% to be sold on the public market. Nothing can explain the rationale behind such an agreement – neither public interest, nor increased productivity, nor the protection of the Italian petrochemical industry, nor the promise of more dynamic research and development – except the greed and ambition of the principals who overlooked the consequences of the creation of this behemoth out of their desire to preside over the largest industrial chemical enterprise in Western Europe. In March 1993, Cagliari was accused of bribery in the original creation of Enimont and imprisoned in the San Vittore jail in Milan. He committed suicide there on 23 July, to be followed within a week by

Raul Gardini, implicated in the same scandal, who preferred to shoot himself rather than face further investigation and trial.

Cagliari and Gardini were not murdered and their deaths can be easily explained. The mystery involves the secrets which they took with them to their graves, the details of secret deals and pay offs which the public may never fully learn. They too join that pile of *cadaveri eccellenti*, the posthumous reminder of an history of the abuse of power and violation of the public trust that pock-marked the 50-year life of the first postwar democratic republic. The corpses referred to include the investigators into abuses, as well as the abusers themselves.

If ever the tangled history of this sorry affair finds its way to the screen, Francesco Rosi is surely the director most qualified for the task. *Tangentopoli* has its heroes as well as its more numerous villains, and they correspond to those who have found themselves at both ends of his spectrum since the start of his career. Since Rosi has always focused on the seductions of power and the corresponding dangers these pose to the democratic functioning of the state, the events unfolding in Italy over the past two or three years reveal him as some form of a prophet, issuing clear-eyed and accurate warnings that have gone unheeded. The fact that these abuses of power have led to the demise of a political establishment and the end of an era can cause him little joy, since he must now imagine the complications and contradictions to come.

In the context in which we can now survey Rosi's earlier work, *The Mattei Affair* assumes an increased status, for it placed its central figure at the outset of a period that has now come to a close in the most demoralising of circumstances. Mattei was a maverick who used and bypassed laws when it suited him; he used public funds for his own convenience; he interfered too often in foreign affairs without authorisation; and he also made some strange political bedfellows. But every action was determined by a consistent agenda, and, in the final analysis, Mattei was a public servant who took the public interest seriously. Expansion and jobs were his top priorities, and Italian industrialists who profited from the relatively cheap supplies of oil and gas that he provided owe him a debt of gratitude. The distinction is between the ethos of the buccaneer and the almost pure self-interest that has since guided the behaviour of the top management of the public agencies, industrialists more adept at moving money on the stock market than at creating new products, and, above all, of party managers whose primary concern was their party's grip on power and influence and the replenishment of its coffers. In *The Mattei Affair*, as in his other major films, Rosi stands out as the major chronicler on film of the political life of the postwar Italian republic.

[1] Sir John Hawkwood (or Giovanni Acuto) (c1320-94), English soldier and adventurer who fought for Edward III in the Hundred Years War and for his son, the Black Prince. After the Peace of Bretigny (1360), he moved to Italy, formed The White Company and entered the service of Bernabò Visconti of Milan. In the next three decades, he and his Company fought for and against the papacy, for and against Milan, and for and against Florence. It was here that he finally settled and was greatly honoured by the Florentines on his death. He is immortalised in a fresco in Florence Cathedral by Paolo Uccello.

[2] Giovanni delle Bande Nere (or Ludovico de'Medici) (1498-1526), took the name of his father, Giovanni, brother of Cosimo de'Medici, and was one of the most distinguished *condottieri* of his day, and the most accomplished soldier in the Medici dynasty. He fought in the defence of the papacy of Leo X (Giovanni de'Medici), and the black banners of his company were assumed in mourning at the Pope's death. He was killed at the battle of Mantua, fighting for the League of Cognac against the German Emperor.

[3] When American forces landed in Sicily in July 1943, they needed contacts in the hinterland to provide local intelligence of German troop movements, to guide troops over mountain passes and to re-establish local government loyal to the allies. Many of these people were members of the Mafia and associates of Luciano, who was still in jail. Despite his incarceration, he was able to provide sufficient information to allow contact to be made with those who could be of service to the US Army, and who would immediately benefit from the invasion. For this, it appears that Luciano's sentence was later commuted.

[4] Clandestine paramilitary organisation formed by dissident French Army officers and right-wing extremists to thwart the attempts of the French government under General de Gaulle to grant Algerian independence. Formed in 1961, it was responsible for a campaign of terror in Algeria and on the French mainland. This lasted for a period of two years, until the arrest of its leaders, including General Raoul Salan, who had been in charge of the French Army in Algeria during the Algerian War.

[5] Ferruccio Parri (1890-1981), Italy's first postwar Prime Minister (June-November 1945), and a founding member of the Partito d'azione (The Action Party), a democratic political group dedicated to the anti-Fascist struggle. Parri was a distinguished Resistance leader. It was during this period that he first met Mattei. He was succeeded as head of government by Alcide De Gasperi. In 1963 he was named Senator for life.

[6] Don Luigi Sturzo (1871-1959), priest, politician and founder of the Partito Popolare Italiano (PPI) in 1919. This was a party that offered all lay and progressive Catholics a chance to participate directly in the political life of the country. Sturzo initially refused to enter into the alliance with the Socialists, which might have prevented the march on Rome and Mussolini's takeover of the government. During the next twenty years, he was a steadfast opponent of the regime, and went into exile, firstly in Paris, then London, and finally the United States. He returned to Italy after the war and

was named Senator for life in 1952.

[7]   Alcide De Gasperi (1881-1954), born in Alto Adige, was a fervent supporter of the movement to have the South Tyrol placed under Italian rule. He joined the Popular Party and became its leader with Don Sturzo's departure for exile. He spent much of the Fascist period in seclusion in the Vatican Library, emerging in 1942 to assume leadership of the newly formed Christian Democratic Party (DC), formed out of the old PPI. De Gasperi succeeded Parri as Prime Minister in November 1945, and remained head of government until his retirement from politics in 1953. He was a firm anti-Communist, and a strong supporter of close ties with the United States and of Italy's membership of NATO.

[8]   Ezio Vanoni (1903-56), economist who began his career as a Socialist during the 1920s, but moved to the Centre-Right in the years after the war. He was appointed Finance Minister in De Gasperi's third Cabinet, and was a strong supporter of Mattei's plans for the development of the Italian oil industry. Mattei's influence in government circles somewhat declined following his early death.

[9]   Mario Scelba (born 1901), one of the founder members of the Partito Popolare Italiano, and a close ally of Don Sturzo. He joined the Christian Democratic Party at its inception in 1942, was in every De Gasperi Cabinet, and named Minister of the Interior in 1947. He gained a reputation as a strict proponent of law and order, and a hard line opponent of trade union militancy. Between 1960 and 1962 he vigorously opposed the movement among moderate elements of the DC towards a political alliance with the Socialists (the opening to the Left).

[10]   In Italian political parlance, the word *liberale* means "conservative", and the Partito Liberale Italiano (Liberal Party; now virtually extinct) has always occupied a place on the Centre-Right of the political spectrum. Rosi identifies Mattei's chief critic as a "giornalista liberale", who not only accuses the chairman of misuse of funds, but also objects to his deals with the Soviet Union, other Eastern bloc countries and those in North Africa. Indro Montanelli was a long-time columnist of the Milanese *Corriere della Sera*, clearly a "liberal" newspaper.

[11]   For Montanelli's broadside against Enrico Mattei and his management of ENI, see the *Corriere della Sera*, Milan, 13-17 July 1962. An edited version in English of the same appears in *Atlas* September 1962. For Mattei's detailed response to those charges, and Montanelli's rebuttal, see the *Corriere* later in July 1962, and the complete translation of the exchanges in *Atlas* October 1962.

[12]   Michele Pantaleone has served as a Socialist member of the Sicilian legislature. Among his best known works on the Mafia are *The Mafia and Politics* (London: Chatto and Windus, 1966) and *Mafia e droga* (Turin: Giulio Einaudi editore, 1966). He also collaborated on he screenplay of the 1970 film on the Mafia, *Un sasso in bocca* (*Stone in the Mouth*), directed by Giuseppe Ferrara.

[13]   The actual words used by Pantaleone on screen are: "Quale supermafia

li protegge?" ("What supermafia is protecting them?"). The term he uses turns the question into an indictment. Pantaleone may be thinking not only of a criminal organisation, but also of a connection between the highest ranks of government and the underworld.

[14] P L Thyraud de Vosjoli, *Lamia* (Boston: Little, Brown, 1970). For the story of Mattei's death, see 271-277.

[15] See "Gian Maria Volonté talks about cinema and politics", *Cineaste* 7: 1 (1975): 10-13. The interview between Volonté and Guy Braucourt was first published earlier the same year in the French film journal, *Écran*.

[16] For Sergio Leone, Volonté starred in *Per un pugno di dollari* (*A Fistful of Dollars*, 1964) and *Per qualche dollaro in più* (*For a Few Dollars More*, 1965). For Paolo and Vittorio Taviani, he was in *Un uomo da bruciare* (*A Man for the Killing*, 1962); for Elio Petri, *Indagine su un cittadino al di sopra di ogni sospetto* (*Investigation of a Citizen Above Suspicion*, 1969) and *La classe operaia va in paradiso* (*The Working Class Goes to Heaven*, 1971); for Jean-Luc Godard, *Vent d'Est* (*Wind from the East*, 1970); and for Marco Bellocchio, *Sbatti il mostro in prima pagina* (*Slap the Monster on Page One*, 1972).

[17] Giuseppe Pinelli, a Milanese railway worker and admitted anarchist, was arrested for the bomb explosion in the Banca Nazionale dell'Agricoltura in Piazza Fontana, Milan, on 12 December 1969. The explosion killed sixteen and left many more injured. On 15 December, Pinelli fell to his death from the fourth floor of a police headquarters building. A neo-Fascist group operating out of the Veneto was later shown to have been responsible for the bombing. The fate of Pinelli is the subject of Dario Fo's political farce, *Morte accidentale di un anarchico* (*The Accidental Death of an Anarchist*, 1970).

[18] Translated from the French: "Pour moi, c'était l'unique acteur qui rendait possible la réalisation du film". *Positif* 140 (July-August 1972): 26 (interview with Michel Ciment and Bernard Cohn).

The other side of glamorous killings: *Lucky Luciano*, Rosi's neo-realistic approach to the Mafia

Claudio Mazzola

Italian filmmakers have always been rather reluctant to bring to the screen the socio-political events that have characterised Italian life in the last 40 years. Whenever a director ventured into this arena, the results have often been characterised by a flat and calligraphic representation of situations whose powerful emotional tones were left outside the film. The only exception to this trend is probably neo-realism, the cinema that came alive at the end of the Second World War. Directors such as Rossellini, De Sica and De Santis registered with great energy and courage the tragic moments that characterised the liberation of Italy by the Allied Forces. They were inspired by events which many of them experienced at first hand, and which they wanted to describe without compromises of any kind. As the writer Italo Calvino explains,[1] while discussing the characteristics of the artistic movement that swept through Italy after the Second World War, what was more important for many was simply the possibility of being able to tell stories which they lived in person. Neo-realist directors developed their own unique style without being too concerned with creating a product that would please the audience. Their political beliefs supported their artistic inspiration throughout the period approximately between 1945 and 1955.

When this urgency to communicate faded away at the start of a new political and economical phase, a new form of artistic conformism took over. A more superficial, "romantic" depiction of the lower classes prevailed, and the socio-political dramas of these people were only marginally presented in a context where solutions came easily and neo-realism became "pink neo-realism". Artistic indifference seemed to dominate Italian cinema at the time when it began to become popular as the so-called *commedia all'italiana*, a genre that included only bland and often ambiguous forms of socio-political criticism. The problems that plagued Italian society in the 1960s and 1970s, such as political corruption, terrorism and the Mafia, remained almost completely ignored by Italian filmmakers.

The great directors of this period, from Fellini to Antonioni, were making very personal statements about Italian society, and their films could hardly be considered politically committed. In a situation of general apathy, Francesco Rosi has always been an exception, because his civic conscience has become the trade mark of films that investigate major socio-political issues of the last four decades. Calling his films "political" could somehow be limiting, because he tries to avoid flat messages or easy answers by raising questions for the audience:

> [M]any of my films – such as *Salvatore Giuliano, Hands Over the City, Lucky Luciano,* and *The Mattei Affair* – are structured as investigations into the relationship between causes and effects. When I devised this method in *Salvatore Giuliano,* this search for the truth became the narrative line of the film. I wanted to pose questions to the audience, questions I either didn't know the answers to or did not wish to give answers to.[2]

Lucky Luciano (1973) is one of the few postwar Italian films directly to tackle one of the greatest taboos of Italian cinema: the Mafia. It is rather surprising how Italian filmmakers have avoided this problem, especially since American directors have become so familiar with this topic that the number of films made in the United States which deal with the Mafia have almost established a rigid codification of its narrative structures. In fact, these films are part of their own genre, distinct from film noir or the gangster movie. Many American directors have attempted to deal with "Mafia movies", also because this sub-genre has always met with the audience's approval and has known no crisis. This success has even allowed some directors to explore comic variations on the brutality of mobsters' activities – from *Some Like It Hot* (1959) to *Married to the Mob* (1988).[3]

This freedom to move around the entire spectrum of narrative possibilities arises from the fact that American directors have always stressed only one side of the issue. They have always been primarily fascinated by the glamorous side of the Mafia, and by the strength and ability of the single individual to surface from mediocrity and become someone to respect and fear. The fascination for the hero of poor origin who conquers the New World has always been part of American society; with the Mafia, the myth of the self-made man takes an even more glorious path. American films tend to encourage identification with the main character, who for this reason is usually presented as monodimensional, and whose positiveness relies above all in maintaining or reaching the higher and most respected position of the social hierarchy. These films do not question the presence of the Mafia at a socio-political level; they come primarily from a structural genre that does not allow any message to be conveyed. The narrative follows an easy pattern with the typical building up of tension that finds a release in the final sequence of the film. Violent and spectacular killings are usually the most important moments of the film.

To Italian directors, making films about the Mafia has always meant something different. Particularly since the end of the Second World War, and with the opening up of new world markets, the nature of the Mafia and its related activities has radically changed. It is no longer strictly a family affair resolved within Sicilian boundaries, but a real business, boosted by drug-trafficking, with interests and connections throughout Italy. The Mafia has become a sad part of everyday life, a serious threat to all Italians and an even harsher reality outside Sicily. To the average citizen, the presence and power of the Mafia are above all the realisation of the impotence of the state in front of an organisation substituting itself to the state, by taking advantage of its weaknesses, and this does not have that "romantic" halo that it has for Americans. Rosi states the situation very clearly:

Mafia grants the respectability to the system and the system gives it back for such 'service' a price that we all pay for and that it is higher for the one who is absolutely in the dark, that is the citizen who is convinced of the old fairy tale of the criminal who does some damage and Justice punishes him.[4]

Rosi's view of the Mafia does not leave much room for hope; he clearly sees the difficulties involved in trying to eradicate the problem when too many private and public interests are at stake. This is the reason why, to Italian directors, discussing the Mafia means necessarily making a political statement, a condition which can be avoided in American films.

In order to understand Rosi's penchant for political films, it should be noted that his formative years are closely linked with the masters of neo-realism, such as Rossellini and Visconti. It cannot be overlooked in fact that, although his first film, La sfida (The Challenge), was made in 1957, his first job in the film industry was as assistant director to Visconti on La terra trema (The Earth Trembles, 1948). There is no doubt that while working for Visconti he absorbed the artistic atmosphere of those years. Aside from some naïve and simplistic statements, neo-realism elaborated technical cinematic solutions and a particular type of plot development that contributed to creating a powerful impression of reality that was going beyond its ontological unity. Neo-realist directors were able to utilise elements of documentary cinema in the typical structures of feature films; this gave the films an unprecedented and shocking feeling of reality which neither documentary nor feature films had previously reached. They employed non-professional actors, outdoor settings, and limited camera movements and editing to make the narrative structure less dependent on the mechanical presentation of the major events. The result is a seemingly uneventful reality that broke with the typical structure of classic films.

Combining different film techniques and journalism, fiction and documentary, Rosi was one of the first directors to bring to the screen with a particularly provocative flavour the rotten side of politicians, policemen and administrators of modern Italian society. In films such as *Salvatore Giuliano* (1961) and *Il caso Mattei* (*The Mattei Affair*, 1972), Rosi does not rely on the schematization of political ideas; his unconventional style allows him to communicate with the audience without being forced to strike the easy emotional note typical of propaganda films. In fact, his films do not present the usual gap between form and content, between good political intentions and the employment of a simplistic cinematic structure. He uses a highly developed cinematic language that refuses to be the vehicle for a particular political idea, but it is political in essence because it makes the subject-matter become part of the active reaction of the audience. Rosi avoids the schematizations of ideas by not supporting a particular thesis, even when this seems fairly safe. In *The Mattei Affair*, there is only a hint at the possibility that the protagonist's death can be attributed to sabotage. Rosi prefers to stress the trouble and contradiction behind a particular event or character. His tendency meticulously to research the subject-matter of each of film convinced him that there can be no other valid political approach than to present the impossibility of reaching absolute truth, even when one is personally convinced of what and who is behind a particular political situation.

In *Lucky Luciano*, Rosi continues the elaboration of the technique employed in *Salvatore Giuliano* and *The Mattei Affair*. The random mixing of objective facts about Luciano's life and a more subjective narration is presented with a style that recalls neo-realism. More than in his previous works, the director takes large risks in view of the fact that he is dealing with a film closely related to the gangster genre. This usually means fast-paced editing, quick action and maximum accessibility for the audience's emotions. As with neo-realist films, Rosi's style has none of the above, because he rejects the easy association between emotions and action. The audience is forced to abandon a purely mechanical reaction to the film[5] in favour of a more active role. As Sandro Zambetti points out, the audience is not asked to identify with the action easily:

Rosi shooting *Salvatore Giuliano* (1961)

Salvatore Giuliano (1961)

Salvatore Giuliano (1961)

Hands Over the City (1963)

Hands Over the City (1963)

Hands Over the City (1963)

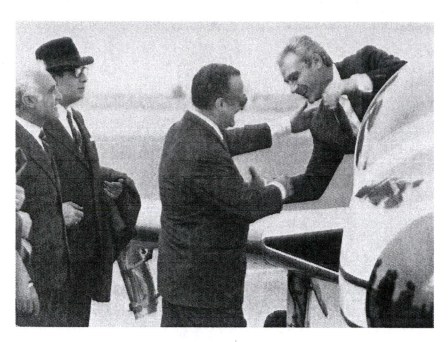

The Mattei Affair (1972)

The Mattei Affair (1972)

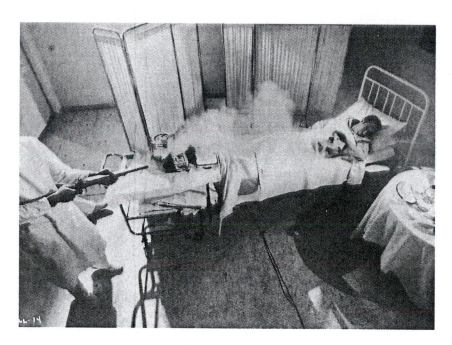

Lucky Luciano (1973)

Lucky Luciano (1973)

Illustrious Corpses (1975)

Illustrious Corpses (1975)

Illustrious Corpses (1975)

Three Brothers (1980)

Three Brothers (1980)

Three Brothers (1980)

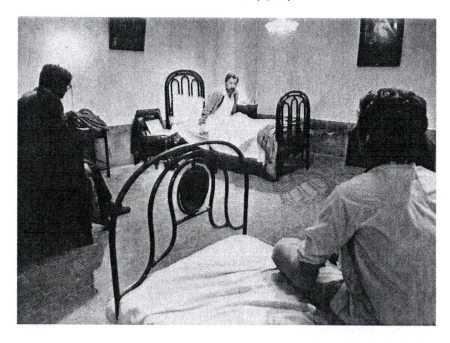

The screen, after all, [should be perceived] not as a mirror of reality which the audience is forced to identify with, but as an *agreed* place of representation of reality in front of which the spectator can remain aware of his being *outside* the representation and on the other hand, *inside* the reality from which it [the representation] has started. For this reason the audience is induced to confront his/her own point of view on the matter with that of the author.[6]

While neo-realist directors depended on an unconventional presentation of the story within a linear development of the plot, Rosi relies on the mixture of three different narrative solutions and the breaking of the time unity to provoke the audience's reactions. The documentaristic part of the film is characterised by the employment of an imposing voice-over, and by subtitles indicating the specific locations and dates of Luciano's whereabouts. The second identifiable section makes use of rather long sequences presenting different meetings concerning the Mafia and drug-trafficking. These sequences are introduced by news reportage technique, with the camera avoiding particularly selected shots that would stress or convey particular emotions. In this section, the information regarding Luciano is somewhat overshadowed by the heated exchange of responsibility commentary that each agency or authority involved has towards Lucky Luciano, and the Mafia in general. Rosi does not take a stand – in fact, he does not follow up the reciprocal accusations with episodes that support or refuse either position. Lastly, there are the purely narrative sections of the film, in which Rosi makes every effort to avoid the typical dramatic solutions of gangster stories in favour of a more low-key tone that can be defined as minimalist in plot development and neo-realist in overall style. The action is very limited, even if the film covers a period of almost 30 years rich with events. The plot progresses mainly in the direction of adding layers of information regarding Luciano's character. Rosi avoids imposing a number of superficial traits, but he allows the narration to reveal Luciano's personality while it progresses. The director is more inclined to explore the other side of the gangster, the Luciano who tries to find time also to search for a normal life, and discovers that he cannot.

The lack of action prevents the audience from becoming too involved in the purely mechanical parts of the narration, and consequently from reducing Luciano to a purely monodimensional character. For example, he is never clearly visually associated with killings. Even when he takes the leading role with the Mafia bosses and eliminates all his rivals in the famous "Night of the Sicilian Vespers", Rosi rejects easy spectacular solutions. The various killings that brought him to power are presented in a fast succession of shots, whilst the voice-over informs the audience of Luciano's role in the killing, and in the background we hear some Italian operatic arias. The images are characterised by medium-length shots and quick editing. It is a highly stylized sequence in which the tension is very low because the shots are completely external to the emotional range of the viewer. The audience may be disoriented at first by the fact that the central figure of the film is not seen in those situations that provide the typical representation of Mafia bosses and glorify their activities: no memorable killing scenes; no love scenes with gorgeous women; no direct confrontation with friends/enemies. Certainly Luciano likes women; he likes to gamble; and he is the brains behind the drug-trafficking in Naples. However, all these activities are not glamorised in the sense that through these sequences his image does not acquire a particular strength. In fact, there seems to be almost a contradiction between the fame that surrounds him and the portrayal given by the director.

The fact that Rosi has always been fascinated by strong, individualistic characters is no mystery,[7] but here, as in *Salvatore Giuliano* and *The Mattei Affair*, the title character provides an excuse for a search of an historical and political nature. Unlike those two previous films, however, there is more room to explore the protagonist's life who comes out as a man who struggles between two cultures, even as a feared Mafia boss, almost to the point of being perceived as a man trapped by his own image. For most of the time, he is described as a mild-mannered man whose only few moments of rage are related to his being forced to leave the United States, the country he has adopted as his homeland. During his farewell dinner speech, Luciano – played by Gian Maria Volonté, an actor who became the flag for left-wing social commitment in the 1970s, and who, as such, could hardly be perceived by the audience as a negative character – shows a very natural calm and an appealing self-control (not the stereotypical arrogant calm of many Mafia leaders of American movies). He only wishes his friends would not leave him in Italy for too long. The man of action is actually a man whose pride has been wounded more by his deportation to Italy than by his being imprisoned in the United States. In this sense, the film develops in two directions: on the one hand, it is an unconventional study of a Mafia leader, while on the other it is an investigation into the circumstances and responsibilities surrounding Luciano's mythical figure at a time when the Mafia was changing its image.

The opening titles of *Lucky Luciano* set the stage for what seems to be a predominantly documentaristic approach to the protagonist's life. A close-up of a newspaper article is read by an authoritative voice-over who informs us of what happened in 1946 when Lucky Luciano was paroled by the New York Governor, Thomas F Dewey, after serving only nine years of a possible 30-50-year sentence. The tone of the brief article is very polemical, stressing in fact the ambiguous role that the very same Dewey had first in persecuting Luciano when he was District Attorney of New York, and later when he freed the Mafia boss for "special services rendered to the USAF" during the Second World War. Sacrificing justice to the logic of politics, the Americans made what the voice-over at the beginning of the film calls "a gift to the Mafia". Such a beginning very clearly underlines the director's point of view and his political opinion. Artistically, the risk is to let emotions prevail and to rely on a superficial attack on the Mafia that could only be regarded as naïve and didactic. Once the action starts, however, Rosi switches mode completely to a more objective narration that gives him the possibility of detaching himself from the subject-matter.

The opening sequence takes place at New York Harbor where Lucky Luciano has embarked on a ship leaving for Italy. On board, there is a gathering of Mafia bosses who come to pay their respects to Luciano. The sequence is presented by Rosi employing two specific types of shot. The first gives a sense of newsreel footage through the use of a hand-held camera kept at a distance outside the pier's gate. The arrival of the Mafiosi in the distance stresses the inaccessibility of the camera to Luciano's activities. The second corresponds to a specific point of view because the camera is positioned inside or near a van from where men of the Federal Bureau of Narcotics are spying on the meeting on the ship. Trapped inside their vehicle, the federal agents observe the arrival of all the big names of New York's organised crime. They are frustrated for being relegated to the role of impotent observers, and they repeatedly express rage at Luciano's liberation. The tone of their remarks is of the same nature as the one contained in the opening inscription. Both these types of shots reveal a specific point of view that it is clearly not that of the director. This solution allows Rosi to distance himself from the subject-matter without having to worry about the label of "political propaganda".

In view of the particular style employed by Rosi, the purely narrative sections of *Lucky Luciano* enjoy a sense of autonomy from the rest of the film and from the director himself. They seem to be randomly selected and self-narrating episodes of Luciano's life that do not impose an interpretation but demand to be interpreted. An example is the very first sequence that shows Luciano in Italy. The predetermined logical sequence of scenes from an action-oriented film would require Luciano establishing contacts with the local Mafia bosses while settling down in a wealthy neighbourhood with all the comforts easily available. Rosi, on the other hand, delivers a sequence where Luciano's activities as a Mafia boss remain peripheral to the narration. Surprisingly, Rosi shows a puzzling visit to the cemetery of Luciano's hometown in Sicily. During the entire sequence, there is basically no dialogue between Luciano and the local authorities who accompany him. While he slowly moves from one tomb to another, a voice-over reads the inscriptions. Most of them describe violent deaths by unknown killers. "His life dedicated to his fellow workers for the cause of Socialism", reads one inscription. Nothing really happens during this visit: no confrontation with people at the cemetery; no discussion or comments with the friends who are with him; he asks no questions, and no one asks him anything. The political nature of the inscription and the lack of a prompt response seem to indicate that Luciano is somewhat outside or at least extraneous to the recent political events in Italy. He is trapped in a situation of which he does not understand all the implications, while at the same time he is alone and completely isolated in his own native land.

The same rejection of the action-oriented plot can be found in three other key sequences. In each, the protagonist faces a moment of confrontation with his new environment and with the new living conditions in Italy. The first describes a press conference in Naples; the second is the visit that his old friend, Gene Giannini, pays to him; and the last is a conversation he has with the local priest. All these sequences are characterised by very unusual narrative solutions in the sense that there is always a lack of communication, so that any form of understanding or conflict among the characters involved is missing. The result is that in each case the plot develops in a rather unexpected direction, and Luciano attracts the viewer's attention through a very unconventional relationship between character and action. During the press conference there is no particular confrontation between the journalists and Luciano; the general atmosphere is rather relaxed. Although some of the journalists are pressing some burning issues ("Is it true that you control gambling houses in Cuba?", asks one) and sometimes Luciano reacts with strong words, the feeling is that there is no particular risk involved, that nothing is at stake. The journalists throw questions on the table with no real sense of confrontation with Luciano's personality. While he denies all the connections with organised crime, the sequence does not really focus on his attempt to establish his innocence. The relevant element is his nostalgia for the United States and his lack of sympathy for the Italian situation.

In the final part of this sequence, the camera is no longer relying on a newsreel quality of shots, with many shaky close-ups of Luciano as at the beginning of the film. In a long tracking shot, the camera goes slowly around the big table where all the journalists are gathered. Luciano says that he is not a rich man, and that the car he owns is a gift of friends back in the United States. This more elaborate camerawork completely contrasts with the previous documentaristic style and underlines Luciano's firmer desire to return to the United States. The tracking shot ends in fact with Luciano saying that he has already bought a chapel in the heart of the Brooklyn cemetery. This particular sequence turns upside down the classical emotional mechanism that is behind a typical public confrontation such as a press conference. The sequence is more an insight into Luciano's character than an opportunity to gather more mundane information about him. The classical clash between Luciano and the journalists is avoided while the viewer becomes more familiar with Luciano's personality. The same approach is used when Gene Giannini visits him. Giannini is caught between the old friendship with Luciano and the pressure that the Bureau of Narcotics is putting on him to help them nail Luciano. The ambiguity of their friendship is well-rendered by their inability to communicate while they move around Pompeii's ruins. Giannini tries to involve Luciano in some future projects, but Luciano does not answer. The camera records the embarrassment of this meeting by creating a sense of void. While the conversation fails to pick up, the camera focuses on the obscene frescos on the wall of the brothel they are visiting. The two friends are unable to agree on any specific plan that involves their activities. Once more, Rosi plays with the structure of the genre, because no particular expectations for a follow-up sequence come out of this meeting. Luciano's only few words of the whole sequence are particularly revealing of his character: "My friends visit here for pleasure".

In these three sequences, Luciano's solitude is investigated at all levels; he reveals to the journalists his longing for the United States, knowing very well that they are deaf listeners – they do not want his confessions, they want scandals. He avoids any contact with Giannini, his former friend, since he knows too well that the friendship Giannini offers is a false one because he is betraying him. Finally, he seeks comfort by talking to the local priest. This scene is different from the others because it is Luciano himself who looks for the priest. Luciano is not a hypocrite: he waits for the priest outside the church because he wants to talk to him as a human being. This becomes the biggest failure in communication.

This sequence is built around two different types of shot. One focuses on the priest eating, and stresses the rather disgusting way he has to eat while Luciano pensively stands near a window looking out. The feeling of separation is already very strong, but it is further enhanced by the next series of shots – almost all close-ups – in which Luciano tries hard to involve the priest in understanding his needs. He tells him that he likes his company because, unlike all the other people who surround him, he does not ask him questions. But the priest does not understand Luciano's cry for help. His behaviour contrasts sharply with the mild-mannered Luciano. It conveys very well the sense of vulgarity and disrespect for human feelings that surrounds Luciano. His very sombre manners are juxtaposed with Don Ciccio's eating and clearing his mouth as if he were an animal. Rather than discussing Luciano's situation, the priest asks him about slot-machines and the possibilities of using them to finance the parish. Luciano's answer and tone of voice quite clearly summarize his failure to obtain something from the only person who, he thought, does not want something from him. With a tone of total disappointment he says, "Leave the little machines alone, that's no stuff for you!" ("Lascia stare le macchinette, non è roba per te!"), and then throws some money to the priest.

These sequences clearly show Rosi's work at presenting characters. Since his interests are also in the investigation of the political struggle proceeding behind the façade of efficiency created for the Mafia and the public, Rosi does not hesitate to operate at other levels of narration. Once Luciano settles down in Naples, he disappears for a while, and Rosi's attention turns to the reciprocal accusation between American and Italian authorities. The Americans make precise remarks regarding the fact that the Italians are ignoring the connection between large pharmaceutical companies and the Mafia's drug-trafficking, while the Italians remind the Americans that the Allied Forces supported the elections of well-known Mafiosi to key positions in local government in the south at the end of the Second World War. In order to make the accusation acquire validity, Rosi interrupts the linear development of the story with flashbacks that take the story back to 1944. While the Italians greet the arrival of the American troops with joy, an arrogant American general arranges the distribution of aid to the population as if he were dealing in some private affair. The American authorities do not care about being surrounded by men well-known for their connection with the Mafia. One of them, Genovese, gives the Americans a list of so-called anti-Fascists to put in key positions in local government in Naples. In a sequence that seems a pessimistic revisitation of Rossellini's *Paisà* (*Paisan*, 1946), a convoy of loaded trucks, led by Genovese himself, leaves the American base for an unknown destination. While, just outside the base, some American soldiers are surrounded by poor, hungry Italians begging for food, the American general and Genovese are taking a tour of the city in a fancy American car that Genovese gives to the general as a bribing gift while they agree on what to do with the loaded trucks.

The strength of this sequence lies in the apparent easiness with which the American authorities contradict themselves abandoning their good propositions at the very moment that they are making them. To end the corruption, the officer calls publicly for more collaboration from the people. "This is a hell of responsibility: all this stuff coming in to Naples must go to the people, not the crooks and the speculators", he says in English, and then adds in Italian, "Abbiamo fatto solo errori in Sicilia, caro Genovese siamo stati troppo buoni" ("We have made too many mistakes in Sicily"). Symbolically, the music is very loud and almost obliterates the officer's speech. The focus is no longer on the fact that the poor and the hungry will not get the food, but that these authorities can behave (and lie) in such a way without remorse.

The ending of the film shows a potential conventional closure with Luciano's death. In reality, this is everything but a typical ending. Rosi has a very clear opinion about the function of the end:

> To be effective, the questions the films ask must continue to live in the viewer even after the film is over. After my first few films, in fact, I stopped putting the words 'The End' at the conclusion because I think films should not end but should continue to grow inside us.[8]

Once more, Rosi rejects the significance that contemporary commercial cinema attributes to the ending, and decides to leave the viewer with many unanswered questions. The only certainty is that the last two sequences of *Lucky Luciano* definitely seal the political defeat of the Federal Bureau of Narcotics and the human defeat of Luciano. The long-awaited confrontation between Lucky Luciano and the police is highly anticlimactic because the two parties seem to be unwilling to support their roles and to face each other. The police arrive at Luciano's house while he is in bed. The officers do not act aggressively and Luciano remains in bed without worrying too much about their searching the house. The few words they exchange are characterised more by a form of superficial politeness than by rage or hate.

The same mood prevails in the lengthy sequence (almost twelve minutes long) at the police headquarters. During the interrogation there are several low-angle shots which enhance the troubling physical presence of Luciano. Some of the shots are also unbalanced: the two characters appear on the side of the frame, while the central part is occupied by objects. These shots create a feeling of non-communication between the policeman and Luciano. The bare office and neon lights (often included in the low-angle shots) help to create an unpleasant atmosphere. The policeman goes over the main accusation with no particular pathos, and Luciano reacts with the same lack of vitality. He remains stiff in his chair without showing any emotion. After a while, the exchange between the two characters loses all interest, while the editing creates a very slow-moving scene that enhances the sense of claustrophobia and voided expectation. When, after what seemed an endless night, the policeman opens the window because Luciano felt ill, the early morning light comes in the dreary office with a sense of relief. Luciano asks to go to the toilet and, in an almost real-time sequence, we follow the walk downstairs where the policeman leads Luciano. In the courtyard of the police station – a location that seems to have been taken from one of Rossellini neo-realist films – the policeman makes the final attempt to get some information out of Luciano. His career is at its end, but once more the film does not seem to have reached an end. The shifting of focus from Luciano to the Mafia in general, and to its connections with the state and the political world, makes Luciano's imminent death only an episode like any other in the everyday desperate fight against the Mafia. Luciano delivers a speech that underlines his detachment from personal interest and contains a broad attack on the hypocritical position that everyone involved in the chase maintains. The very last sequence at Naples Airport is shot as if the camera happened to be there by accident. Luciano's death is emptied of any emotional tone. During the entire film we do not see him doing anything related to illegal activities and the police do not catch him red-handed. His sudden death provides no impetus for relief. Luciano's body laying on the floor of the airport has the anonymity of anyone's death. His body is shown in a quick series of shots from various angles that conveys the brutality of police pictures of unknown corpses.

The game played by the authorities at the UN, and then the internal struggle between the American government, with Governor Dewey behind it, and the Bureau of Narcotics are what remain beyond Luciano's death. Earlier in the film, during a conversation, a member of the Bureau of Narcotics points very clearly to the fact that it is an endless game of power from which Luciano is the only one to benefit: "What do I do now?". "Well, you keep chasing Luciano, Dewey will keep on chasing us and Cafaldo will keep on chasing Dewey, and when all this running around is over everybody will find themselves back at the same goddamn place where he started." "Not everyone...not Luciano". These very same words are recited by a voice-over at the very end of the film. Symbolically, this time, Luciano is not mentioned; he has not been able to get out of the circle, even he has been trapped somehow in this game. These words stress the no-win situation in which everyone is caught, where even Luciano loses – not simply because he is now dead but because as a human being he has been unable to establish any contact with his fellows.

In a recent article on Rosi, Gary Crowdus defines Rosi's combining different formal elements and styles as "postmodern neorealism".[9] No matter how empty and fashionable an expression such as this is, it is surely an indication of the difficulties encountered by critics in labelling Rosi's works. Beyond this definition, there is the undeniable fact that his filmmaking transcends time and trends, and "his films are finally as much political for the way they are structured as for the choice of subject matter".[10] His constant search for an original approach to his subject-matter has put him in the position to elaborate what was valid in neo-realist language within a contemporary socio-political context. In an interview, Rosi complains about the fear that young Italian filmmakers have in approaching whatever is labelled "political".[11] Such a fear can easily be justified by the state of chaos that dominates in Italian politics in the first half of the 1990s, but it also hides the lack of courage and of control of the medium that young directors show whenever they face political issues. It is sufficient to remember Rosi's versatility and his ability to include – in the sometimes vague political label – films tackling a wide range of problems, in order to understand that we can only wish that he will be the one to give us a provocative view of the recent events in Italian society.

Notes

[1]   See the preface Calvino wrote in 1964 to the second edition of his first novel, *Il sentiero dei nidi di ragno*. On this occasion, Calvino points out very clearly that in literature, as well as in cinema, neo-realism was, above all, a group of voices, a chorus, that needed to express themselves about what they experienced.

[2]   Gary Crowdus, "Investigating the Relationship between Causes and Effects. An Interview with Francesco Rosi", *Cineaste* 20: 4 (1994): 26.

[3]   The only recent comic variation in Italy on this subject is the very successful but rather flat film, *Johnny Stecchino* (1991), directed by Roberto Benigni.

[4]   Translated from the Italian: "La mafia costituisce la garanzia della rispettabilità del sistema e il sistema le corrisponde per tale 'servizio' un prezzo che paghiamo tutti, e che più caro lo paga chi è assolutamente ignaro, e cioè il cittadino convinto della vecchia favola del criminale che fa il male e della Giustizia che lo punisce" (Sandro Zambetti, *Francesco Rosi* [Florence: La Nuova Italia, 1976]: 3).

[5]   See how Gilles Deleuze defines neo-realism, tying it with the "build-up of purely optical situations" and departing from the sensory-motor situations which characterised old realism and which audiences are used to. (Gilles Deleuze, *Cinema 2: The Time-Image*, translated by Hugh Tomlinson and Robert Galeta [Minneapolis: University of Minnesota Press, 1989]: 2.)

[6]   Translated from the Italian: "Lo schermo insomma, non come specchio della realtà in cui il pubblico sia spinto a identificarsi, ma come luogo *convenuto* di una rappresentazione della realtà di fronte alla quale lo spettatore possa mantenersi consapevole del proprio esser *fuori* dalla rappresentazione stessa e *dentro*, invece, alla realtà da cui questa ha preso le mosse, e si senta quindi indotto a confrontare il proprio punto di vista al riguardo con quello dell'autore." (Zambetti: 12.) Emphasis in original.

[7]   As Zambetti (13) states: "C'è anche, indubbiamente, una predilezione per le personalità forti e combattive, spiegabile sia a livello di affinità psicologica fra l'autore e le sue creature, sia – e più ancora, forse – col fatto che per un uomo di spettacolo vien naturale puntare su personaggi di questo tipo per stabilire un più immediato aggancio con il pubblico". ("Doubtless, there also is a predilection for strong, combative personalities, which can be explained at a level of psychological affinity between the author and his creatures, and also – even more, perhaps – by the fact that for a showman it is natural to count on characters of this kind in order to establish a more immediate contact with the public".)

[8]   Crowdus: 26.

[9]   Gary Crowdus, "Francesco Rosi. Italy's Postmodern Neorealist", *Cineaste* 20: 4 (1994): 19-25.

[10]   Ibid: 20.

[11]   In the interview with Carlo Testa in this volume, Rosi says: "I think that today in Italy the time has come for us to start again to take a good look around ourselves, looking at the problems of Italian society – something which Italian cinema has always done, and which has been its characteristic trait. The great masterpieces of the Italian cinema of the past, from the postwar period onwards, *did not* neglect individual problems; but they did interweave them with the problems that ran through society and that had to do with collectivity. Films such as *Umberto D* [1951], *Ladri di biciclette* [*Bicycle Thieves*, 1948], *La terra trema* [*The Earth Trembles*, 1948], *La dolce vita* [1960], and many others, testify to just such an attitude...[This] has nothing to do with the cinema labelled 'political cinema'. That is not what it is. In some young *autori* there is a slight fear to be catalogued as belonging to a 'political cinema' from which they may well have attempted to distance themselves. One should not be afraid of labels, however. What one should instead be afraid of is the idea of not being close enough to a truth in which the collectivity may recognise itself." Emphases in original (152-153).

Dancing with corpses: murder, politics and power in *Illustrious Corpses*

Salvatore Bizzarro

Everything which was in the past and is now, will be in the future; but the names change, and the outward appearance of things, so that any one who lacks perspicacity does not recognize them and cannot draw conclusions or form an opinion from what he observes. (Francesco Guicciardini)[1]

I.

Francesco Rosi is probably one of the least known filmmakers emerging from the ashes of the postwar and post-neo-realist cinematic world. Never particularly well-known in the United States, his obscurity is even more perplexing in light of such outstanding films as *Cristo si è fermato a Eboli* (*Christ Stopped at Eboli*, 1979), *Lucky Luciano* (1973), and *Tre fratelli* (*Three Brothers*, 1980) which, like *Cadaveri eccellenti* (*Illustrious Corpses*, 1975), presents a contemporary view of corrupt, absolute power in Italy and touches upon the effects of terrorism on Italian society. Rosi's films have had little success in the United States, if we exclude the film he made as assistant director to Visconti, *La terra trema* (*The Earth Trembles*, 1948), or his cycle on the Mafia, which also includes *Salvatore Giuliano* (1961) and *Le mani sulla città* (*Hands Over the City*, 1963). Yet, even these played better in smaller art cinemas than in larger theatres, and appealed more to Italian-Americans than to other Americans in cities such as New York, Chicago and San Francisco.

Rosi is predominantly a storyteller, and myths, legends and superstition whisper through his films. He likes wide screens and vast settings as much as close-ups, and his films feel polished and patterned even when they are jumping hectically between mythical geographies, time zones and flashbacks. Common to all his films is the ability to move viewers in mysterious ways, sweeping them along without completely revealing what it is that is moving them. Rosi uses the resources of film so powerfully that we feel a profound transformation in our relation to the historical drama which we are witnessing. As is the case with *Illustrious Corpses* and *Christ Stopped at Eboli*, literalization inevitably accompanies cinematic adaptations of novels. Rosi's scripts beg to be read, as well as seen. Nevertheless, his film adaptations of literary texts are always as good as they can possibly be. His camera's movement is free and invigorating, and experimentation is not new to his work. Fiction has power in his films, but it can also represent a reality that is oppressive and unjust, as shown in *Illustrious Corpses*. Rosi is unique among Italian directors in that he is less interested in commercial success than in the quality of his films and the integrity of his story. He is a showman who does not shy away from box-office failure. Movie history is full of ringmasters of every description, but not one – not even Fellini – has Rosi's instinctive need to hang around and see the big tent come down.

The underlining premise in Rosi's films is that the search for historical truth, although extremely difficult, is at times possible. If most of Rosi's characters are always static and never-changing, the truth that surrounds them is always subject to innumerable adjustments and discriminations. For Rosi, truth corresponds to reality, but truth is not static. It is a co-creation of self and object, an "I" and "thou" relationship, a fusion of the artist with his art. This union leads to action, because truth is not self-contained bliss. As Inspector Amerigo Rogas (Lino Ventura) discovers in *Illustrious Corpses*, even if you could look truth straight in the face, it would not be worth trusting.

Illustrious Corpses is a political thriller set in the 1970s, but in retrospect it is also a visionary film foreshadowing the recent political scandals that have rocked the pillars of Italian democracy to its foundations. Just how close Italy came to suffering a *coup d'état* is hard to determine from the film, which prefigured the political troubles which the country would undergo in the 1990s. If the story is vintage Rosi, pitting a spirited outsider against a tiny-minded bureaucratic establishment, this time the stakes are much higher than the fate of a mere handful of individuals. It is an entire system built on a house of cards, where the deaths of prosecutors and judges by unknown assassins threaten to bring it down.[2]

II.

Based on Leonardo Sciascia's novel, *Il contesto* (*Equal Danger*),[3] and set in a town in the south, Rosi's film links political power with corruption. The deaths bring onto the scene Inspector Rogas, the story's apparent hero, who gropes to find the solution to the crimes. The inspector resembles Sherlock Holmes in the power of his imagination and intelligence; Rogas almost has everything figured out before all the facts are with him. However, he also speaks with a Watsonish tone; he embodies common sense and has a mind that refuses to prejudge any set of circumstances. Thus, we have a dualistic approach to finding the criminal(s), two radically different ways of looking at the haphazard events that face the inspector as he leaves every morning to work on his case. Rogas is supposed to act as a link between the locals and the authorities in the capital, but in truth he seems stranded in a twilight of his own making. He is a recluse who understands the laws of society and how they should be implemented.

The force of the film lies in the tension it creates; the more the tension grows, the better it transmits the filmmaker's direction. The action – if it may be called that – takes place in the south and in the capital over a period of several days. The stylization implicit in the act of filming gives us the camera as a second narrative voice in counterpoint to that of the inspector. The camera's eye tries to document a sinister plot, break down the world of appearances, and reveal another level of reality that the unknowing inspector could not have imagined before.

Who is responsible for the killings? No one seems to know. A paranoid archbishop tells the inspector that, in the past, townspeople came to talk and dance with the corpses. "You come from the capital, you will not be able to understand such things", he tells Rogas. The inspector, however, from the very beginning suspects a deranged pharmacist named Cres, who has spent several years in jail for allegedly attempting to murder his wife. As it turns out, the conviction of the pharmacist is arbitrary and based on questionable evidence given in court by Signora Cres (Maria Carta) about the poisoning of her cat.

In the opening scene of the film, the camera shows a crude gallery full of cadavers, a long tunnel of sombre humans caught in the moment of their death. The prosecutor Varga (Charles Vanel) continues the tradition of talking to the corpses, and still believes that the dead are the only ones capable of keeping secrets. Moments later, Varga, who knows the secrets of all the people in the town, meets a violent death as he picks a jasmine flower from a tree. At first, the Mafia is suspected, but the inspector quickly discards this hypothesis. Death is ever-present in the film and is not the action of a lone assassin, as Inspector Rogas thinks at first. Even if it were, Rosi seems to suggest to us that the societal power structure is responsible for pulling the strings.

The pragmatic inspector, with his rational mind, initially does not accept the idea of a conspiracy, as one judge after another and even the President of the Court meet their deaths, allegedly at the hands of the pharmacist/executioner Cres. As long as Rogas does not accept the conspiracy theory, he is allowed to proceed with his investigation. The inspector's fatal error lies in his impulse to derive secret meanings from a series of events that clearly implicate a political motivation on the part of the power structure, which is using the killings for its own concealed purposes. It is not clear at the start if one or more executioners are involved.

The Minister of the Interior (Fernando Rey), tells the inspector that Italy is on the verge of an historic compromise between members of his own party, the Democrazia Cristiana (Christian Democrat Party), which has wielded power since the end of the Second World War, and the Communists, who are driven by international forces alien to the Italian system. It is clear from what the minister says that he is against such a future for the Italian state, and that his views are shared by the Armed Forces, the police, and the security forces, set on defending Italian constitutionality as they interpret it. It is ironic that, less than two years after the film's release, Italians witnessed the abduction of Aldo Moro, a Christian Democrat who was in favour of bringing the Communists under the umbrella of the national government. Taken prisoner by the Brigate Rosse (Red Brigades), the Italian terrorist group of the Far Left, Moro became a tool in the state of war that existed between the terrorist organisation and the Italian government. Like the inspector, who met his death when he came too close to discovering a political conspiracy (whether real or imagined), Moro became a tragic symbol around whom the political drama was played out.[4]

III.

Both novel and film seem to remind us of the delicate balance between facts as they are known to us, and facts as they are imagined by us. This is the same dilemma facing the inspector in his search for individual truth and historic truth. After the death of Varga, another judge is killed on a road a few kilometres from the first homicide, and under mysterious circumstances. Rogas begins to see the murders as the workings of the criminal and vengeful mind of the pharmacist Cres.

The death of judge Sanza (Francesco Callari) is investigated, but potential witnesses "saw nothing, heard nothing, knew nothing".[5] Rogas, with his obsessive sense of deductive reasoning, is not satisfied that the murders of a prosecutor and a judge are merely coincidental; the two crimes make him suspect the pharmacist out of three people who had been wronged by the judicial system. His thesis is not taken seriously by the local Chief of Police (Tino Carraro).

The killing of another judge at the National Bank is attributed by the local powers to the acts of a crazy man. With a third magistrate killed, Rogas concludes that all the murders are the work of a lone assassin. Judge Calamo is killed with the same gun and bullets used in the two other homicides. "What could possibly link the three killings?", Rogas asks himself. The answer is that all three magistrates have been involved in the incarceration of Cres. Strangely, every photograph of Cres has been removed from his abandoned palace, where an eerie song playing on a victrola, the tango "Jeanne y Paul" (composed by Astor Piazzolla), increases the Inspector's solitude and sense of estrangement, and is a presage of what will happen to him in the days to come.

The pharmacist has disappeared. In fact, he never really appears as a character in the film; only his "shadow" is felt throughout the investigation. Rogas seems to spot him at a party attended by the elite of the Italian political apparatus and Italian society. But Cres's presence, if he is there at all, is fleeting and evanescent.

At the party of ship magnate, Patos (Alexandre Mnouchkine), every possible political group is represented together with the Armed Forces, the diplomatic corps, the police and the security forces. The party itself becomes a metaphor for corrupt power and for the country's political and societal ills, where both the Far Right and the Far Left "sleep" in the same bed and "dance" with the living and with the dead. Rogas begins to suspect that, while the Left is accused of making the revolution, it may be the Right that is preparing a coup to overthrow the democratic state.

While looking for a suspect in what seems to be an unlikely place, the inspector becomes an inadvertent witness to sensitive political discussions. He sees an altercation between Nocio (Alfonso Gatto), a Communist writer, and Galano (Paolo Graziosi), the leader of the Gruppo Zeta, a Far Left group waging a "permanent revolution" intent on bringing down the multi-party system governing Italy. The Communists smell an illusory victory which would bring them to share power with the Christian Democrats, while the Gruppo Zeta envisions revolutionary uprisings that would result in the demise of the bourgeois state.

Several people at the party are baffled about the murders and the murderer(s); seeing both the inspector and the Minister of the Interior there, they theorize that those in power are spying on them and that their telephones are tapped. The inspector, too, is beginning to ask for further explanations about the legality of these extreme security measures. The Minister of the Interior reassures him that if some telephones are tapped, this is done with the explicit consent of the courts in order to protect the government.

Rogas is convinced that a fourth magistrate is about to be removed, and he tries to reconstruct the events leading to the murder. The police pay no heed to his speculations, and purposely state that the Left has a hand in the killings of the magistrates in order to cause a political crisis which will eventually bring down the government.

Rogas disregards the police's complicated theories, opts for an obvious outcome, and correctly predicts the murder of the alternate judge, Rasto (Alain Cuny). The fourth murder opens the door to the conspiracy theory at the highest level of government. The police cover-up threatens democracy itself, and Rogas must take on the system by himself, becoming more and more isolated from his chief and from those who are in control. The voice of the Chief of Police is heard saying in a recorded tape: "questi giudici, stiamo un po' attenti con questi giudici. Abbiamo addosso Rogas che ha già annusato troppo" ("these judges, let us be careful with these judges. Rogas is on to us and he has already sniffed too much"). From this moment, Rogas is a condemned man; from pursuer he becomes pursued.

What happens here is so rich in strangeness that the whole film begins to feel like a voyage: the characters, never fully developed, are jammed together (at the party; at the Justice Department; at the Commissariat) and swept along by unmanageable forces towards a destination which they cannot imagine. Only the newly-appointed military leaders, the Chief of Police and the plotters know what is going on. Even location, whether it is the province or the capital, becomes indistinguishable in the film and in the story-line. The only hints come from shots of the architecture: rich, adorned and baroque in the province; cold, geometric, orderly, neo-Fascist in the capital.

As the film proceeds, the political implications of the story gain strength. Ambiguity and ambivalence become part of the *mise en scène*. As a Communist journalist friend of Rogas tells him, "one murder needs an inspector; four murders become a political question". Here Rosi is least patient and most inventive, as the camera-narrator moves around with brisk tempo. Orders come from the capital; the Communists are blamed for the instability in the country and for the unions' call to strike; the inspector is told that he should become subordinate to the political squad, which he refuses to do. Shortly afterwards, Rogas is relieved of his duties. Fear and panic set in; Rogas is threatened and pursued, but his ironic narrative voice continues to be heard in the conversation with the Chief of Police, and later with the President of the Court, Richès (skilfully played by Max von Sydow).

The country seems to be on the brink of revolution with mass arrests taking place, the suspension of habeas corpus, the torture of political prisoners, the tapping of telephones, and the installation of listening devices on the part of the state apparatus to protect a corrupt government. The Armed Forces name a new Commander-in-Chief, and the country begins increasingly to resemble a police state, not unlike the one established in Chile during the violent *coup d'état* by the military, which saw the overthrow of the democratically-elected president, Salvador Allende (Gossens) in 1973.[6]

Before he abandons the investigation, Rogas decides to warn Richès, telling him that he is likely to be the fifth victim. When asked why he wants to see the President of the Court, Rogas replies that the President faces grave danger from the pharmacist Cres. Rogas is told to return the next evening at 8.00. However, as he leaves the palace, he sees several government cars abandoning the premises. All the powerful are in their cars: several ministers, the Secretaries of the Navy, Army and Air Force, the Commander-in-Chief of the Armed Forces, and the Chief of Police. The inspector also spots the Mercedes with Swiss licence plates reported by a prostitute at the scene of the second murder.

The Chief of Police urges Rogas not to scare Richès by warning him that he may be harmed, since Richès is well-protected. Rogas ironically replies that the entire government seems to have been guarding the palace – a reference to all the government cars he had seen leaving the mansion. However, Rogas also begins to suspect the role of the political leaders in keeping "the truth" from him and from the people.

In Rogas's ensuing conversation with Richès, Rosi deconstructs the parameters of truth, using, on the one hand, the discourse of Richès, and, on the other, his fanaticism in defending the infallibility of the judiciary. The President of the Court gives us his views on the innocence of Cres, and his opinions about judicial error. Richès personally attacks Rogas, lecturing him on how useless the job of inspector is in a country on the verge of chaos – "Il suo mestiere, mio caro amico, è diventato ridicolo" ("Your job, my dear friend, borders on the ridiculous") – and then goes on to criticise Voltaire and other writers such as Bertrand Russell, Sartre and Marcuse for their political views and for protecting the "innocent" against the court's judgment. He especially attacks Voltaire's *Traité sur la tolérance* (*Treatise on Tolerance*), and the state of warfare that exists in the country. But, in his attacks, Richès gesticulates excitedly, moves about theatrically, and shows a mounting nervousness that makes him lose all credibility.

The inspector is likewise parodied in his belief that a lone assassin is responsible for the murders of the judges, when a roving camera shows the machinations of those in power to hide the truth. By deconstructing the story of the film, Rosi forces the viewer to think, while at the same time satisfying audience expectations in a suspense film. Throughout the film, Rogas remains true to his double role as a "speaking narrator" (*sujet énonciateur*) and the "narration's subject" (*sujet de l'énonce*).[7] Upon leaving Richès's palace, the eerie tango plays once again, symbolising the inspector's increased isolation. The corruption of the ruling class, the compromise of political leaders, and the "conspiracy" to destabilise the government all point to an invisible, omnipresent power that "investigates, listens".

Rogas is now pursued relentlessly and the camera flows effortlessly in the same direction, its movements driven by an overpowering sense of historical inevitability. The Mercedes follows Rogas as he leaves the party alone; lights flash on and off his face, then are turned off; Rogas is almost hit by the car. He quickly jumps on a bus, but jumps off when he realises that he is being followed. As the tension mounts, he finds refuge in a café. But even here there is a suspicious man eying him. Rogas summons a policeman friend and escapes. When Rogas hears the tape with the voice of the Chief of Police confirming that he is getting closer to the "truth" and therefore in danger, he writes a letter to the person in charge of security and secretly meets his journalist friend. Their conversation revolves around a possible political plot. The journalist tells him that there are plots every day, but that this time it will end badly. He convinces Rogas to meet with Amar, the leader of the opposition Communists, while all the time their conversation is being recorded and listened to by Richès and "others".

As predicted, Richès is killed, and Rogas has come to the realisation that he is a marked man. He learns that his apartment is bugged and ponders what he should do next. Not fully conscious of his actions, he moves from room to room and goes to the kitchen to make some coffee. He wanders to the bathroom, splashes water on his face and dries it, trying to avoid the eyes of the man in the mirror. As with Judge Rasto, who washes his hands and looks at himself in the mirror before being shot, we sense that the inspector will suffer a similar fate. The mirror represents self-referentiality, and knowledge is revealed to the inspector through the visual experience of looking at himself. As he finishes drinking his coffee, the room that hides him from danger suddenly assumes the guise of an infinitely more secret, remote, even more tenebrous place than it really is: a spot, lost in an immense space, in a cold and impersonal city. He leaves the flat and goes to sleep in the car, assuming that the car park is a safer place than his apartment.

Ironically, the next day, Rogas meets Amar secretly, going over to the Communist enemy in order to defend the "truth" and the principles which have always governed his actions. When both are killed in the Museo di Civiltà Romana in the EUR (this time, plaster casts of Roman Emperors are the only witnesses to the crime), the mystery is not resolved within the parameters of the film. The official version is that Rogas first killed Amar, because he saw conspiracies everywhere and suspected the extreme Left and the Communists of plotting a *coup d'état*, and then killed himself. To add irony upon irony, the word "civiltà" means "civilisation, public spirit, civic virtues", all of which are absent in the cold-blooded murder of the inspector and of the Communist leader.

The assassination of the inspector and the Communist Party leader makes us reflect on the opening scene of the film at the Capuchin Monastery in Palermo. There, the mummified corpses, like the statues of Roman Emperors now in the art museum, seem to be unwitting witnesses to murder and political power-plays. Both represent the notables during two different periods of Italian history, and exclude the peasants and the plebeians from their ranks. In fact, the only peasant in Rosi's film has a very brief but significant appearance. Interrogated by the inspector as to what type of man the murdered judge Sanza was, the peasant simply replies, "come questa città. Sono loro che l'hanno voluta cosí" ("just like this city. It is they who wanted it so"), a reference to the judge's monetary gains with the city's development at the expense of the beautiful orange groves that the building replaced. The viewer is left wondering how many murders both the corpses and the Roman emperors witnessed and approved of when they lived as notable citizens.

IV.

The juxtaposition of two concepts of historical truth – one that aspires to liberty and justice, and one that draws its strength from the force and abuse of power – is present in both film and book. If Rogas predicted the fourth and fifth murders of judges, why was he incapable of preventing them? And, if he foresaw his own death, why did he trust the Minister of the Interior, in charge of the same security forces who were enmeshed in the conspiracy, to save his own life by writing him the letter? Firstly, Rogas probably realised that he could not do anything at this point to save the judges. Secondly, he began to see that everything was closing in on him because of what he had discovered. Driving the viewer/reader relentlessly from a detective story-line to a political conspiracy and its conclusion, both Rosi and Sciascia deprive the viewer/reader of any intellectual or moral satisfaction from the *dénouement* of the film and of the book. The story ends without a solution or, in typical Rosi fashion, it does not end.

The recurrent theme of corrupt power makes Rogas the expiatory victim of a system gone awry. Decency, truth and justice, symbolised by Rogas, are defeated by a state apparatus embodying evil. The investigative journey Rogas had willingly undertaken can only end in his own death: "Ma Rogas aveva dei principi, in un paese in cui quasi nessuno ne aveva" ("But Rogas had principles, in a country where almost no one had any"), writes Sciascia at the end of his novel. The labyrinth, which Rogas and others like him enter, does not have exits, only trapdoors.

At the end of the film, the journalist talks to a Communist Party bureaucrat telling him that he does not believe that Rogas has killed himself, and that he believes there was a plot to overthrow the government. The state had been held prisoner, and Rogas himself was a prisoner of those who wanted to hold the state hostage. The bureaucrat advises "non bisogna scatenare la piazza" ("we cannot allow a revolt to break out"), to which the journalist replies, "allora la gente non dovrà mai sapere la verità" ("hence the people should never have to know the truth"). "La verità non è sempre rivoluzionaria" ("Truth is not always revolutionary"), says the bureaucrat, and these are the last words spoken in a film that significantly concludes without the traditional "The End". The film's final images are of the "masses" mobilising against government repression, as tanks, helicopters, gunshots and mayhem break out. We are faced with a saga of the continuing problem of what Italy is, as well as – perhaps – a mixture of fact and fiction in the deconstruction and reinterpretation of given moments of Italian history.

Through Rogas, Rosi introduces the theme of deception and illusion into the film. Rogas is transformed from a capable inspector into a misled figure not worthy of the fate that awaits him. Dying searching for the truth presents a brand of heroism quite different from that which evolves from the Manichean struggle between the forces of good and evil. Since there does not seem to be any good in the capital or in the province, the political ambivalence of the system is called into question by Rosi. When the inspector leaves his apartment for the last time, Rosi's fluid camera movements, panning up and down the outside and inside of the apartment, are in juxtaposition to the jarring soundtrack of the blaring clatter of a country in turmoil.

Illustrious Corpses dares to bring to the screen a specific criticism of the Italian polity. The inspector moves through a bureaucratic jungle in an attempt to get someone to make a simple statement of fact and arrive at the truth. The police and members of the power-elite are depicted as corrupt men, using illegal means to maintain power. If the viewer feels no sympathy for the judges, it is because they too, at the moment of their death, show undesirable idiosyncrasies: Judge Rasto washes his hands when he comes into contact with anyone; Varga knows the secrets of everyone in town; Sanza acquires wealth through urban development; Calamo has hundreds of millions stashed away; Richès fanatically defends law and order without any regard for justice. Rogas is their opposite: an honest citizen caught in a web of intrigue, who believes that the police are the safeguard of citizens' rights, and not the tool of a repressive state.

Terrorism and terror can be attributable to outside forces, as well as to internal ones. Rogas attempted to find the truth of the official lie in his headlong rush to attempt to understand the facts and meditate on their significance. Both the book by Sciascia and the film by Rosi widen their scope to concentrate on the very fabric of Italian society: what was threatened beyond mere individuals was the very polity of the state. Perhaps the author's and the filmmaker's pessimism hides a note of optimism. The country, having been reduced to unscrupulous self-interests, where all that counts is power for its own sake, may now start anew and opt for liberty and justice for all its people. The measures taken in Italy against the Mafia and against iniquity, however, all proved to be promising but ineffectual (save for the recent capture of Mafia boss, Giovanni Brusca, the alleged killer of Judge Giovanni Falcone). The 1996 elections that brought in a new government still leave many Italians sceptical about the ability of the state to rebuild and reconstitute a society mired in corruption. What the Prince of Lampedusa used to say, "bisogna che tutto cambi, perché nulla cambi" ("it is necessary for everything to change, so that nothing will change"), seems to reflect the political and social realities of the country.[8]

V.

The film's release, like the book's publication, gave rise to polemics and to much speculation by journalists and politicians as to its meaning. Many critics pointed to the heavy ideological content of the story, as aptly demonstrated in the compilation of reviews by Francesco Bolzoni and Tom O'Neill.[9] Yet, the chronology of the film is quite linear, accumulating a heavy dose of political interpretation only at the end. Sciascia considered the film faithful to his book, which was a requiem for revolution and a warning – a warning echoed by Rosi. The film is an example of how fine acting, original camerawork and the use of sound can provide a simple indictment of the Italian political system more devastating than the overblown ideological films of the 1970s.

Rosi's superb cinematography in *Illustrious Corpses* brings Sciascia's book to an even greater audience. Rosi deconstructs reality through the camera-narrator; through the video, using images to chronicle political unrest; through the appearance of a "screen-within-a-screen"; and through the insertion of still photographs in the unfolding of the story. When the film takes on documentary features, Rosi realises that colour could never hope to match the expressive timbre of the black-and-white.

Ultimately, the question posed by Rosi is: does art have the metaphysical and moral power over reality? And can it ever re-create the truth? Although the film's language is disarmingly simple and straightforward, we find ourselves "reading" between the lines. While the surface of the story is crystal clear, intangible forces are building up underneath. The semantic possibilities of language are manipulated by the narrator, Rogas, and by the poignant camera.[10] For Rosi, art constitutes the ultimate reality, and it acquires such suggestiveness that we leave the film questioning our simple assumptions about the nature of truth. The film thus becomes an extended metaphor with a clear message: creativity in a work of art is capable of representing social problems, but not of resolving them. The only thing the artist can hope for is that images and ideas may move the viewer to social action that will change the world.

Speaking about his book, Sciascia said that he started writing *Equal Danger* as a parody for fun, but ended up no longer enjoying it: "ho cominciato a scriverla con divertimento, e l'ho finita che non mi divertivo più" ("I started writing it for fun, and ended up no longer enjoying it"). Rosi's adaptation of the book to the screen remains true to the author's purpose, using the detective motif as a vehicle for social and political commentary and not as a means for solving a mystery, and all the while focusing on the universal desire of all people for a government which is responsive to the well-being of those it governs. The camera moves quickly from interpreting the work as a mere *divertissement*, and instead considers Sciascia's text with the high seriousness its author had intended.

Both author and filmmaker reflect a personal vision of their own making. If they seem increasingly less optimistic about changing the status quo, it is because they are well aware of the gap between the ideals dear to them and reality. Nevertheless, they are willing to dance with corpses in order to remind the living that they must be active participants in ridding Italy of a decomposing system. They want to redeem the sickness of contemporary Italy, washing away its nasty taste. In so doing, they become the repository of Italian hopes for social justice and for genuine radical change. With narrative boldness, visual audacity and emotional directness, Sciascia and Rosi seem to be telling us: "expect the worst, and hope for the best". Only then can we stop dancing with corpses, and learn once again to scrutinise our individual conscience and collective identity so that we can see who we are with clarity, and have the courage to speak out.

VI.

   – Far from a scournful world of jeering crowds
     and peering magistrates,

sleep in peace, lovely enigma, sleep
in your mysterious tomb (Charles Baudelaire)[11]

Thus ends the story of an honest inspector. In Italy, Silvio Berlusconi and the Far Right briefly establish a new government, which strangely resembles the old one, only to be replaced in 1996 by the first Left-of-Centre coalition to govern Italy in 50 years (already envisioned by Aldo Moro before he met his tragic fate two decades ago).[12] And History continues.

Notes

[1] Francesco Guicciardini, *Selected Writings*, edited with an introduction by Cecil Grayson, translated by Margaret Grayson (London: Oxford University Press, 1965): 23.

[2] When *Illustrious Corpses* was made, Italian democracy operated overwhelmingly through the political parties. The killing of judges and magistrates in the late 1980s and early 1990s became a serious threat to the system, and elicited voter rejection of most of the political forces operating in the country since 1947. Despite the fact that the Communist Party and the Christian Democratic Party tried to recycle themselves by changing their names, rightist and extremist parties, such as Forza Italia, the Lega Lombarda, and the Alleanza Nazionale (formerly the Movimento Sociale Italiano), have made strong showings in recent elections and even produced a Prime Minister.

[3] The country depicted by Sciascia in the book is purely imaginary, but resembles the same Italy represented in the film. Leonardo Sciascia, *Il contesto*, edited and introduced with notes and vocabulary by Tom O'Neill (Manchester: Manchester University Press, 1986). The English translation of this book is by Adrienne Foulke, *Equal Danger* (New York: Harper and Row, 1973).

[4] The Red Brigades killed Aldo Moro less to show that the state was weak than to goad it into taking repressive action. Their fear was that citizens, and especially Communists – who should have favoured political change – were too complacent towards the status quo. Other political scandals that followed are prefigured in the film by the actions of those judges who loved money and power. Money in Italy often changes hands under questionable circumstances. This was the case with the secret Masonic lodge, Propaganda 2, involved in shady dealings with the Banco Ambrosiano in 1981, and with the Ferruzzi-Montedison Group in 1992, which resulted in several suicides of businessmen and politicians who embezzled money at the highest levels of government. Even the brother of Italy's Prime Minister, Silvio Berlusconi, Paolo, was under house-arrest in 1994 accused of political corruption, bringing the investigation perilously close to the Prime Minister who later resigned.

[5] In Sicily, no witness dares testify against a crime possibly committed by the Mafia. Among the many characteristics of the Sicilian Mafia is the self-protecting law of "omertà", which is a conspiracy of silence. The punishment for breaking the silence is death.

[6] Although the threat of a *coup d'état* was present in Italy in the late 1960s and early 1970s (this was documented by the CIA), it never reached the violence or the repression that was evident in Chile in the first few days of the *coup d'état* of 11 September 1973, where, in Santiago alone, some 2000 people lost their lives. In the first three months of the Chilean coup, more than 30 000 died, according to sources from the Church and human rights organisations. See Salvatore Bizzarro, "Chile", in *Encyclopedia of Developing Nations* (New York: McGraw-Hill Book Company, 1982); "Chile Under the Jackboot", *Current History* 70: 413 (1976): 57-60, ff. 81; and "Rigidity and Restraint in Chile", *Current History* 74: 434 (1978): 66-69, ff. 83.

[7] See Linda Coremans, "De intertextuele relaties tussen een literaire tekst en een filmtekst", *Cadaveri eccellenti* van Fr. Rosi naar de roman *Il contesto* van L Sciascia. *Spiegel Der Letteren* 29: 1-2 (1987): 119-126. For more on intertextual analysis, see her book *La transformation filmique du:* Il Contesto à Cadaveri Eccellenti (Berne: Peter Lang, 1990). See also Michel Ciment, *Le dossier Rosi* (Paris: Editions Ramsay, 1987).

[8] At the time of this writing, magistrates in Milan continue to issue arrest orders for Italian businessmen, government tax inspectors accused of trading bribes for lenient or fraudulent tax audits, and corrupt judges and magistrates. Silvio Berlusconi himself is under investigation for his dealings with several private television stations that might have violated anti-trust laws.

[9] For several newspaper articles written on *Illustrious Corpses*, see Francesco Bolzoni, *I film di Francesco Rosi* (Rome: Gremese Editore, 1986): 114-115. Of particular interest are the articles by Francesco Savio in the weekly *Il Mondo* 4 March 1976, in which he calls Rosi's film a "Poli-fizione" ("Poli-fiction"), and that by Lino Micciché, in the daily organ of the Socialist Party *Avanti* 14 February 1976, which later appeared in the book, *Cinema italiano degli anni '70* (Padua-Venice: Marsilio Editori, 1980). For criticism of Leonardo Sciascia's *Il contesto*, see the "Bibliography" in the book of the same name edited by Tom O'Neill (Manchester: Manchester University Press, 1986). Also of note are the following articles: Tom Baldwin, "Leonardo Sciascia, l'uomo, il cittadino, lo scrittore", *ATI Journal* 30 (1980): 30-51; and Marcello Strazzeri, "L'ideologia di Sciascia: dalla critica meridionalista alla critica dello stato", *Critica Letteraria* 11: 2, 39 (1983): 299-312.

[10] An example of the semantic manipulation of language is found when Rogas indicates that the early court conviction sending Cres to jail is arbitrary, but what the inspector really wants to communicate is that Cres is innocent. In this matter, tension is created between what is said (*énonce*) and the matter in which it is said (*énonciation*), which makes us aware of the presence of a storyteller and of what the storyteller means by what he says. Similarly, the camera-narrator gets a close-up of Judge Varga picking a jasmine flower at the moment of his death. We are told by the priest that

the flower symbolises life, but in the case of Varga it means death. Furthermore, by picking this flower, Varga is also taking the life of the flower. Another example of language being manipulated occurs when the Chief of Police tells Rogas that all the dignitaries gathered in the palace were attending a reception at the Portuguese Embassy. Rogas calls the embassy to discover that the Chief of Police had lied. The inspector arrives at the truth by way of a falsehood.

[11] Charles Baudelaire, *Les Fleurs du Mal*, translated by Richard Howard (Brighton: The Harvester Press, 1982): 123. The quotation comes from the poem, "A Martyr: drawing by an unknown master".

[12] The new government headed by Romano Prodi includes two former prime ministers (Lamberto Dini and Carlo Azeglio Ciampi), a former prosecuting magistrate (Antonio Di Pietro), and several long-standing political wheeler-dealers. Of particular interest are the pledge by Prodi to continue going effectively after the Mafia, and the question of the secession of the North from the South, favoured by Umberto Bossi and the Lega Lombarda. Bossi wants to create a separate country for the Padana (all the Northern regions on the Po Valley). But it is clear that what Bossi and the North really want is political and economic independence from Rome.

Beyond *cinema politico*: family as political allegory in *Three Brothers*

Millicent Marcus

Towards the middle of *Tre fratelli* (*Three Brothers*, 1980), Raffaele, a judge, leafs through a photo album of slain corpses, including those of the presumed perpetrator and the victims of the type of terrorist attacks to which he also could be subject, were he to agree to preside over a trial of left-wing extremists. As he falls asleep, the photographs modulate into a nightmare about his own assassination at terrorist hands. This sequence reads like a self-quotation: it could be an extract from a number of Rosi's earlier films – from his very first, *La sfida* (*The Challenge*, 1957), whose protagonist is gunned down at the conclusion; from *Salvatore Giuliano* (1961), which begins and ends with blood-soaked corpses; or from *Cadaveri eccellenti* (*Illustrious Corpses*, 1975), whose title is self-evident. Raffaele's dream serves as a micro-history of Rosi's film career up to *Cristo si è fermato a Eboli* (*Christ Stopped at Eboli*, 1979) – a career dedicated to *cine-inchieste*, cinematic investigations into cases involving power relationships between charismatic individuals, corporations, criminal organisations and the state. Rosi labelled this approach a second phase of neo-realism,[1] replacing the immediate postwar cinema of objective witness with a new "critical realism with overt ideological intentions",[2] and thus anticipating the *cinema politico* of Costa-Gavras and Elio Petri of the late 1960s and 1970s. Although never a documentary filmmaker, Rosi nevertheless sought to expose the operations of a univocal, partisan truth beneath the surface of events. To that end, he employed a non-linear, investigative style whose editorial violence reveals the inner-relationships and hidden complicities underlying the official version of the facts.

However, the terrorist sequence in *Three Brothers* departs from its cinematic precedents in several crucial ways, and signals the new direction which Rosi's work would take in the 1980s. Had he made *Three Brothers* in the mid-1970s, while still bound to the monolithic ideological truths of his *cine-inchiesta* period, the film would have been dedicated entirely to the terrorist question, and would have been more properly entitled *The First Son* or *The Only Son*. But, by 1981 Rosi seems to have come around to a more subtle and nuanced approach to "the Italian case":[3]

The problem of terrorism? It is a problem to which a whole film should be devoted, and it's not as though I haven't given it some thought...But I always recoiled because I found myself facing problems of knowledge: if I, as a director, had not been able to disentangle the logic of terrorism, both in its human and in its political reality, in what way could I help the public?[4]

Daunted by the magnitude of the "problems of knowledge" posed by terrorism, and aware that to understand its logic one must live its "human and political reality", Rosi chooses to inscribe the phenomenon in the experience of one of his characters, thus refusing to endow his representation of the issue with the presumed objectivity of a third-person perspective, or to arrogate the authority of an omniscient one. In so doing, Rosi acknowledges the limits of a purely abstract, cerebral approach to the problem, and defers to the superior power of personal witness. In addition, his decision to make the film only *in part* about terrorism might reflect a conscious, anti-terrorist strategy – i.e. not to place the phenomenon centre-stage, not to give it the full press which only serves to promote terrorist objectives, and not to single it out as the privileged symptom of the diseased body politic of the 1970s. By making terrorism one of three manifestations of social disorder (the others are embodied by the younger brothers, Rocco and Nicola), Rosi seeks to demystify and delimit his subject-matter, rather than surrender to terrorism's tyrannical hold over national attention.

Another measure of Rosi's shift from the ideological filmmaking of his *cinema politico* period is the decision to employ multiple centres of consciousness in his film, and, with them, to entertain a plurality of perspectives on "the Italian case", rather than insisting on one totalizing approach: "The three brothers are all parts of myself", Rosi explains, "I don't identify with one rather than another".[5] As the brothers discuss, argue and dream, Rosi's reluctance to take sides makes his film a virtual symposium of views on the plight of contemporary Italy, prompting such approving reactions as those of Pauline Kael: "Earlier, full of theory, Rosi imposes his vision; now, he searches it out – he goes deeper down into himself, and much further into his subject".[6]

Most indicative of Rosi's evolution beyond *cinema politico* is the fact that the terrorist attack is embedded in a dream. It is highly subjective and personalised, leaving behind the realm of documentary, albeit highly manipulated, factuality for the inner recesses of human consciousness. Such a movement had already been foretold in his previous film, *Christ Stopped at Eboli*, where Carlo Levi's subjective experience of the peasant world had been translated into the film's own language of long takes, sweeping panoramic shots of the landscape, slow pacing and an emotional musical score. But, in that earlier film Rosi scrupulously respected Levi's personal privacy, never entering into the interior spaces which the writer's own text had so jealously guarded. Dreams, fantasies and memories are never explored in *Christ Stopped at Eboli*, whereas *Three Brothers* depends heavily on such psychic incursions to reveal the inner lives of characters, whose reticence in some cases borders on solipsism. To dramatise this move into subjectivity, the film begins in the mind of one of the brothers, Rocco, who dreams about a junkyard teeming with rats, and wakes up to find that the "rats" are the boys in his reformatory who have been routinely escaping and pillaging all night. By anticipating and interpreting the bad news that he is about to learn from the police, Rocco's subjectivity is privileged in the film, inviting us into his nightmarish foreknowledge, and providing us with metaphoric terms for thinking about the plight of contemporary urban "scavengers", as he will call them later, while leafing through a UNICEF report on disadvantaged children.

Piero Piccioni's soundtrack is extremely important to the development of the characters' inner lives. By introducing Rocco's nightmare with the sound of the dreamer's heartbeat, Piccioni immediately locates the viewer *within* the human organism, suggesting the primacy of internal experience over its external causes. Rocco's heartbeat then modulates into the sounds of string tremolos, miming the swells of emotion brought on by the dream itself. Heartbeats will be heard once again in the film during Raffaele's assassination nightmare, while the string tremolos will continue throughout *Three Brothers* to link the film's emotionalism to a unitary familial source.[7]

A second character to be introduced through a subjective experience is Donato, the aged father of the family. Walking down a country road, he comes upon a rabbit, which an elderly woman (presumably his wife) urges him to capture. "I wanted to cook it for tomorrow", she explains, "but it escaped. It was afraid of dying." When Donato seizes the animal and hands it to his wife, she lets it go, walks away and herself disappears, rematerializing behind him against the background of their farmhouse. All this remains quite cryptic until the next scene, when Donato telegraphs his sons with the news that their mother has died, and we realise, retroactively, that the hallucination had been a poetic re-enactment of her death. By making us privy to the subjective experience before the information that would give it factual meaning, Rosi privileges the private, interior world of signs over their objective referents, and implicates us imaginatively in Donato's loss. So compressed is the poetic language

118

of this daydream that it condenses an entire lifetime of domestic routine – of hunting, meal planning, cooking and general nurturing – into one simple exchange between husband and wife. Where the rats of Rocco's dream were bearers of all the negativity of contemporary urban life, Donato's rabbit is the repository of his wife's posthumous consolations. In releasing the animal, Caterina tells her husband all he needs to know about her death: it may have been a capture, but it was also a liberation. Later in the film, this insight is affirmed by Raffaele's ancient wet-nurse, Filomena, who reports that she, too, had dreamt of the dead Caterina, and had found her "well and content".

By endowing the subjective sequences with both cognitive and moral authority, Rosi opens up his film to multilevelled poetic interpretation. Whereas metaphor governs the relationship between dream images and their referents (Rocco's juvenile delinquents are rats; the dead Caterina is a rabbit), it is allegory which determines the signifying mode of the narrative as a whole. Thus, the Giuranna family as a disintegrating corporate unit allegorises the plight of the Italian body politic in the postwar era. From their origin in the Murgie region of Apulia, the three sons migrate to Rome, Naples and Turin, respectively, in a re-enactment of Italy's demographic shifts from agrarian to urban centres, from south to north. True to the universalizing thrust of allegory, the family's geographic origin is never named – it remains the generic southern Italian town whose populace is composed predominantly of card-playing elderly men. The one visible young woman in the town, Rosaria, is married to a guest worker in Germany, who returns home twice a year. When Raffaele encounters an old schoolfriend in the town bar, this lone specimen of non-geriatric manhood is apologetic about not having migrated elsewhere. Like the emblematic Tara in Bertolucci's *La strategia del ragno* (*The Spider's Stratagem*, 1970), an entire generation is absent from this Pugliese town and, by extension, from rural Italy itself, whose population will not be replenished once the elderly have died off. Thus, the funeral of Caterina serves to allegorise the death of the rural Italian past, and offers the occasion for the brothers, representatives of the new social order, to take stock of a national identity now cut off from its source.

Like so many Italian films of the postwar era, *Three Brothers* found its most sympathetic audiences abroad.[8] The problem with the domestic reception seemed to reside in the film's allegorical structure, which provoked a Crocean resistance to Rosi's didacticism as "non poesia" ("non-poetry") – as uninspired, sterile and programmatic. Foreign audiences, on the other hand, seemed willing to accept the film's pedagogy as an integral part of its visionary mode. Since the allegorical method in modern fiction will only succeed when the literal

119

level is sufficient unto itself – expressive in its own autonomous terms – detractors of *Three Brothers* were obviously insufficiently engaged at the narrative level to move beyond it in search of ulterior meanings. Hence such critics' resentment of a significance which they perceived to be imposed from above or, as Francesco Bolzoni put it, "just as he had done in his earliest films, it seems that here Rosi first sought a sociologically interesting datum, and then constructed around it the semblance of a character".[9]

On the other hand, admirers of the film, such as Pauline Kael, defended it in suggestive terms: "even though the structure is schematic", she argues, "the film moves on waves of feeling".[10] I think therefore that the viewer's disposition to accept or reject Rosi's allegorical superstructure is established in the first few moments of *Three Brothers*, in the subjective sequences of Rocco's nightmare and Donato's daydream – sequences which either succeed or fail in carrying us on those "waves of feeling" so necessary to our engagement in the film's literal level. Thus, Rosi's privileging of subjectivity is the necessary precondition for his allegorical mode, whose failure for Italian audiences may be attributed either to its low threshold of tolerance for terrorist treatments, or to its Crocean impulse to dismiss allegory as "non-poetry".

In accepting the allegorical justification for the film's structure, a series of schematic correspondences emerge. The three brothers each personifies a facet of the modern Italian condition; they embody the cities to which they have emigrated; and they experience mid-life crises of a personal or professional nature. In terms of narrative symmetries, each brother enacts his characteristic relationship to the town of origin, and each has a dream or wish-fulfilment fantasy which reveals that individual's hidden self. The allegorical schematism even extends to the brothers' modes of return to their birthplace: Raffaele, the family celebrity, arrives by airplane and then by taxi; Nicola, the car worker, by car, appropriately; and Rocco, the semi-monastic reform school teacher, on foot. If Bolzoni is correct in arguing that "Rosi's cinema rather belongs to the character novel" and that his dramatis personae are "character-functions"[11] who guide viewers through the vicissitudes of recent Italian history, it would behove us to attend carefully to Rosi's portraits of his family members.

Raffaele, the first-born, in professional terms is the most successful of the brothers. Donato's obvious pride in his distinguished son emerges in the post office scene, when he instructs the clerk to send a telegram to "Raffaele Giuranna, *judge*", and repeats this appellation with obvious pleasure at the conjunction of name and title. Based in Rome, Raffaele embodies the professional power establishment, and the various spaces with which he is associated (a car in rush hour traffic; the office he shares with an assistant; his austere but elegant apartment; the corridors of the court house) define life in the centre of things – in the geographic mid-point of Italy, of class structure, of family, and of the judicial system. But his is a centre that will not hold: his son is having an affair with an older woman and is absent from home when most needed; his own marital relations are sorely tried by the terrorist threat; and his government's hold on power is tenuous at best, given the impact of leftist extremism on all social institutions.

Rosi, who did not presume to fathom the logic of terrorism, experiences through Raffaele "its human reality and its political reality" ("la sua realtà umana e la sua realtà politica") by showing its concrete effect on an individual life. Raffaele carries a gun, receives death threats, can maintain no fixed schedule, must always try to blend into a crowd, takes separate holidays from his wife and son, and cannot bring his family to his mother's funeral. In the paranoid dream discussed earlier, a photograph album of terrorist victims modulates into a nightmare of his own assassination, culminating in the flash of the police camera documenting his own bloodstained corpse. The image of his body will now enter the chain of signifiers which constitute the book of terror, to be read by the next prospective judge of a politically sensitive trial.

Although an embodiment of the power establishment, Raffaele is not uncritical of it. As such, he may be said to occupy the Centre-Left of the political spectrum (*pertiniano* [Pertinian], according to the critic Valerio Caprara),[12] advocating constructive, gradualist reform from within the system. In a remembered or imagined dialogue with a judicial colleague prior to his paranoid dream, Raffaele argues that punishment alone is insufficient to resolve the problem of terrorism, and that government must address its root cause by deterring youths from political lawlessness through a programme of preventive action.

Will Raffaele agree to preside over the trial? Although the film begs the question, and one critic argues categorically that he will refuse,[13] Rosi drops a series of cogent hints to the contrary. "I can't imagine someone like you not accepting" ("Figurati se uno come te non accettasse"), snaps Raffaele's wife to him on the telephone in the wake of a death threat sent to their home. Immediately after hanging up, Raffaele engages in a spontaneous seminar in the local bar on the subject of bearing witness against political crimes. "Terror defines itself", Raffaele claims. "It substitutes persuasion with fear. Society can't be founded on fear. The only answer is faith, or all is lost." Events soon undermine Raffaele's institutional confidence, however. In the same bar, late that night when Nicola goes in for cigarettes, a television newscast reveals what happens to witnesses who turn state's evidence, such as the one about to testify at a murder trial who is gunned down on his way to court.

But Raffaele's faith in the system resists such empirical proofs to the contrary. Very early in the film, a fellow magistrate explains why he resigned from the terrorist case that has now been assigned to Raffaele. "I would have risked my life if I thought I could change something", his predecessor admits. Were the above sentence to be rewritten in the light of Raffaele's faith in the system, the conditional and subjunctive verbs of the contrary-to-fact construction would be replaced by indicative verbs expressing simple causality: "I will risk my life because I think I can change something". By linking willingness to undergo personal sacrifice with a belief in the perfectibility of institutions, Rosi makes Raffaele's choice a foregone conclusion. In the paranoid nightmare and in the telephone booth where Raffaele can barely hold himself up for fear as he receives the news about the death-threat, we see the enormous price that the judge must pay for his faith. The dream and the anxiety attacks are measures of what Raffaele must fight in himself, indexes of the internal resistance against which he must struggle to maintain his idealistic resolve.

If the family as a corporate unit functions as a microcosm of the body politic as a whole, we would expect the Giurannas to express the conflict between radicalism and the power establishment that plagued Italy throughout the 1970s. Although no terrorist, Nicola is the next best thing – a militant unionist who does not shrink from the use of violence to redress the abuses of the capitalist system. Hence the strategy of physically beating department heads joins the repertory of labour's more benign tactics – those of protest marches, strikes, picket lines and absenteeism – to promote the quest for worker justice. In terms of official party allegiances, Nicola would belong to the militant wing of the Partito Comunista Italiano (Italian Communist Party – PCI) or to the more radical Partito Democratico di Unità Proletaria (Democratic Party of Proletarian Unity – PDUP), a post-'68 organisation advocating radical social change, which, while not overtly supporting terrorism, did not condemn the use of violence for revolutionary ends.

Predictably, Nicola engages in constant polemics with Raffaele, the embodiment of the status quo within the family unit. As the oldest and youngest siblings, respectively, Raffaele and Nicola are twenty years apart, so that the former would have come of age during the political *restaurazione* of the 1950s, while the latter would have matured in a post-1968 climate of anti-bourgeois revolt. This means that the Raffaele-Nicola conflict verges on the generational, resembling no less than a traditional father-son struggle for dominance. It also means that, while Raffaele would have migrated to Rome in an era of relative openness, which would have given him access to a university education and good professional advancement, Nicola would have arrived in Turin during the massive onslaught of southern migrants to the industrial north. Rosi thus goes to some pains to show how the difference in their perspectives is historically and economically conditioned. Like the pitiful, disoriented protagonist of Ettore Scola's *Trevico-Torino: Viaggio nel Fiat-Nam* (*Trevico-Turin: Journey in Fiat-Nam*, 1972), cited by Nicola as the cinematic prototype of his own experience, this young Pugliese transplant found himself alienated, ghettoized and exploited in the inhospitable north. Against such cultural and economic violence, Nicola felt that he had no other recourse than that of militant syndicalism. Yet, in his polemics with Raffaele, the younger brother insists on maintaining a distinction between the violence sponsored by the unions and that practised by the *brigatisti*: "Demonstrations, strikes and pickets are separated by an abyss from terrorism", Nicola claims. "There are protest marches and protest marches", Raffaele quibbles. "It is called self-defence when protesters carry P-38s and Molotov cocktails. How many kids began terrorist careers this way?". While Nicola argues that there is a qualitative difference between union militancy and terrorism, Raffaele holds that it is merely a question of degree. Once violence enters into the equation, distinctions become arbitrary and thrashings escalate into killings with appalling ease.

For all Nicola's political ranting and raving, however, his fantasy life reveals preoccupations of a far different sort. It is his marital situation which obsesses Nicola when he is not busy arguing with Raffaele, although the sexual and the political in the film are by no means distinct orders of experience. Through his troubled marriage to a Turinese woman, Nicola encounters in his erotic life the regional divisions and tensions that beset the Italian body politic as a whole. "She's a typical northerner", he complains to Raffaele. "We even argued over pasta – with tomato sauce, as I say, or with butter, according to the Signora". Nicola's use of regional stereotypes, however, is far more insidious and morally suspect than this petty charge of culinary incompatibility would suggest. "She had a fling", he confesses. "I'm from the south. I can't stand to be two-timed." When Raffaele counters with reminders of Nicola's own sexual truancy – "I'm sure she's stood a lot. I know you." – we realise that the outraged husband is using his regional identity as an alibi. The double standard, it seems, is Nicola's birthright as a southern Italian male.

Thanks to the virtuoso cinematography of Pasqualino De Santis, the best expression of the north-south dichotomy is the visual form it takes in Nicola's daydream of reconciliation with his estranged wife, Giovanna. Although the institutional gloom of the Neapolitan sequence and the rush hour chaos of the Roman ones stand in sharp contrast to the pastoral setting of Apulia, the Turinese sequence seems to occur on another planet.[14] As Nicola lies on his boyhood bed in the house where the brothers grew up, and his mind travels north to Turin, he imagines himself in a surreal space – an ultra-modern arcade leading to Giovanna's apartment building. As if in a de Chirico painting, Nicola traverses this dreamscape, whose architectural masses cast geometric shadows in shades of greens and greys. With oneiric arbitrariness, a young girl roller-skates in a zigzag pattern before the advancing figure of the dreamer. In terms of lighting, colour, resolution of image and *mise en scène*, nothing could be further from Rosi's visualisation of Nicola's homeland, characterised by "the harsh and arid white of a certain South", according to Gian Luigi Rondi. "A white that, with neat lines and dry, precise contours, clashes with the black, both in the extreme close-ups of faces, and the dilated expanse of the long shots".[15]

The surreal entrance to Giovanna's apartment building does little to prepare the viewer for the fluorescent brightness and sterile anonymity of her kitchen, where she and Nicola tentatively reconnect after a six-month period of separation. Shot frontally, this rectilinear space tells the whole story. This is *Giovanna's* jurisdiction and, having merely entered it, Nicola implicitly accepts her terms for being there. Although his movements are aggressive and proprietary, especially when he unceremoniously raids the refrigerator or helps himself to her wine, she is clearly in control. Only when the camera slowly closes in on him as he discusses his feelings about emigration, does Nicola temporarily command his place within the *mise en scène*. Moreover, since his newfound insights will be the basis for a reconciliation with Giovanna, as well as the construction of a new, non-regional identity, we must consider Nicola's revelations to her in some detail. "How was it at home?", Giovanna asks. He answers:

> Beautiful, but also a disaster. For the first time, I discovered a new thing. More painful than the death of a mother. Sorrow for a mother is something that you carry with you for the rest of your life. I discovered that my home town was no longer a part of me, nor I of it. You know what the true trauma of the emigrant is? He lacks the ground under his feet. He returns to the town looking for happiness and he doesn't find it. Then he returns to the 'city', to Germany or America, and he feels homesick.

Unable to revert to his culture of origin because he has experienced too much, and unable to assimilate into the new social context, the emigrant is doomed to live betwixt and between, never at home, always drifting in search of an impossible rootedness. In the face of this dilemma, the emigrant has two choices: to rail against his lot, venting his anger in futile gestures of violence or self-destruction; or to create a compromise space in which he assumes responsibility for the pain of exile and seeks a revised definition of self.

Having confided in Giovanna, Nicola is now offered the possibility of such a space – not in the harshly lit, rectilinear kitchen, but in the blue-tinged, heavily curtained bedroom along the corridor. Even the camerawork changes accordingly, from the static takes and subdued movements of the kitchen scene, to the smooth, 180° pan that follows Nicola as he circles the bed and undresses in increasingly less than tentative acceptance of Giovanna's invitation to stay the night. Even the dialogue shifts register, from the direct, referential comments of the kitchen scene to the oblique, elliptical language of mutual desire. "How hot it is in this room", she begins. "It's the walls", Nicola responds, "at night they radiate the heat they retained from the day". "You wanted a southern exposure", she rejoins.[16] "You're right, I wanted us to get some sun". Nicola's attempt to create a compromise space by incorporating southern elements into a northern setting, understood now in the light of his discovery that he can never return home, suggests a therapeutic approach to the emigrant's plight.

Is the imagined lovemaking of Nicola and Giovanna only a temporary solution, or does it signal Nicola's permanent willingness to forego the double standard which he considered a form of regional inheritance? Although one critic argues for the transience of this marital truce,[17] the film hints at the possibility of a more lasting resolution to their domestic troubles. Nicola daydreams of returning to his wife after having renounced the opportunity for a sexual encounter with Rosaria, the childhood sweetheart who had married another man while Nicola was doing military service. It takes little to reignite Nicola's passion for her – a few sultry glances are sufficient to send him prowling around Rosaria's house like the lovesick cat patrolling her neighbourhood that night. After a passionate embrace, however, the couple decides not to make love – Rosaria refuses to defile her husband's bed, and Nicola does not insist. The reasons for his uncharacteristic restraint are significant, suggesting that his sexually self-serving definition of southern Italian manhood has undergone a radical change. Rather than avenge himself on the love rival who had succeeded in wooing her away from him in the past, Nicola chooses to identify with Rosaria's absent husband, himself an emigrant in the north. Nicola's restraint also reflects an awareness that he cannot simply take up where he left off with his fiancée of so many years ago – that he has undergone irreversible changes as an emigrant whose "home town was no longer a part of me, nor I of it". In Nicola's case, it is entirely appropriate that this truth be played out in sexual terms.

When Nicola and Raffaele engage in their endless polemics on the night before the funeral, it is Rocco who finally puts a stop to the proceedings by insisting that his brothers shift to more private, personal concerns. "Let's talk about us", he implores, "your families, your kids". Rocco, who has neither a wife nor children of his own, remains the most enigmatic of the brothers, and although he is the only character to have two dreams, they do little to reveal his inner self. This could be explained by the fact that Rocco is indeed selfless, lacking the monadic, ego economy that defines identity in a more conventional sense. As director of a Neapolitan reform school, Rocco is altruistically committed to the cause of rehabilitating youthful offenders before they are beyond reclamation. Accordingly, both his dreams relate directly to his sense of social mission. The first, about a rat-infested cityscape, provides Rocco with the metaphor for the disadvantaged children of the world, turned *topi*, or scavengers, through desperation and neglect: "We must sacrifice, for humanity. Not just family, our own people. It means changing man's heart. We have to be gentler towards mankind, nature. If not, these rats will do us in, here and everywhere." This apocalyptic scenario is only reinforced by Rocco's description of an incident involving subproletarian encampments outside Naples, where lawlessness had invited massive police mobilisation: "They intervened with tanks, tear gas. A war." Consequently, Rocco's second dream involves another type of assault on social misery: a one-man clean-up campaign to rid young people of the syringes, rifles and easy money that turn their lives into the human debris of contemporary urban existence. If the other brothers' dreams parody a given cinematic genre – the *cinema politico* of Raffaele's terrorist nightmare, or the "adult" melodrama of Nicola's reverie – Rocco's dream may be said to derive from musical comedy. Set to the music of Pino Daniele's Neapolitan pop song, "Je so' pazzo", the dream action involves clean-up squads of kids against stylized theatrical backdrops of New York City, Moscow and Naples. Rocco experiences a virtual apotheosis at the end of the song as he climbs a mountain of swept-up debris and raises his arms in triumph with a painted Vesuvius arising in the background on the painted shores of the Bay of Naples. The brazen artifice of Rocco's dream, in contrast to the more realistic modes of his brothers' imaginings, makes explicit its status as pure wish-fulfilment fantasy, and only heightens the sense of his inadequacy in the face of such incurable social ills.

When Rocco intervenes in his brothers' ideological debate, he does so both because he is by nature a peacemaker, and because he harbours a congenital distrust for political solutions. For Rocco, slogans, programmes, party platforms and elected officials are not the key to social justice. As far as he is concerned, the answer lies in a deeply personal notion of *caritas* involving "changing the human heart", and as such it associates Rocco's code of ethics with a Christian humanist, or even a Franciscan, approach to correct action in the world. It is therefore not surprising that Rocco's interaction with the town is confined to the parish church. No sooner does he arrive at the house and pay his respects to the dead than Rocco visits the local sanctuary where the priest has been awaiting him. "I knew you'ld come", Don Vincenzo remarks, as if his advent were somehow foreordained, a necessary element in the providential scheme of things.

Rocco is the brother most closely bound to the world of his parents. He is the only sibling to experience a flashback of his mother as a young woman, and he is inextricably linked with his father through a casting strategy whereby the same actor, Vittorio Mezzogiorno, plays both Rocco and the young Donato. Arriving at the family farm on foot, along the same path down which Donato had walked after fantasizing about the meeting with his dead wife, Rocco stops and seems to connect with the landscape in a way which his siblings' automated arrivals necessarily precluded. The casting choice also suggests that of the three brothers, Rocco remains closest to the Utopian values of the land and, in so doing, Rosi naturalises this character's Christian humanist approach to social injustice.

No study of *Three Brothers* would be complete, however, without consideration of the literary source for Rosi's inspiration. Although the filmmaker goes to great lengths to minimise his debt to the textual model, Rosi's screenplay, written in collaboration with Tonino Guerra,[18] owes a great deal to Andrei Platonov's 1936 short story, "Trety syn" ("The Third Son"). Rosi explains:

> Platonov's story, which is very short, served us as a starting point...the mother's death, the telegram, the brothers who arrive (in the short story there are six of them; here, three), and the relationship that arises between the old man and the child. We also took the child's tears as she realises that her grandmother is dead. All the rest was invented by us.[19]

Although Platonov's seven-page story could provide only the barest of skeletons for Rosi's screenplay, the filmmaker is unfair to reduce his debt to mere elements of plot. What Rosi fails to acknowledge here is the way in which Platonov's text authorised not only the narrative structure of the film, but also, more importantly, its allegorical mode. If Rosi's great achievement in *Three Brothers* is to link familial chronicle to social history, to construct in the family microcosm a compelling reflection of events on the national level, Platonov's "The Third Son" offers the richest of literary precedents. "An old woman died in a small country town", the story begins, and with the death of this shrivelled-up, biologically exhausted body, Platonov considers the radical changes that take place in the familial body, as a corporate entity, and in the body politic of post-revolutionary Russia. Through a series of focalizers – the old husband, the country priest and the third son – Platonov delivers a powerful social commentary whose subtleties and ironic reversals merit close scrutiny in order to fathom the workings of Rosi's own allegorical mode.

The opening passages of the story are centred in the consciousness of the old man, whose sense of loss permeates all his perceptions, creating a natural and social environment in synchrony with his grief. When an aged female telegraph worker performs her duties with shocking ineptitude, the old man projects onto her his own psychic disarray. "It seemed to him that the elderly woman had a broken heart, too, and a troubled soul that would never be quieted – perhaps she was a widow or a wrongfully deserted wife".[20] Nature, too, reflects his loss – as he waits for his sons by his wife's cold body, the "solitary grey bird" hops about its cage, flakes of "wet, tired snow" fall outside, and the sun shines "cold as a star".[21] If the pathetic fallacy conjures up a natural world in harmony with inner psychic experience, such a device has special appropriateness to the organic coherence of rural life.

With the arrival of the sons, however, this natural cohesion is shattered – even the prose style suddenly shifts to express the disruptive effects of their advent. From the long, flowing, paratactic sentences describing the old man's experiences, the style abruptly changes to one of short, straightforward statements of fact: "The eldest son arrived by aeroplane the very next day".[22] Technology intervenes, and we soon learn that all six of the sons have done extremely well in the various lines of work that define the new, post-revolutionary state. The oldest is department foreman of an airplane factory; two sons, both sailors, have achieved the rank of captain; another is an actor in Moscow; another is a physicist (and a Communist); and the youngest is a student of agronomy. Such accomplishments in the fields of industry, transportation, science, agriculture and the arts justify the old man's obvious pride in his "powerful sons" – a pride which eclipses his widower's grief: "Their father was not crying any more. He had wept his full alone and was now glancing at his half-dozen powerful sons with concealed emotion and a delight that was quite out of place in the circumstances".[23] As mobile, productive, cosmopolitan and technologically evolved individuals, the brothers exemplify the glorified self-image of the modern Soviet state. In addition to the proud father, another character responds to these "six powerful men" in a way which suggests that their generational significance is ideologically fraught. Of all people, it is the country priest who views them as "representatives of the new world which he secretly admired but could not enter. On his own he used to dream of performing some sort of heroic feat to break his way into the glorious future with the new generations".[24] Platonov reserves his most withering satire for this priest, whose aspirations to heroism combine elements of *deus ex machina* with the latest aviation technology. In this spirit, "he had even applied to the local aerodrome asking to be taken up to the highest point in a plane and dropped by parachute without an oxygen mask, but they had not replied".[25]

"The Third Son" therefore involves two temporalities: that of traditional, agrarian, natural time (the time of birth, death and seasonal cycles) and that of progressive, linear, historical time (that of irreversibility and change). Corresponding to these temporalities are two conceptions of space – those of continuity and rupture – as signified, respectively, by the two bedrooms of the story. Together in the room with the coffin is the marriage bed, occupied now by the old man and his granddaughter. This room is illuminated by the glow of moonlight reflected by the falling snow outside, as befits a space of generational continuity and natural process. Next door, in a room electrically lit, the six brothers are housed as they had been in childhood, but their talk is of metal propellers and voyages to foreign ports. They wrestle, laugh and boast, in keeping with a need to perform their adult identities for one another. The inappropriateness of such behaviour does not seem to bother the old man, so smitten is he by his powerful offspring that he would never dare to question their conduct. But one of the sons is clearly distraught – the third son of the title – and it is he who shames his siblings into a decorous silence which suits the occasion. Crossing the boundary from the sons' bedroom to the room with the coffin, the third brother stands over the corpse for a moment, and then faints from emotion. It is his example of unbridled grief which frees his brothers to mourn at last: "One by one they slipped off to different parts of the house, through the yard and the night that surrounded the place where they had spent their childhood, and wept".[26]

There could be no more poignant proof of the disintegration of the family unit than the separateness of this fraternal grieving, and Rosi puts Platonov's insight to powerful cinematic use in his film's corresponding scene. When Rocco wakes up from his dream and goes into the kitchen to make coffee, he looks out of the window to see his siblings mourning in the courtyard below. Photographing the two brothers from behind Rocco's shoulders, the camera reveals Nicola in long shot, sobbing against the back wall, and Raffaele, huddled apart from him, also mourning in solitude. The spectacle of his brothers' grief triggers Rocco's own outpouring of sorrow – sorrow as much for the death of their mother as for the emotional distance figured in this *mise en scène*.

In the Platonov story the writer goes to some lengths to express the sons' perception of loss, and its implications for a cultural history of the post-revolutionary age. The third brother experiences most acutely what all the siblings had mourned when they first beheld the corpse of their mother: "the lost happiness of love which had welled continuously and undemandingly in their mother's heart and had always found them, even across thousands of miles. They had felt it constantly, instinctively, and this awareness had given them added strength and courage to go about their lives".[27] Read etymologically, this mother is the *matrix* – the principle of the land, rural life, the humus in which their identities are rooted, the basis of all their subsequent accomplishments in life. If, in diachronic terms, the mother allegorises the agrarian Russian past, Platonov's argument is that the successes of the present regime are predicated on the strengths of this ancestral culture. It is of the utmost significance, therefore, that the son most stricken by the death of the mother is the physicist (who is also, importantly, the only Communist Party member in the family) and, as such, the most "evolved" of them all. Yet, it is he who suffers most intensely from the loss of the matrix, and who is most aware of the need for connection to a source. Although we are excluded from his sorrowing – we do not overhear the words with which he silences his brothers, nor do we enter a mind about to lose consciousness before the object of its grief – the third son's reaction becomes normative. Neither the father, blinded by paternal pride, nor the priest, a prey to ideological mystification, can offer reliable judgments on the post-revolutionary age; as such, they serve as foils for Platonov's own judgment, implied in the mute and anguished mourning of the third son.

Motivated by a similar impulse to condemn the rise of industrial, urban culture at the expense of its rural matrix, Rosi fully appropriates Platonov's allegory. The three brothers "belong to a generation that has in some way failed", remarks Rosi, "and for this there is the grandfather and little girl to close the circle, to give sense to the film".[28] Rosi's use of the phrase "close the circle" ("chiudere il cerchio") is significant in this context, for it suggests the notion of temporal continuity which governs the natural world, and anticipates the image of the wedding ring which heralds the film's Edenic theme. Donato's memories of marriage merge with a vision of the agrarian past as earthly paradise – a blessed site of innocence and rest. To heighten the sense that this is a privileged space, Donato's flashback occurs immediately after the film's most violent moment: that of Raffaele's imagined assassination at terrorist hands.

At the centre of Donato's garden of memory reside a man and a woman – Adam and Eve before the Fall. Although one critic faulted this sequence for its sentimentality, such a reaction fails to acknowledge that this is indeed a flashback, embedded in the idealising consciousness of the newly bereaved.[29] Shot in slow motion, through the diaphanous cloth of the bridal veil, the opening frames of this reminiscence explicitly announce its "soft focus" take on memory. Once the pace increases to normal speed, the camera moves to medium distance to reveal a country wedding party, about to be rained out. Although the proverbial "rained-on bride, lucky bride" ("sposa bagnata, sposa fortunata") may be trite, it is indeed predictive of the long course of happy marriage that awaits the newly-weds. After a brief glimpse at the couple's honeymoon journey in a horse-and-buggy, the flashback reaches its culmination in a scene of surpassing lyricism. Lingering on the beach, Donato tends to the horse while Caterina amuses herself by burying her feet in the sand and sifting great handfuls of it through her fingers. At a certain point she realises that her wedding ring is gone: "Donato, aggio perduto la fede" ("I lost my wedding ring"), she announces in dialect. "We won't go until we find it", he reassures her, and manages to retrieve the ring after cleverly resorting to the help of a sieve. When Donato puts the ring back on her finger and kisses her, we realise that this is the true wedding – Adam and Eve alone in the garden. Without mediations, in an untainted, natural setting, the newly-weds reconsecrate their marriage in their own private state of grace. Against this ideal of marital bliss, all other relationships in the film are measured and found wanting: Raffaele's strained marriage, threatened from without, and Nicola's troubled one, destabilised from within.

Read as political allegory, this lapse has important implications for the course of postwar Italian history, suggesting that contemporary Italy has indeed fallen away from the Eden of its provincial, agrarian past. There is another moment in the film, also associated with the mother, which serves to mark the specific historical coordinates of Italy's fall from a prior state of perfection. I am referring here to the film's first flashback, embedded in the memory of Rocco as a way of linking this particular son to his parents' Utopian context. As Rocco beholds the image of his dead mother, to the accompaniment of the nenia, or dirge, of the neighbourhood women, the scene dissolves into a close-up of his face as a child amidst the sounds of shelling and prayer. Called to his young mother's side, Rocco peeks out from her protective embrace to see the rosary dangling before him, amongst his family members and neighbours who have sought refuge from the advancing front. At a certain point, the artillery sounds give way to the joyous pealing of bells, and the camera pans the townscape, bespattered with Fascist graffiti: *Duce, Vincere, Vinceremo*. Now a lone tank approaches as the little community emerges from hiding. A camouflaged army vehicle, like a strange, alien creature, crests the hill, broadcasting the sounds of American jazz from its depths: "I can't give you anything but love, baby". Nothing could be more incongruous than the apparition of this hi-tech equipment, spouting an incomprehensible musical language on a primeval Italian landscape. Moreover, to compound the indecipherability of the event, Donato and his neighbours interpret this as an enemy assault, raising their hands in surrender. When a living human being jumps out of this machine, kisses the ground, introduces himself in English as "Galatti, Salvatore", and then switches into Italian to announce "pure io sono italiano, paisano" ("I too am Italian, countryman"), the reversal of expectations could not be more violent. In an appropriate end to this scene of incongruities, the soldier then embraces every civilian in sight.

By synthesizing a series of oppositions – Italian vs. American; agrarian vs. technological; enemy vs. ally – this scene invests the Liberation with the highest Utopian significance. It is no accident that the liberator in this episode is an Italian-American named Salvatore, himself a synthesis of the old and the new, returned to his homeland to redeem it from the sins of its past. As Salvatore hugs the young Caterina, their composite image fades into the present-tense scene of mourning, accompanied by the *nenia* of the neighbourhood women. By framing this reminiscence with prayer – the prayer for the dead, here and now, and the rosary on the eve of the Liberation – Rosi associates Caterina's youthful maternal role with the promise of national-popular rebirth, and her death with the disappointment of that promise.

As the moment of highest political idealism, when the military victory against Fascism meant that the new Italy could pursue its agenda for domestic self-renewal, the Liberation also had important consequences for the cinema. In films such as Rossellini's war trilogy (*Roma, città aperta* [*Rome, Open City*, 1945], *Paisà* [*Paisan*, 1946] and *Germania anno zero* [*Germany Year Zero*, 1947]), the experience of the Second World War gave rise to the cinematic form of neo-realism in order to express the revolutionary power of its subject-matter. Rosi has made no secret of his enthusiasm for neo-realism as a form of political action – itself an outgrowth of the domestic agenda of the Resistance:

We were all desirous and aware of participating in the reconstruction of the country and we thought that with the cinema we could do something. This, in fact, occurred because those films, all told, accomplished a great deal. This is neo-realism, for me, as a fact of life.[30]

It is therefore not surprising that the canonical neo-realist treatment of the Liberation – that of Rossellini's *Paisan* – should be explicitly invoked in this flashback, where the mutual misunderstandings which plagued encounters between Italians and American GIs in the earlier film would undergo "a neat reversal" in Rosi's decision to make the liberators Italian-Americans.[31] Thus, by alluding to the Liberation in his film's first flashback, Rosi is invoking both the political idealism of this historical moment and its privileged mode of cinematic expression. The Liberation and neo-realism thus serve as twin indicators of contemporary Italy's fall from grace.

However, paradise is not entirely lost. In Nicola's daughter, Marta, child of the urban north, the dead Caterina seems to be reborn, closing the circle to which Rosi had alluded in his commentary on the current generation. A series of details suggests that Marta is indeed the very incarnation of her grandmother: she sleeps in Caterina's old bed; receives her grandmother's earrings as an inheritance; is juxtaposed with her image in the family photograph collection; and buries herself in the grain, just as the new bride had done on the beach in Donato's honeymoon reminiscence. In one scene, a mystical bond between grandmother and granddaughter is established as Marta views the corpse from a secret window high above the place of mourning. From this hidden vantage point, Marta appropriates an omniscient view suggestive of Caterina's own perspective from beyond the grave.

Most important to her role in establishing continuity is Marta's acquisition of her grandfather's rural wisdom. Without an alarm clock, Marta wonders, how does he know when to get up in the morning? "Peasants regulate themselves by the stars and the animals", Donato explains. "The rooster crows two times, first at 1 am and then at 4. Old folks get up at the second crowing. Children wait for the donkey to bray at 7. Three stars line up at dawn, called the dipper. The morning star precedes them by half an hour." "If I stay with you", the child observes, "I'll learn all these things. In Turin there are neither donkeys nor roosters." "But there are the stars", her grandfather reassures her. What Marta learns from Donato, and what she will take back with her to Turin, is the cosmic connectedness of things, the bond between the heavens and the earth, between the natural world and the world of men. As the repository of her grandfather's wisdom, Marta represents genealogical continuity, reversing the effects of the family diaspora and the anti-traditionalism of her father's generation. Such continuity is perhaps best expressed in the image of the egg which Marta offers to her grandfather after the funeral cortège makes its way offscreen.

If *Three Brothers* is about mothers as signifiers of origins, it is important to note that the film's only child, Marta, is literally motherless. Giovanna is off in Turin and there is no maternal surrogate within the reconstituted family in the south. Yet, we do not sense that Marta is in any way bereft or incomplete. In connecting with her culture of origin, she is gaining the metaphorical mother that Nicola regretted losing as emigrant – "he feels the earth vanish from under his feet" ("gli manca la terra sotto i piedi"), as he told Giovanna in his daydream of reconciliation. Marta's discovery of her matrix is rendered in specifically cinematic terms in one of the film's most lyrical moments. Sent off by Nicola to play in the barn, Marta leads our gaze through a labyrinth of miscellaneous farm implements which De Santis's camerawork succeeds in endowing with the magic of childhood curiosity. In one long, fluid take, the camera precedes her into the barn, cranes up and down again, filming her behind the very carriage which the newly-weds had taken on their honeymoon (another connection with the young Caterina), then follows her as she moves left to examine an array of cowbells suspended on the wall, then circles her and cranes up as she moves through the archway into an inner chamber at the end of the take. Now Marta begins to ascend to successive levels of the barn, stopping to play with the chickens housed on the next storey, and then climbing to the uppermost floor of the granary, where she disrobes and buries herself in the grain as if she had finally found her true element.

In one of the film's most significant departures from the Platonov story, the old man and his granddaughter do not follow the coffin to the grave site, but remain behind to give their own meaning to Caterina's demise. Where Platonov's mystified old man was less grief-stricken than "proud and content that he too would be buried by these six strong men, and just as finely",[32] Rosi's widower transforms his loss into a poetic reaffirmation of his marriage vows. Back in the room where her corpse had lain, he finds Caterina's wedding ring and places it on his own finger. This is, of course, the second time he had found the ring, and recalls that Edenic moment when he had reconsecrated their marriage on the beach. With this farewell gesture Donato reweds Caterina, now in the presence of Marta who will "close the circle", to use Rosi's own metaphor for generational continuity. Nor is this ring devoid of political significance, for the Italian word for wedding ring is *fede*, recalling Raffaele's plea for a society based on faith and hope, not violence and fear. If marriage serves as a microcosm of the ideal society – the synthesis of opposites figured in the Liberation scene – the analogy between the wedding band and the social bond is easily drawn. In the image of the circle, Rosi is issuing a plea that Italy keep its *fede* with the ideals of its rural past, and that it seek to recover the matrix, if not in the historical order, at least in memory and art. When Marta returns to Turin, she may not be able to see the stars in the industrial night sky, but at least she will know that they are there.

Notes

[1] See Gary Crowdus and Dan Georgakas, "The Audience Should Not Be Just Passive Spectators: An Interview with Francesco Rosi", *Cineaste* 7: 1 (1975): 6.

[2] Peter Bondanella, *Italian Cinema: From Neorealism to the Present* (New York: Continuum, 1991): 170.

[3] "Il caso Italia". This is Francesco Bolzoni's term in *I film di Francesco Rosi* (Rome: Gremese Editore, 1986): 129.

[4] Translated from the Italian: "Il problema del terrorismo? È un problema su cui bisognerebbe fare tutto un film, e non è che non ci abbia pensato... Ma ho sempre arretrato perché mi sono trovato davanti a problemi di conoscenza: se neanche io avevo capito bene la logica del terrorismo, la sua realtà umana e la sua realtà politica, in cosa potevo aiutare il pubblico?". Quoted in Franca Faldini and Goffredo Fofi, *Il cinema italiano d'oggi: 1970-1984* (Milan: Arnaldo Mondadori, 1984): 531-532.

[5] Translated from the Italian: "I *Tre fratelli* sono tre parti di me stesso... Non mi identifico con questo piuttosto che con quello". Ibid: 531.

[6] Pauline Kael's review of *Three Brothers* is in "The Current Cinema: Francesco Rosi", *The New Yorker* 22 March 1982: 160.

[7] On Piccioni's contributions to the soundtrack of *Three Brothers* and to Rosi's work in general, see Ermanno Comuzio, "Quando diventa esemplare il rapporto regista-compositore: La musica di Piccioni nei film di Rosi", in Sebastiano Gesù (ed), *Francesco Rosi* (Acicatena: Incontri con il Cinema, 1991): 64-73.

[8] For a compilation of appreciative foreign reviews, see Bolzoni: 132-133.

[9] Translated from the Italian: "Sembra che, qui, come ai suoi lontani inizi, Rosi abbia cercato prima un dato sociologicamente interessante e, in seguito, vi abbia costruito intorno una parvenza di personaggio". Bolzoni: 132. For other typical examples of such objections, see the comments of Mino Argentieri, Morando Morandini and Sauro Borelli, quoted in Gesù: 243-244.

[10] Kael: 160.

[11] Translated from the Italian: "Il cinema di Rosi rientra, piuttosto, nel romanzo di carattere" (Bolzoni: 14) and "personaggi-funzione" (Bolzoni: 15).

[12] Cited in Bolzoni: 133. Sandro Pertini (1896-1990) was an anti-Fascist and a moderate Socialist. Imprisoned and then exiled under Fascism, after 1945 he was Secretary of the Partito Socialista Italiano (PSI – Italian Socialist Party; now defunct), President of the Chamber of Deputies, and finally (1978-85) an enormously popular president of the republic.

[13] Ibid: 132.

[14] As Kael notes in her review, the cinematography of this scene enables us to "*feel* the difference between North and South": 161. Emphasis in original.

[15] Translated from the Italian: "il bianco arido e aspro di un certo Sud. Un bianco che, con linee nette e contorni secchi e precisi, si scontra con il nero; sia nei primissimi piani delle facce, sia nella dilatata vastità dei totali". Quoted in Gesù: 244.

[16] Here the English subtitler supplied a witticism lacking in the more prosaic Italian: "volevi un appartamento in questa posizione".

[17] See Bolzoni: 132.

[18] On Guerra's contribution to Rosi's screenplays, see Nino Genovese, "Le fonti letterarie del cinema di Rosi", in Gesù: 62.

[19] Translated from the Italian: "Il racconto di Platonov, che è molto breve, ci è servito come spunto...la morte della madre, il telegramma, i fratelli che arrivano (nel racconto sono sei e qui tre), e il rapporto che nasce tra il vecchio e la bambina. Abbiamo anche preso il pianto della bambina quando si accorge che la nonna è morta. Tutto il resto è inventato da noi." Faldini and Fofi: 531.

[20] Andrei Platonov, "The Third Son", translated by Kathleen Cook, in *Fro and Other Stories* (Moscow: Progress Publishers, 1972): 64.

[21] Ibid: 65.

[22] Ibid.

[23] Ibid: 65-66.

[24] Ibid: 68.

[25] Ibid.

[26] Ibid: 72.

[27] Ibid: 66.

[28] Translated from the Italian: "Ma penso che tutti e tre appartengano a una generazione che è in qualche modo fallita, e per questo ci sono il nonno e

la bambina a chiudere il cerchio, a dare il senso del film". Faldini and Fofi: 531.

[29] For his objection to this scene as eliciting an "easy heart-tug", see Stanley Kauffmann, "Stanley Kauffmann on films: Good Intentions", *The New Republic* 21 April 1982: 25.

[30] Translated from the Italian: "Eravamo tutti quanti desiderosi e consapevoli di partecipare alla ricostruzione del paese, e pensavamo che con il cinema si potesse fare qualche cosa, come in effetti è stato perché quei film tutto sommato hanno fatto molto. Questo è il neorealismo, per me, come dato di vita". Quoted in Aldo Tassone, *Parla il cinema italiano* (Milan: Il Formichiere, 1979): 282.

[31] For this insight, see Bondanella: 333. It should be noted that in the first episode of *Paisan*, an Italian-American soldier, Tony, is included among the liberating forces. But the entire landing in Sicily is met with anxiety and suspicion by the natives, and Tony's command of the Italian language does little to assuage their fears.

[32] Platonov: 72.

Interview with Francesco Rosi

Carlo Testa

Interview conducted in Rome, 24 May 1994. Transcript translated and edited by Carlo Testa.

In your filmmaking, what inspiration have you drawn from the American cinema?

American cinema – the cinema of Hollywood and American cinema in general – has always been an important one, extremely well-represented in Europe during both the best and the worst periods of its artistic production. It would have been difficult for a person enthralled with film ever since his youngest years, such as I always was, to escape its charm and influence.

All great countries have enjoyed, in cycles, a period of splendour in their cinematographic production; this depends, I believe, on the fact that cinema bears witness to, and is a mirror of, the society and the reality which produce it. I am thinking, for example, of the American social cinema of the 1950s, as well as of the musicals of a few years earlier, which involved me very much. In the realm of Italian cinema, the same happened with postwar film, "neo-realism", which changed the way cinema is made throughout the world.

The way people make films takes place by means of a general communication and circulation, a general attention which the practitioners of cinema pay to the ways in which others practise it. Therefore, *there is* communication, and thus *there is* influence. Without a doubt, many filmmakers – North American, South American, French, Spanish, German; the British less so, I believe – have been influenced by postwar Italian cinema. Similarly, there is no doubt that Europe has been influenced by American cinema, and recently this influence has increased considerably.

This happens even within those cinematographic traditions which may, in a sense, appear to be relatively more isolated: the Indian one, for example. Clearly, there have been great Indian filmmakers for whom – as they themselves stated – the Italian cinema of the immediate postwar period was a fundamental point of reference. Those who carry out creative work always have a comparative approach to creativity worldwide.

Having commented on what could be called a constructive dialogism with Americans, do you feel that there are, on the other hand, also elements of difference between that type of cinema and yours?

Elements of difference are to be found in the cultural identity of a given work of art. And the more a work of art is identifiable as belonging to the culture of a specific country, the more authentic it is. This is an argument which needs to be especially stressed for cinema, because a film is *always* a testimony to the social reality in which it lives.

I would say that a film in general is truly the mirror of a country, of an entire reality. I would say that it is the most immediate form of expression by which one can portray the cultural identity of a country. While, on the one hand, this causes a film to belong to a specific culture and to a specific society, on the other hand it also makes it universal, to the precise extent that the film in question manages to deal with particular problems by means of a universal language. De Sica's *Ladri di biciclette* [*Bicycle Thieves*, 1948] is a *very* Italian film; but it is also a film whose problems are understood the world over. This can happen thanks to the force of its images and emotions.

Through emotions, images manage to portray problems and human beings, as well as historical moments and social occurrences. Thus, many a time even the spectator who does not understand what *is being said* in the film can nevertheless understand what it is that the film *wants to say*. And this is the great strength of cinema.

Lately there has been concern about Italian cinema being "in a crisis" after the generation of filmmakers from the 1950s-1960s and that from the 1970s-1980s – let us say, broadly, the generations of 60- and 40-year olds, respectively. Firstly, I would like to ask you whether you think it is true that there is, in fact, a crisis of this kind. Secondly, assuming that this is the case, does this potential crisis depend on the artists, or is it due instead to Italian society?

This is a major question, to which I have devoted an entire article published a few weeks ago in *la Repubblica*. I would like to refer you to it for full details.[1]

Free trade vs. interventionism. In the United States the government does not subsidise filmmaking; in Canada and in Italy – in Europe – it does, however partially and inadequately. What are the advantages and the disadvantages of this practice?

I would say, firstly, that we need to be more specific, because in Italy cinema has never been "subsidised"; it has received financial support – and I must add that, to tell the truth, what support it has received has been *very* small – so small, in fact, that we have recently worked very hard to obtain a new law intended to provide support for Italian cinema. This law has been voted on and passed, but it must now go through the development of regulations for its implementation.

In Italy financial support for filmmaking is extended above all through a system of loans at preferential rates. If the film is unable to repay its debt, the state eventually becomes co-owner of the film's negative. In addition, there are other forms of support for low-budget films to be made by young directors. However, these are all regulations that are currently in a phase of implementation, so they do not yet have a definitive status.

Generally speaking, I believe that European cinema does have the right to certain forms of support, especially when its goal is that of "practising culture" [fare cultura]. France, to take one example, has already managed to pass a good law on this subject a long time ago. I consider this type of intervention entirely legitimate; I see no reason why research in the field of industry and business should be partially financed by the state – in some cases even in the form of sunk capital – with nothing of the sort happening in the case of a cultural activity.

Over and above carrying out a specific study for the cinematographic tradition of each country, I believe that Europe needs to develop a platform of mutual support among all Member States, so as to increase and facilitate production and exchange, to facilitate European production. That is the only way to meet successfully the challenge of the competition coming from the American cinema, which is much more active and much richer than European cinema. The only answer is for Europe to create opportunities for reciprocal support that may increase the production and distribution of European cinema. Needless to say, the criteria by which support is granted *must* be based on a very careful assessment of the projects submitted.

Allow me to ask you in more detail about this issue. Europe and Canada see 1994 as the year of the great debate on GATT, the international agreement on tariffs and trade – the debate, that is, on what is described by some as "cultural protectionism", and by others as a "fair levelling of the playing field". (It is, of course, paradoxical that the term "levelling of the playing field" should have been coined in the United States at the time of the American polemic against "excessive" industrial exports from Japan towards the US market.) The Canadian/European argument is that Americans can, to all intents and purposes, practise commercial "dumping" to the detriment of foreign producers, because they have already absorbed certain costs. In your opinion is it good or bad to try for a "correction" of this situation?

On this issue, I do not see that we have a question of good vs. evil; I think it is a matter of having a very realistic view of things. Firstly, the cinema of Hollywood has a definite advantage over European cinema, because for its distribution around the world it can count on a language that is spoken in many countries – the English language. Secondly, since its inception the cinema of Hollywood relies on a very carefully developed system of commercial distribution of its products throughout the world. Americans – or rather, American entrepreneurs – have long ago perceived the need to attend to the commercial distribution of their product as much as, if not more than, to its creation. This is only to their credit as entrepreneurs; but it *has* created a situation of commercial privilege, which corresponds precisely to a protectionism of sorts.

As a consequence, an American film enjoys a globally privileged, much stronger commercial life than a European film does. Throughout the countries of the world, a Hollywood film is marketed in a version that is dubbed in the language of the country in which it is being distributed. This establishes an undisputable commercial advantage, insofar as an American film arriving in Italy and being dubbed in Italian has chances that are the same as, if not greater than, those of an Italian film; the reason being that it is spoken in the same language as that of the audience, on top of having actors of an international reputation, and greater financial means.

By contrast, an Italian, French, Spanish or German film going to the United States is destined to remain, in a sense, in a cultural and commercial ghetto, because all these films are distributed there in their respective original languages, with English subtitles.

Nor can we accept the justification, voiced by American producers and distributors, that the American public rejects films dubbed in their own language; this simply is not true. There are cases of Italian films, for example, which were dubbed in English and had a very brilliant commercial life. They were not "rejected" at all by the American public. The truth is that, wilily and skilfully, American producers and distributors have *defended* themselves and their product. On this basis, the accusation of protectionism which they address at European cinema has no basis in truth. In the case which I quoted, that of dubbing, the only real protectionism is the one practised by American cinema.

In other words, what in law is called *par conditio* does not obtain here. If an American film were distributed in Italy exclusively in English with Italian subtitles, that film's commercial life would be enormously diminished. Clearly, the public – let us say, average movie-goers – prefer to hear their own language spoken when they go to see a film. Watching a subtitled film always entails a certain effort, because the attention required to read the subtitles obviously causes spectators to sacrifice, in exchange, a part of their fruition of the images. Only a section of the public, not the majority of it, is ready to do this. Therefore, when some people describe protectionism as an "imposition" meted out or attempted by Europeans against American cinema, this is not the truth.

Let me broach the same theme from a different angle. One of the most shocking experiences for a North American visiting Italy (at any rate, for a North American Italianist visiting Italy) is the relative difficulty in obtaining videocassettes of the classics of Italian cinema. At the same time, there are innumerable American videocassettes flooding video rental shops. It is almost as if the average Italian renting a videocassette necessarily equates renting with renting American. Why?

Frankly, I am not very knowledgeable in the field of the rental of videocassettes. What I do see is that today there are many collections of classics being produced, Italian films being released for *home video.*[2] However, there is a lot of confusion and no clear-headed planning in this way of marketing the cinematographic product. Italian film production is different from that of the American *majors.*[3]

On a previous occasion, I mentioned to you the case of the Italian journalist who was looking for the videocassette of my film, *Il caso Mattei* [*The Mattei Affair,* 1972]. Because it was made many years ago and has not been reprinted to date, this cassette can be procured on the market only at an extremely high price.

We also talked about your Uomini contro (Just Another War, 1970*), which today is nowhere to be found.*

Precisely. There are videocassettes that simply cannot be found anywhere, whereas American films certainly enjoy greater circulation – a greater circulation which depends on the greater commercial success those films have enjoyed. This is obvious.

We notice so many American films circulating in video form, and may therefore receive the erroneous impression that those films are taking over the market, that they are endowed with longevity and durability. But it could be that this is, in fact, an optical illusion; it may be by no means true that a specific American film from, let us say, twenty years ago is any easier to find than its Italian counterpart from the same years.

Sure. However, that film will be aired more frequently on local television stations, both public and private. Televisions, of course, quite literally *live off* films, especially in Italy, where there are few rules. The field of television in Italy can be described as a real and true jungle, with no rules. It has become possible to view, whether during the day or at night, an incredible number of American films, both very beautiful and absolutely dreadful, both old and new. By contrast, the Italian films that are most interesting from an historical point of view, firstly, are aired to a lesser extent, and, secondly, are relegated to the nightly hours, at impossible times. It is obviously very unlikely that a young person will take the trouble to watch such a film at 3 am.

Your remarks point precisely in the direction of our next topic: television. In your opinion, what are the ways in which the spread of multichannel television can change the very nature of the filmmaker's profession and influence the process of artistic creation? All private television channels practically feed on ready-made films. This is a usage which, historically, comes after the fact. In the knowledge that such television stations now exist, does it seem to you that the new films currently being made are *conceived by the director in a different way* – can *be and perhaps* ought *to be conceived in a different way?*

It is a self-evident fact that today competition from television influences very heavily even such things as the creativity of the cinematographic product – the decision as to which film to make, and when to make it. I will mention a banal example. Here in Italy there was a time, let us say about 25 years ago, when certain films on Italian society were able to make up, among other things, for the inadequate, distorted, limited or incorrect information then available to the public. So it was that *those* Italian films managed, among other things, to correspond to what has become the characteristic trait of television information.

Films such as my *Salvatore Giuliano* [1961] or *Le mani sulla città* [*Hands Over the City*, 1963], just to mention two examples, or even my first film, *La sfida* [*The Challenge*, 1957], shared information of a social nature and thus with time acquired an historical value as well. During that period they at times made up for the unwillingness shown by the press to speak out, or substituted for the information not given on television. Back then, television was not that global medium, that instrument of information, which it has since become.

In Italy those were the "golden times" of Democrazia Cristiana (Christian-Democrat) monopoly on information.

Yes, exactly. The newspapers, too, ran into trouble at times. Take, for example, a film such as *Salvatore Giuliano* – a film denouncing a certain type of collusion between politics, the Mafia and certain institutions within the state. The fact that Giuliano may have been killed in a manner other than that mentioned in the government's official report was hypothesized in a famous article by a great journalist of *L'Europeo*, Tommaso Besozzi, entitled: "Di sicuro c'è solo che è morto" ["The Only Certain Thing Is That He Is Dead"].[4] Ten years after the killing, thanks to the wider audience enjoyed by films with respect to newspapers, and thanks to the effectiveness of emotionally charged images, my film managed to bring to the attention of the great mass of the public things which the powers that be had previously kept carefully hidden from general awareness. The film acted as a denunciation: it put the official version of facts face to face with the contradictions entailed by the latter in actual reality, as well as with the objections raised by different hypotheses. *Salvatore Giuliano* acted as a testimony to the historical moment when the events had taken place, in the framework of the general political situation of the times and in the framework of the social, political and human conditions of Sicily.

Returning now to your question about the impact of television, it must be said that today television has obviously become an immediate and all-pervasive instrument of information. As a consequence, certain types of film must inevitably take into account the fact that information is now immediately being brought to viewers' homes; and not only the information, but also the discussion. Therefore, today more often than not a film that deals with a social topic, a film of denunciation, reflection or discussion about everyday problems, and so on, is having to gain a certain distance from the facts at the narrative level and to focus instead on the poetic level. From a certain point of view, that is all for the good, because this situation may force directors to make films that de-emphasise the narration of facts [*cronaca*] and attempt to emphasise creation instead.

Today's edition of la Repubblica *publishes an interview with you, in which you state that you might be interested in making a film on the circumstances surrounding Gardini's suicide in 1993 (the Ferruzzi family, the Montedison scandal, bribes and illegal financing for political parties, and so on).*

That is a subject which, given the films I have been making up to now, certainly intrigues me. At the same time, this is precisely one of those cases corresponding to the analysis I was developing moments ago. Events such as those surrounding Gardini's death have recently filled Italy's television screens and continue to do so. Immediately making a film on the same subject might well result in people thinking that they have seen it all already. Besides, there remains the obligation to interpose a certain distance between us and the events, so as to set up an historical filter allowing for a better knowledge and a deeper acquaintance with the facts. This is, after all, what I have always done with my other films in the same genre.

Surely, if a film such as this should ever be made, who better than Francesco Rosi to direct it?
Today there are plenty of talented young people. The only real issue is the direction in which they wish to develop their talent: this is the point. It seems to me that in Italy, at this particular time, the talent of young directors is not especially focused on the analysis of society or the problems that affect the community. What can be detected is an interest in problems of an individual nature, rather than in those of a collective nature.

To a filmmaker, to an artist, what may be the difference between making a film based on a pre-existing text, and one based instead on a free creation, or on a social theme, in which no literary work pre-exists? One could perhaps name Just Another War, *inspired by* Un anno sull'altipiano [One Year on the Plateau] *by Lussu, or* Cristo si è fermato a Eboli (Christ Stopped at Eboli, 1979), *inspired by Carlo Levi – contrasted with* Hands Over the City *or* The Mattei Affair.
Let me begin by saying that, as far as I am concerned, whenever I shoot films drawn from works of literature I always try to transpose those books which (with all the due, respectful distance I acknowledge between myself and the authors of those books) I could have "written myself", or at the very least I would have been *interested* in writing myself. I have never chosen a book on the basis of it being a good commercial platform for the launching of the corresponding film. Instead, I have always chosen books that echoed my own way of seeing and perceiving the problems dealt with by their authors.
Having said that, there certainly *is* a difference between the two patterns. That comes across in the very way a film is written. The script of a film arising from the direct observation of reality, such as *Hands Over the City* or *The Mattei Affair*, clearly enjoys a freedom that comes to fruition by the use of all available sources of information and inspiration. For example, when I made these two films, just as was the case when I made *Tre fratelli* [*Three Brothers*, 1980], I not only drew upon the observation of reality, but also turned to a narrative form derived from journalism, from television, from various sources of information – from the news, to put it briefly.
By contrast, a novel or book has *already* carried out its own process of historical sedimentation of a given topic. Therefore, when one turns to a book by a great author, one is forced to move within narrower, predetermined bounds. One cannot choose a masterpiece such as Levi's *Christ Stopped at Eboli* and then use it exclusively as a source of raw material. That simply would not be a legitimate way to

proceed. Using a book as a source and as a point of reference carries with it the obligation to respect a certain narrative structure. Surely, this narrative structure will eventually, when translated into images, have to muster the specific demands made upon it by the images themselves, which are different from those imposed by words. Thus it is that the film also eventually becomes an act of writing [*scrittura*], to the extent that the creative process involved in a film is autonomous with respect to its literary antecedent.

Another possible example is the film I made from the book *Il contesto* [*Equal Danger*] by Leonardo Sciascia – *Cadaveri eccellenti* [*Illustrious Corpses*, 1975]. There one can certainly find a great respect for the spirit of Sciascia's book, but at the same time also a great degree of freedom on my part. For example, to mention just one circumstance, Sciascia's book makes no precise reference to Italy as the country in which the plot unfolds. I, on the other hand, felt the need to identify that country as Italy in the film, because otherwise the story I was telling by means of images would not have had the same force it came to have once the public could recognise the country in which it is set. I would not have been able to talk about political parties and institutions, had I not identified a precise, specific society, and had I not shown Italy. It would not have been possible to make the film otherwise; it would have come out as something completely abstract.

Literature can afford to be metaphorical or even metaphysical, but it is very difficult for cinema to be metaphorical. As for metaphysical, I believe that I have managed, by way of the choice of locations, the scenes, and my treatment of them (with the lenses, lighting, and so on), to attain a certain metaphysical dimension. But what is most germane to cinematographic composition [*scrittura*] is realism. And then, of course, there is the *interpretation* of reality. The interpretation of reality allows for poetry to arise; but reality is at the basis of every film, to the extent that every film is a mirror of society and bears witness to it.

Then surely Platonov's short story, "Trety syn" ["The Third Son"] is a slightly exceptional case in your œuvre? Three Brothers *is neither exclusively inspired by reality, nor solely drawn from Platonov.*

Certainly. I have always said that Platonov's short story offered me the key necessary to "unlock the door" to the plot of *Three Brothers*. *Three Brothers* was written by myself and Tonino Guerra on the basis of the stimulus offered to us by Italian reality, in which the situation in Platonov's novella fits well. Out of fairness, out of intellectual and professional honesty, I considered it my duty to make an explicit reference to Platonov; but what has remained from the novella is only the initial situation – that is to say, the death of a mother and the consequent reunion among brothers who have lived for years far away from each other, in very different professions and in very different areas of their country.

As a student, you were a law major. Are you therefore now called Dottore *in the world of cinema?[5] On the same theme, I noticed that some people in the milieu call you* Professore. *How does that strike you?*

I could never quite figure out why. Who knows?! Even people who hardly know me, who know nothing about me... "*Professore*"! Maybe because I do not like to be called *Dottore* to begin with...

...Italian-style...

Yes! They may think that in order to make certain films one must also have a certain deeper, more historical knowledge of the issues at hand; and so, naturally the term *Professore* goes hand in hand with this idea. And nowadays some people have started calling me *Maestro. Maestro* bothers me even more than *Dottore.*

But the fact remains that, in order to be able to make a certain type of film, one needs the unquestionably pugnacious spirit that can be typical of a prosecution attorney. Is there, in your opinion, an interpenetration between the world of the legal profession and Francesco Rosi's artistic world? Or, at the opposite extreme, has cinema been a way for you to break away and into something new? Between the practice of law and the practice of art, do you feel that there was continuity *or* opposition *in your life?*

For me, getting into filmmaking was the fulfilment of an aspiration, of a dream, of a desire which I had nourished ever since I was very young, probably as a consequence of the fact that my father was a great fan of cinema and of photography. My father was the director of a sailing company, but he was also a fairly well-known and very skilful caricaturist. And he was a passionate fan of cinema ever since its inception. I remember him always taking pictures, developing them himself, and then printing his own photographs. I remember him with the camera and Pathé projector ever since I was a very small child (I was born in 1922). In short, since around the age of two, I have had this memory well-delineated in my mind.

I saw my first films with my father when I was a very small child. He would always take me to the movies, and so I have always lived in a constant *contact with images* and with cinema. Cinema has always enthralled me.

Later, of course, I enrolled in the Faculty of Jurisprudence because, as all parents do, my father advised me to choose an activity that might offer more security by comparison with the relative insecurity of an artistic career. I wanted to sign up for the Centro Sperimentale di Cinematografia, but dad advised me to take a degree in law first.

Then I did not finish my degree after all, because in the meantime the Second World War had broken out. I was drafted and when I came back from the war, from military service, I no longer felt the desire to study and I started working instead; firstly, I worked for Italian radio, then in the theatre. Then, finally, I made it into the world of cinema.

Therefore you have not gone through a sequential development from law to art; the two paths have been parallel for you.

Perhaps that is so. Certainly, however, I had a passion for facts of a social nature, for history. Without doubt, that is what impelled me above all to practise a certain type of cinema.

When you consider the ways in which the public and the critics react to your films, respectively in Italy, Europe and North America, does it ever seem to you that your films are viewed, read, understood and interpreted in different ways in these three areas, or does that thought not occur to you?

No, I would say that it does not occur to me. I would say that, whenever these films had a chance to be screened and viewed in the United States, the reactions were very, very similar to those they had encountered in Italy. I was very surprised, for example, on the day my film *Christ Stopped at Eboli* was screened at the Chicago Film Festival. I was very concerned – partly on account of the rhythm of the narration, and partly on account of the very story it told – that the film perhaps could not be received there as it had been received in Italy. Contrary to that expectation, I found myself faced with a public that was, I should say, enthusiastic, very warm. The public understood that film right away. In fact, they had understood it perfectly; they were touched.

This happens to echo what I was alluding to before. When a film is able to preserve its own well-defined cultural identity, but at the same time it *also* broaches and treats problems in a universal manner, then all differences between one country and another are overcome. On the one hand, the cultural identity remains; but on the other, there arises the possibility to open up debates that involve nations throughout the world.

Has there ever been a moment in your career when your reputation as a possibly "austere" and "demanding" filmmaker has been a burden to you, or has seemed to you in any way inaccurate?

Firstly, rather than "austere" I would say *rigorous,* because I do not recognise myself in austerity. What I do recognise myself in is the rigour with which I tried to develop some arguments that *demanded* rigour – and they demanded it because they demanded respect for truth. One cannot make films such as *Salvatore Giuliano, Hands Over the City, Just Another War,* or *Lucky Luciano, Illustrious Corpses, Three Brothers* or *Christ Stopped at Eboli* without expecting from oneself respect and rigour, respect for a certain cultural identity, on the one hand, and for a certain historical truth, on the other.

This in no way detracts from the freedom which creativity is to enjoy. Quite on the contrary, one can allow creativity to roam perhaps even more freely, once one has made sure to abide by the historical platform, the social platform, the general "platform of truth".

When I was shooting *Salvatore Giuliano,* I was *extremely* respectful towards elements of truth of a social and historical nature. This is why I demanded of myself and of the producer that we shoot on the very locations where the original events had taken place. This was not a director's whim. It was a necessity – it was an imperative need for historical reconstruction, to be fulfilled by the participation and the involvement of the people who had witnessed those events no more than ten to fifteen years before. By way of that involvement and thanks to that respect, I managed to *add emotion* to the film, causing a form of trauma of an emotional nature which allowed local Sicilians to cooperate. Reproducing that emotion served as a basis for images that could get closer to the truth. Therefore, the question as to whether this "rigour" of mine has ever hurt me, or felt like a burden – no, it has not.

What may have been a burden, if anything, was the fact that I have sometimes taken longer in my attempts to convince people to shoot films according to this method than would otherwise have been the case. However, starting from the moment when the plan was ready, from then on carrying it out, actually making it happen from the director's viewpoint, was exactly like shooting any other film – a film of total invention, I mean. For example (if we count from the moment when an idea was first generated to the moment when the corresponding film was finished and released), I must say that *Salvatore Giuliano* was perhaps the film that was completed in the shortest time span.

The criminal investigations on governmental parties' involvement in bribery and corruption scandals, the so-called "Mani pulite" ["Clean hands"] inquiries, which are affecting the Italian political and industrial worlds as we speak, are foreshadowed in your œuvre:

149

Salvatore Giuliano, Hands Over the City, The Mattei Affair, Illustrious Corpses, *and so on. What feelings have you nourished recently – have you perhaps felt morally vindicated in the two years since the investigations began?*

No, no vindictive feelings. However, what I have indeed found in the "Clean hands" investigations was a confirmation of what I and my cooperators had intuited as we were grappling with certain stories. I sensed a confirmation that our "stories" had smelled *the truth* and had guessed right. After all, those stories did not invent any of their situations. My stories aimed at seeing, with objective and attentive eyes, what was going on, what was actually there, in the reality that surrounded us.

You should not think that, for example, *Hands Over the City* was born out of a particular talent for clairvoyance. Far from that, the film simply featured that which *was there* in Neapolitan society (and around the world – we should not forget that real estate speculation, characterised by collusion between economic power and corrupt political power, was something that occurred globally, not just in Italy). I chose Naples as an example because it was my city, the city I knew best. Certainly, it was a city where this type of real estate speculation, with attendant collusion between the various forms of power, was much more in evidence than elsewhere; the famous "sack of Naples"[6] was something absolutely obvious. What one did need to have was, in the first place, the political determination to denounce the misdeeds. Other than that, a pair of eyes was all that was required.

Then time went by. When, 30 years later, the bubble burst at a generalised national level, suddenly a film such as *Hands Over the City* started to be recognised as having anticipated the situation. But, I repeat, the film was an anticipator simply because in it there was the *determination* to see that which was already perfectly visible by itself.

Now, many years later, your current project is based on Primo Levi's La tregua [The Truce]. *Here another major theme emerges: Nazism and the reconstruction that followed it. What prompted this choice for your latest project?*

The Truce introduces an element of, let us say, novelty with respect to the films that deal with the Holocaust. The novelty is that *The Truce* recounts the return to freedom and to life. *The Truce* is a wonderful book by Primo Levi characterised by a special irony and gusto for the grotesque. In certain situations and at certain moments it even reaches into the comic register, no less, precisely because it portrays the return to life and to freedom, and the successful struggle against all intervening obstacles. In practice, *The Truce* begins at the exact moment when *Schindler's List* ends. Its return to life is narrated with the full outburst of hope and joy that quite naturally accompanies it. The film portrays the return to life in the full awareness of the fact that life is "a truce" between one sorrow and the next, between a war and the following one.

This is the theme to which today's events, with tragic urgency, once more draw our attention, both in Europe and throughout the world. Think only of the events in the former Yugoslavia to relate to what I am mentioning. So *The Truce*, a project that had already captivated my interest a number of years ago, occurred to me again three to four years ago, precisely on account of its *urgency*. I felt that urgency intensely, I experienced it as a reason for again proposing that book, that story, to the public. The demise of the Berlin Wall, which on the one hand opened up human hearts to hope, has on the other hand meant a disappointment of hope, because that hope was a hope for peace and fraternity among the peoples. Today, unfortunately, this brotherhood has experienced a throwback, it has been disappointed and betrayed; and we are all searching for ways to reconstitute it. To me, this seems to be the most interesting aspect in the project for *The Truce*, the reason that makes it necessary.

What makes *The Truce* so applicable for our time, therefore, is on the one hand the rush towards freedom, towards the joy of being alive; and, on the other hand, the awareness of a threat that is ever-impending, of a war that can flare up again at any time, and of the intrinsic difficulty of thinking and believing that a feeling of brotherhood can prevail in the world.

The fact remains that you interpret and exemplify this theme by having recourse to episodes dating from almost 50 years ago – almost as if you wished to say that the present times would not be able to recognise and identify a great theme, if they were to experience it cloaked in the "everydayness" of our life.

This is not so. The story of *The Truce* is a story that plays 50 years ago, to be sure; but although the narration is based on events that took place half a century ago, in practice it portrays feelings that are eternal. The theme of returning home [*l'Anabasi*] is an eternal feeling.

Almost 200 years ago, the German poet Hölderlin pondered on the purpose of poets, artists, in times of political oppression and intellectual misery. German culture has had – unfortunately – ample opportunity to debate this theme in the course of our century. I would update the question in the following terms: what is the purpose of engaged and rigorous directors in an epoch such as ours, which is not only an epoch of "garbage TV" [TV-spazzatura] but also, even worse, one in which such a large part of the population actually seems to desire *to be thus demeaned?*

Our purpose is to ensure that it will continue to be possible for us to feel confident that we can express ourselves and that we can profess our belonging to the world of hope, to the world of respect for the fundamental values of human life. These values are: respect for life, respect for the rights of others, and respect for truth.

I believe that cinema, the type of cinema to which you are referring, the type of cinema that respects the human being and human values, is indispensable if we want to continue to believe in the possibility for human beings to respect their fellow human beings. Even more importantly, I believe that it is indispensable if we want to keep alive the idea of our obligation to respect the fundamental values of life.

This is, of course, what art is needed for. Art conveys not only emotions, but also a moral experience. It conveys the need for us to identify with a world in which we may hope to fight successfully in order to assert fundamental values, *and* respect for human life, *and* respect for human *dignity.* I believe that through an "engaged" cinema (a label which, by the way, I do not like very much), through a cinema that *attempts as much as possible to rub shoulders with truth* and with the real values of life, one can succeed in conveying the urgency of respecting human dignity. Many times the respect for human dignity is even more important than the respect for human life itself.

What advice do you give, or would you like to give, to today's autori *– whether real or imaginary, the choice is yours – who wished to claim to be, in whole or in part, pupils of yours, who stated that Rosi is one of their masters?*

I believe that the most important thing for the young *autori* of today is to resume dealing with individual problems by paying careful attention to the collective picture. I think that today in Italy the time has come for us to start again to take a good look around ourselves, looking at the problems of Italian society – something which Italian cinema has always done, and which has been its characteristic trait. The great masterpieces of the Italian cinema of the past, from the postwar period onwards, *did not* neglect individual problems; but they did interweave them with the problems that ran through society and that had to do with collectivity. Films such as *Umberto D* [1951], *Bicycle Thieves*, *La terra trema* [*The Earth Trembles*, 1948], *La dolce vita* [1960], and many others, testify to just such an attitude.

In support, I could mention many instances, even films *apparently* far removed from focusing on collectivity: for example, Antonioni's *L'Avventura* [1960]. Apparently, Antonioni is an *autore* who is more distant than others from probing into the collective self – but on closer inspection this turns out not to be the case. It is not the case precisely because Antonioni's films, however focused on extremely individualised facts they may have been, in the end were inscribed within a collective sentiment. In short, I think that, after a long period of distance from a certain way of feeling, the Italian cinema of today shows signs of a return to it.

All of which has nothing to do with the cinema labelled "political cinema". That is not what it is. In some young *autori* there is a slight fear to be catalogued as belonging to a "political cinema" from which they may well have attempted to distance themselves. One should not be afraid of labels, however. What one should instead be afraid of is the idea of not being close enough to a truth in which the collectivity may recognise itself.

The problems of each of us can reverberate authenticity only when these problems can be felt by *many* at one time. That is what universality as the *value* of a work of art is all about. Making films that express only very intimate and very specific problems, without creating this type of *resonance* all around – this, I believe, is, broadly speaking, the danger incurred by some of the young *autori* who made their debut in the reality of Italian cinema during the last few years.

As I point out in my article in *la Repubblica*, I believe that this situation was the inevitable result of a moment of great tragedy which our country has experienced, and which has brought in its wake a form of disarray, a confusion. We have been the only European country with such a bloodshed-minded, such an ideological terrorism, and one that lasted for ten years. Young people have had ten years of that terrorism, which Italian cinema so far has not been able to retell – except with partial[7] works. For example, I believe that in 1980 I was myself one of the first who broached the theme; but I did so obliquely, with *Three Brothers*. However, there are few films which have tackled this problem. And perhaps they have not yet tackled this crisis in the way it should be, that is to say, as a general crisis of cultural, political and human values in society. I believe that in some of these new *autori* it will certainly give rise to the desire of going back to the theme of the experience of terrorism and attempting to narrate it.

It would not be the first time that the history of a society and the history of its art live on different "clocks": suffice it to mention the Leopard, a figure portrayed with such accomplishment in Tomasi di Lampedusa's novel (and then filmed by Visconti, only with a full century's delay). Perhaps terrorism too will have to wait a long time. However that may be, do you have other particular topics in mind for the younger generations?

Aside from terrorism, today there is an Italian society that is in rapid transformation; there is an Italian society to which one must pay great attention – which one must try to narrate, I mean. Aside from many violent films and many questionable films made with an eye on box-office spectacularism more than anything else, American cinema produces every year at least 20-30 films which in one way or another reflect the social reality of the United States and are attentive to all the problems of their country.

We may therefore conclude this conversation by exhorting the young to bring back cinema, if not to politics, certainly to history...

...and to the social. Even through a political lens, if that is what they want – as long as this happens without any schematic notions of an ideological nature, but, rather, with respect for truth and freedom.

Notes

[1]   See Rosi's article in *la Repubblica* of 20 April 1994, reprinted on pages 155-158 of this volume.

[2]   In English in the original.

[3]   In English in the original.

[4]   *L'Europeo* 16 July 1950: 1-2.

[5]   In Italy the honorific title *Dottore* is often used to show politeness in addressing educated, powerful or otherwise influential persons.

[6]   The reference is a paraphrase and adaptation of the name given to the historical event of 1527, the "sack of Rome" – a pillage perpetrated by the Imperial troops of Charles V.

[7]   *Partial* not as the opposite of "impartial", but as the opposite of "comprehensive".

The future of Italian film: for a cinema of memory and identity

Francesco Rosi

In the March 1994 issue of *The New Yorker*, Clive Barnes made a reference to Federico Fellini, and in the context wrote about the Italian cinema of the 1960s and 1970s: "In those times, Italy was the world capital of cinema; and this fact, apparently pertaining only to the artistic sphere, has had an immense impact on the political and economic image of Italy abroad".

This statement suggests some reflections on present times. Without a doubt, the last few years have witnessed a weakening in the creativity of our cinema which continues to this day. For a while now, much less has been produced in Italy than was produced before; moreover, it is a self-evident fact that, the fewer films are made, the fewer opportunities there are for a certain number of outstanding ones to be counted upon. The system by which Italian television pre-finances films has reduced the threshold of risk, but, by the same token, it has also greatly reduced the producers' entrepreneurial role.

The rule of money-making

The philosophy of box-office receipts – a sacred one, as long as it does not paralyse film directors – has flattered the taste of the Italian public by pursuing well-trodden artistic paths of often doubtful quality, instead of encouraging movie-goers to accept the stimuli for reflection that may have come to them from the screen.

Together with the rule of money-making, the lack of an adequate law offering incentives, support and a clear regulation of the relationship between cinema and television has been the other reason why Italian directors have been forced in recent years to invest the greatest part of their energy in activities other than artistic ones directly related to rousing the emotions on which the success of a film is based. Far from that, they have had to retrain themselves as fund-raisers, or even as financial mediators and accountants. They have thus reduced their creative space to moments of emergency, characterised, if anything, by haste, difficulties and approximation, ever-haunted by the fear of going over-budget.

Listing these reasons does not claim to be a justification for a slackening in inspiration; it merely describes the *de facto* situation which anyone attempting an analysis of Italian cinema today must take into account. The point is that, according to the individual director's personality, the situation causes either dejection or rebellion, or even an outright self-censorship prompting the *a priori* suppression of those themes that are guaranteed not to meet the financiers' approval. It has been widely recognised that the very latest generation of Italian directors and authors have produced many films which show indisputable talent, but which are characterised on the whole by the choice of a minimalist approach. Such a choice was encouraged by producers, by the Italian state television (RAI), and by the appropriate state agency. In doing so, all these agencies forgot that cinema is an industry, and that competition on the international front against the strongest and best-equipped companies is lost in advance if one gives up fighting them on their very terrain.

To make matters worse, a contributing factor in the authors' choice was the difficulty of interpreting Italy's ever more confused political situation, upset by ten years of terrorism, weakened by shady, tit-for-tat deals and apportioning of power among political parties [*consociativismo*], and riddled with deadly bombings and unresolved political mysteries. Together with competition from television, this has caused a distinct break with the features typical of Italian cinema as referred to by Clive Barnes – a cinema which, both in its dramatic films and in its so-called *commedia all'italiana*, had previously been a mirror of the collective themes of Italian national life. On more than one occasion, the paralysing difficulty of finding financing, and the further reasons I indicated in my attempt at an explanation, finally caused today's directors to abandon all attempts at "flying higher" than they actually did.

It is our duty to probe the causes for the laziness of sorts which seems to have befallen all of us who practise cinema in Italy. This laziness can eventually turn into stagnation of the spirit, and thus also of the will. I believe that this has happened because we have lost confidence in our points of reference and in ourselves.

We live in a society that we do not like. Because cinema is a reflection of the society in which it develops, and because it is (compared to all other artistic mediums) the instrument most liable to make people aware of a given issue, as well as the one best capable of stimulating a debate among different ideas, it follows that when a society is struck by disease, so too is cinema. Leonardo Sciascia once described his native Sicily as a living metaphor; likewise, one could argue that the Italian cinema of today is a metaphor for Italy as a whole. Enthusiasm has gone from it, whereas it had been the state of mind of authors, directors, producers, actors and technicians from the immediate postwar years until recent times.

My generation outlived Fascism, which it had opposed and defeated, and it survived the physical and moral ruins of the war. It nourished a true craving for reconstruction, a craving which made us all feel that, ideological differences notwithstanding, with each other's help we all intended to practise cinema as an active participation in public life. We all wanted to interpret the life that was growing back under our very eyes, and we wanted to recount it without the constant concern of having to please everyone at all costs. Quite on the contrary, we had a provocative determination to open the eyes of those very people who would have preferred to keep them shut.

Let no one tell me that all those cinema artists were Communists. That simply is not true: Rossellini was no Communist, nor was De Sica; Visconti claimed to be one, but really was not. While Zavattini did in fact profess to be a Communist, and Giuseppe De Santis was one, Suso Cecchi D'Amico was not. Nor were Fellini, Antonioni, Germi and many, many others whom it would take too long to list. What is true is that in the Italian cinema of those times there was a wave of volunteer idealism whose importance had been well understood by the Communists (among whom there were many followers of Benedetto Croce's philosophy) and by Nenni's Socialist Party. Such idealism was defended by those two political groups, against the open hostility of governmental officialdom.

Had the governments of the time not been hostile to that enthusiasm, they would have had to acknowledge that, more than in the actions of their political representatives, the Italian people recognised themselves, their own anxieties, hopes and disappointments in the works of the three great fathers of neo-realism – who had changed the way of practising cinema throughout the world – as well as in those of their artistic heirs.

It was an enormous mistake on the part of the Italian governments of those years, and of those that came later, not to realise just how much resonance across the world Italian cinema would give to its country – and still gives to it today, despite the present crisis in creativity and productivity.

Actors and spectators of the collapse

Today, in the face of a collapse in which we are all actors and of which we are all spectators, the official attitude is still unchanged. To experience this at first hand, one need only take a look at the choice of Italian films aired by Italian television stations, both public and private, and at the time of day (or of night!) that they are being aired.

Cinema means History and continuity. My urge to make Italian cinema available for the younger generations does not merely strive to defend an artistic past, however glorious. By means of the emotions aroused by images, it aims to make the young acquainted with what Italy was in the past, showing them images of their fathers, and of their fathers' fathers.

The first channel of RAI recently aired Second World War Allied war footage under the title *Combat Film*. However cruel and loaded with pathos, such documentary material will never be able to convey to young people the feelings that can be conveyed to them by a Rossellini film from the same years – a film that is art rather than news, and narration rather than episode. Young Italians of fewer than twenty years of age not only do not know who Badoglio was, but also do not even know who Rossellini was and what he accomplished – which, to my mind, may be an even greater shortcoming. Umberto Eco made a public statement to the effect that it would be more appropriate to redirect the funds earmarked for the Milan celebration of Liberation Day on 25 April towards the printing of a booklet, to be sold at a dollar a copy, explaining to the young what Fascism was and what the Resistenza was. Then why not air on all public and private channels, at prime time, Rossellini's *Paisà* (*Paisan*)?

Films such as *Paisan* were born not only out of a unique historical moment, but also out of enthusiasm. This enthusiasm we must all recover, in the name of our determination to voice a collective interest responding to issues that affect everyone's life. In order for this to happen, it is necessary that we rediscover lost moral values, and that we conquer those never previously attained. It is necessary that we identify with a society that is morally reunited, rather than with one made up of a myriad stray monads, as could be the case if we fail to act. The great fathers of Italian neo-realist cinema did not preach solidarity; they practised it in their art.

* * *

[Originally published in *la Repubblica*, 20 April 1994, under the editorial title "C'era una volta il cinema". Edited and translated by Carlo Testa.]

Francesco Rosi: filmography

Compiled by Carlo Testa

The following abbreviations have been used in this filmography:

FR	Francesco Rosi	*ed*	editor
		ep	executive producer
ad	art director	m	mins
bw	black and white	*m*	music
col	colour	*p*	producer
cost	costumes	*pc*	production company
d	director	*ph*	cinematography
dist	distributor	*sc*	scriptwriter

La sfida
The Challenge
Italy/Spain 1957 120m bw 35mm feature
ep Enzo Provenzale *p* Franco Cristaldi *pc* Lux-Vides, Cinecittà, Rome/Suevia Film (Madrid) *d* FR *sc* FR, Suso Cecchi D'Amico, Enzo Provenzale *ph* Gianni Di Venanzo *m* Roman Vlad *ed* Mario Serandrei *ad* Franco Mancini *cost* Marilù Carteny
main cast José Suárez (Vito Polara), Rosanna Schiaffino (Assunta), Nino Vingelli (Gennaro), José Jaspe (Raffaele), Tina Castigliano (Vito's mother), Pasquale Cennamo (Ferdinando Ajello), Elsa Valentino Ascoli (Assunta's mother), Elsa Fiore (Vito's sister), Ubaldo Granata (Califano), Ezio Vergari (Antonio), Concetta Petito (aunt Rosa), Rosita Pisano (washing-woman).
dist Lux Film
awards Special Prize of the Jury, 29th Venice Film Festival; Nastri d'Argento (Silver Ribbons) for original story, producer (Franco Cristaldi) and supporting actor (Nino Vingelli); Noci d'Oro prize for director.

I magliari
The Swindlers
aka The Dry Goods Dealers
Italy/France 1959 107m bw 35mm feature
ep Orazio Tassara, Gino Millozza *p* Franco Cristaldi *pc* Vides *d* FR

sc Suso Cecchi D'Amico, Giuseppe Patroni Griffi, FR *ph* Gianni Di Venanzo *m* Piero Piccioni *ed* Mario Serandrei *ad* Dieter Bartels *cost* Graziella Urbinati
main cast Alberto Sordi (Ferdinando Magliulo, *aka* "Totonno"), Belinda Lee (Paula Mayer), Renato Salvatori (Mario Balducci), Linda Vandal (Frida), Aldo Giuffré (Armando), Nino Vingelli (Vincenzo), Nino Di Napoli (Ciro), Pasquale Cennamo (Don Gennaro), Aldo Bufi Landi (Rodolfo Valentino), Carmine Ippolito (Don Raffaele), Joseph Damen (il signor Mayer).
dist Titanus
awards Nastro d'Argento (Silver Ribbon) for cinematography.

Salvatore Giuliano
Italy 1961 125m bw 35mm feature
ep Enzo Provenzale *p* Franco Cristaldi, Lionello Santi *pc* Lux-Vides-Galatea *d* FR *sc* FR, Suso Cecchi D'Amico, Enzo Provenzale, Franco Solinas *ph* Gianni Di Venanzo *m* Piero Piccioni *ed* Mario Serandrei *ad* Sergio Canevari, Carlo Egidi *cost* Marilù Carteny
main cast Frank Wolff (Gaspare Pisciotta), Salvo Randone (President of the Court), Federico Zardi (Pisciotta's lawyer), Pietro Cammarata (Salvatore Giuliano), Giuseppe Teti (young shepherd), Cosimo Torino (Frank Mannino), Giuseppe Calandra (plainclothes under-officer of the *carabinieri*), Pietro Franzone (separatist leader), Giovanni Gallina, Vincenzo Norvese (*picciotti*), Sennuccio Benelli (journalist), Bruno Ukmar (spy), Max Cartier (Francesco), Fernando Cicero (bandit), Tullio Kezich (parish priest of Montelepre), Federico Wertmuller (lawyer), Accursio Di Leo (Concetto Gallo), Francesco De Felice (Member of Parliament), the inhabitants of Montelepre.
dist Lux Film
awards Silver Bear, 12th Berlin Film Festival; Nastri d'Argento (Silver Ribbons) for direction, music and cinematography; Grolle d'Oro (Golden Grail) for direction.

Le mani sulla città
Hands Over the City
Italy 1963 110m bw 35mm feature
ep Enzo Provenzale *p* Lionello Santi *pc* Galatea Film *d* FR *sc* FR, Raffaele La Capria, Enzo Provenzale, Enzo Forcella *ph* Gianni Di Venanzo *m* Piero Piccioni *ed* Mario Serandrei *ad* Sergio Canevari *cost* Marilù Carteny
main cast Rod Steiger (Edoardo Nottola), Salvo Randone (De Angeli), Guido Alberti (Maglione), Angelo D'Alessandro (Balsamo), Carlo Fermariello (De Vita), Marcello Cannavale, Alberto Canocchia, Gaetano Grimaldi Filioli (friends of Nottola), Terenzio Cordova (prosecutor), Dante Di Pinto (president of the inquiry committee),

Dany Paris (Maglione's lover), Alberto Amato, Franco Rigamonti (city councillors), Vincenzo Metafora (mayor), Pasquale Martino (head of the archive), Mario Perelli (head of the technical office), Renato Terra, Renzo Farinelli (journalists).
dist Warner Bros.
award Leone d'Oro, 24th Venice Film Festival.

Il momento della verità
The Moment of Truth
Italy/Spain 1964 110m colour 35mm feature
ep FR, Antonio Cervi *p* Angelo Rizzoli *pc* Federiz (Rome)/AS Films (Madrid) *d* FR *sc* FR, *with the cooperation of* Pedro Portabella, Ricardo Muñoz Suay, Pedro Beltràn *ph* Pasqualino De Santis, Gianni Di Venanzo, Aiace Parolin *m* Piero Piccioni *ed* Mario Serandrei
main cast Miguel Mateo Miguelin (Miguel, the matador), José Gomez Sevillano (impresario), Pedro Basauri Pedrucho (Pedrucho), Linda Christian (herself), Luque Gago, Salvador Mateo, Manuel Ruiz Serrana, Francisco Caño, José Rodriguez Matia, Manolo Perez Moratilla, José Vizcaino (bullfighter's *cuadrilla*).
dist Cineriz
award David di Donatello for direction.

C'era una volta...
Cinderella - Italian Style
aka Once Upon a Time
Italy/France 1967 115m colour 35mm feature
ep Gianni Cecchin, Claudio Mancini *p* Carlo Ponti *pc* C C Champion (Rome)/Les Films Concordia (Paris) *d* FR *sc* Tonino Guerra, Raffaele La Capria, Giuseppe Patroni Griffi, FR *based on the book by* G B Basile, "Lo cunto de li cunti" ("The Story of Stories") *ph* Pasqualino De Santis *m* Piero Piccioni *ed* Jolanda Benvenuti *ad* Piero Poletto *cost* Giulio Coltellacci
main cast Sophia Loren (Isabella Candeloro), Omar Sharif (Prince Rodrigo), Georges Wilson (Monzù, the cook), Leslie French (brother Giuseppe da Copertino), Dolores Del Rio (princess mother), Carlo Pisacane (first witch), Marina Malfatti (Olympia, the enterprising princess), Anna Nogara (impatient princess), Rita Forzano (miserly princess), Rosemary Martin (pretentious princess), Carlotta Barilli (superstitious princess), Fleur Mombelli (haughty princess), Anna Liotti (*infante*), Renato Pinciroli (signor Capaccio), Giovanni Tarallo (shepherd), Valentino Macchi (Mariano), Giacomo Furia (monk in the convent), Chris Huerte (Spanish soldier), Gladys Dawson, Kathleen St. John, Beatrice Greack (witches), Pietro Carloni (priest), Pasquale Di Napoli, Vincenzo Danaro, Salvador Runo, Luciano Di Mauro, Francesco Coppola, Luigi Criscuolo (six *scugnizzi*),

161

Francesco Lo Como (young black servant).
dist Interfilm MGM

Uomini contro
Just Another War
Italy/Yugoslavia 1970 101m colour 35mm feature
ep FR, Luciano Perugia *p* Marina Cicogna *pc* Prima Cinematografica
(Rome)/Jadran Film (Zagreb) *d* FR *sc* Tonino Guerra, Raffaele La
Capria, FR *based on the book by* Emilio Lussu, "Un anno
sull'altipiano" ("One Year on the Plateau") *ph* Pasqualino De Santis
m Piero Piccioni *ed* Ruggero Mastroianni *ad* Andrea Crisanti
cost Franco Carretti, Gabriella Pescucci
main cast Mark Frechette (Under-Lieutenant Sassu), Alain Cuny
(General Leone), Gian Maria Volonté (Lieutenant Ottolenghi),
Giampiero Albertini (Captain Abbati), Pier Paolo Capponi (Lieutenant
Santini), Franco Graziosi (Major Malchiodi), Mario Feliciani (medical
Colonel), Alberto Mastino (soldier Marrasi), Brunetto Del Vita
(Colonel Stringari), Luigi Pignatelli (Lieutenant Avellini).
dist Euro International Film, Warner Bros.

Il caso Mattei
The Mattei Affair
Italy 1972 118m colour 35mm feature
ep Gino Millozza *p* Franco Cristaldi *pc* Vides-Verona *d* FR *sc* FR,
Tonino Guerra *with the cooperation of* Nerio Minuzzo, Tito De
Stefano *ph* Pasqualino De Santis *m* Piero Piccioni *ed* Ruggero
Mastroianni *ad* Andrea Crisanti *cost* Franco Carretti
main cast Gian Maria Volonté (Enrico Mattei), Luigi Squarzina
(liberal journalist), Peter Baldwin (William McHale, *Time* journalist),
Gianfranco Ombuen (engineer Ferrari), Franco Graziosi (minister),
Elio Jotta (commander of the investigation panel), Edda Ferronao
(Mattei's wife), Luciano Colitti (Bertuzzi), Accursio Di Leo (Sicilian
politician), Giuseppe Lo Presti (Sicilian politician), Felice Fulchignoni
(Sicilian politician), Camillo Milli (money-exchange agent), Terenzio
Cordova (policeman), Aldo Barberito (officer), Dario Michaelis
(officer of the *carabinieri*), Jean Rougeul (US civil servant), Furio
Colombo (Mattei's assistant), Blaise Morrissey (US oilman), Alessio
Baume (journalist from *Time* magazine), Vittorio Fanfoni, Sennuccio
Benelli, Ugo Zatterin, Gianni Farneti, Umberto D'Arrò, Salvo Licata,
Giuseppe Rosselli (journalists), Ferruccio Parri, Michele Pantaleone,
Arrigo Benedetti, Thyraud de Vosjoli, FR (themselves).
dist Cinema International Corporation
awards Grolle d'Oro (Golden Grail): Valdostana Cup (Franco
Cristaldi); Nastro d'Argento (Silver Ribbon) for new actor (Luigi
Squarzina).

Lucky Luciano
Italy/France 1973 115m colour 35mm feature
ep Gino Millozza *p* Franco Cristaldi *pc* Vides (Rome)/Les films La
Boétie (Paris) *d* FR *sc* FR, Lino Jannuzzi, *with the cooperation of*
Tonino Guerra *ph* Pasqualino De Santis *m* Piero Piccioni *ed* Ruggero
Mastroianni *ad* Andrea Crisanti *cost* Marisa Crimi, Luciana Fortini
main cast Gian Maria Volonté (Lucky Luciano), Edmond O'Brien
(Harry J Anslinger), Rod Steiger (Gene Giannini), Charles Siragusa
(himself), Vincent Gardenia (Colonel Poletti), Charles Cioffi (Vito
Genovese), Jacques Monod (Commissioner of Police), Karen
Petersen (Igea), Magda Konopka ("Countess"), Larry Gates (Judge
Herlands), Silverio Blasi (officer of the *Guardia di Finanza*), Dino
Curcio (Don Ciccio).
dist Titanus

Cadaveri eccellenti
Illustrious Corpses
Italy 1975 120m colour 35mm feature
p Alberto Grimaldi *pc* PEA (Produzione Europee Associate) (Rome)/
Les Artistes Associés (Paris) *d* FR *sc* FR, Tonino Guerra, Lino
Jannuzzi *based on the novel by* Leonardo Sciascia, "Il contesto"
("Equal Danger") *ph* Pasqualino De Santis *m* Piero Piccioni; tango
"Jeanne y Paul", composed by Astor Piazzolla *ed* Ruggero
Mastroianni *ad* Andrea Crisanti *cost* Enrico Sabbatini
main cast Lino Ventura (Inspector Rogas), Fernando Rey (Minister of
the Interior), Max von Sydow (President Richès), Charles Vanel
(District Attorney Varga), Tino Carraro (Chief of Police), Marcel
Bozzuffi (former inmate), Paolo Bonacelli (Doctor Maxia), Alain
Cuny (Judge Rasto), Maria Carta (Signora Cres), Luigi Pistilli (Cusani),
Tina Aumont (prostitute), Renato Salvatori (commissioner of police),
Alfonso Gatto (Nocio), Paolo Graziosi (Galano), Anna Proclemer
(Signora Nocio), Carlo Tamberlani (archbishop), Enrico Ragusa
(Capuchin friar), Corrado Gaipa (Mafia boss), Claudio Nicastro
(general), Francesco Callari (Judge Sanza), Mario Meniconi
(mechanic), Accursio Di Leo (Rogas's assistant), Ernesto Colli (night
guard), Silverio Blasi (head of the political squad in the police),
Alexandre Mnouchkine (Patos), Giorgio Zampa (Amar), Florestano
Vancini (Communist Party leader).
dist United Artists
awards Grolle d'Oro (Golden Grail) for direction; Valdostana Cup
(Alberto Grimaldi). David di Donatello for film and direction.

Cristo si è fermato e Eboli
Christ Stopped at Eboli
Italy/France 1979 160m colour 35mm feature

p Franco Cristaldi, Nicola Carraro *pc* RAI-TV 2/Vides Cinematografica
(Rome)/Action Film (Paris) *d* FR *sc* FR, Tonino Guerra, Raffaele La
Capria *based on the book by* Carlo Levi *pb* Pasqualino De Santis
m Piero Piccioni *ed* Ruggero Mastroianni *ad* Andrea Crisanti
cost Enrico Sabbatini
main cast Gian Maria Volonté (Carlo Levi), Paolo Bonacelli (Fascist
mayor or *podestà* Luigi Magalone), Alain Cuny (baron Rotundo), Lea
Massari (Luisa Levi), Irene Papas (Giulia), François Simon (Don
Trajella), Luigi Infantino (driver), Accursio Di Leo (carpenter),
Francesco Càllari (Dr Gibilisco), Antonio Allocca (post office
employee), Tommaso Polgar ("sow-healer"), Vincenzo Vitale (Dr
Milillo), Muzzi Loffredo (exiled Mafiosa), Giuseppe Persia (tax
collector), Frank Raviele (officer of the *carabinieri*), Stavros Tornes
(city secretary), Giacomo Giardina (undertaker), Francesco Capotorto
(exiled Communist), Vincenzo Licata (Italo-American), Maria Antonia
Capotorto (donna Caterina), Lidia Bavusi (widow), Antonio Jodice
(*carabiniere*), Paolo Di Sabato (Italo-American), Francesco Palumbo
(barber), Rocco Sisto (peasant with goat), Francesca Massaro
(peasant woman with chicken), Carmelo Lauria (Carmelo).
dist Titanus
awards Golden Trophy, 1979 Moscow Film Festival. Nastro
d'Argento (Silver Ribbon) for supporting actress (Lea Massari). David
di Donatello for film and direction. BAFTA award for foreign film.
Prix Moussinac for foreign film.

Tre fratelli
Three Brothers
Italy/France 1980 113m colour 35mm feature
ep Franco Ballati *p* Giorgio Nocella, Antonio Macri *pc* Iter Film
(Rome)/Gaumont (Paris) *d* FR *sc* FR, Tonino Guerra *based on the
short story by* Andrei Platonov, "Trety syn" (The Third Son")
pb Pasqualino De Santis *m* Piero Piccioni *ed* Ruggero Mastroianni
ad Andrea Crisanti *cost* Gabriella Pescucci
main cast Philippe Noiret (Raffaele Giuranna), Michele Placido
(Nicola Giuranna), Vittorio Mezzogiorno (Rocco Giuranna/Donato as
a young man), Charles Vanel (Donato Giuranna), Andrea Ferréol
(Raffaele's wife), Maddalena Crippa (Giovanna, Nicola's wife), Sara
Tafuri (Rosaria), Marta Zoffoli (Marta, Nicola's daughter), Simonetta
Stefanelli (wife of Donato as a young man), Gina Pontrelli (old-age
wife), Tino Schirinzi (Raffaele's friend), Pietro Biondi, Ferdinando
Greco (judges), Cosimo Milone (Raffaele's son).
dist Gaumont
awards Nastri d'Argento (Silver Ribbons) for director,
cinematography and actor (Vittorio Mezzogiorno). David di
Donatello for director, screenplay, cinematography, editing and

supporting actor (Charles Vanel). Nomination for Academy Award®
as Best Foreign-Language Film.

Carmen
Italy/France 1984 152m colour 35mm feature
p Patrice Ledoux *pc* Gaumont-Marcel Dassault (Paris)/Opera Film
(Rome) *d* FR *sc* Tonino Guerra, FR *based on the libretto by* Henri
Meilhac and Ludovic Halévy, *of the opera by* Bizet, *inspired by the
novella by* Prosper Mérimée *ph* Pasqualino De Santis *m* Georges
Bizet *ed* Ruggero Mastroianni, Colette Semprun *ad* Enrico Job
choreography Antonio Gades *cost* Enrico Job
main cast Julia Migenes Johnson (Carmen), Placido Domingo (Don
José), Ruggero Raimondi (Escamillo), Faith Esham (Micaëla), Jean-
Philippe Lafont (Dancaïre), Gérard Garino (Remendado), Susan
Daniel (Mercédès), Lilian Watson (Frasquita), John Paul Bogart
(Zuñiga), François Le Roux (Morales), Julien Guiomar (Lillas Pastia),
Accursio Di Leo (guide), Maria Campano (Manuelita), Cristina Hoyos,
Juan Antonio Jimenez (dancers), Enrique el Cojo (old dancer,
innkeeper), Santiago Lopez (stuntman for Escamillo during the
corrida), Aurora Vargas, Concha Vargas, Carmen Vargas, Esperanza
Fernandez, Lourdes Garcia, Maria Gomez, Pilar Becerra (Carmen's
friends), and the participation of the Antonio Gades Dance
Company.
dist Gaumont
awards César for sound. Nastro d'Argento (Silver Ribbon) for
costumes. David di Donatello for film, director, cinematography,
editing, art director, costumes. Alitalia Trophy (FR).

Cronaca di una morte annunciata
Chronicle of a Death Foretold
Italy/France 1987 110m colour 35mm feature
ep Jean-José Richer *p* Carlo Lastricati, Yves Gasser, Francis von
Büren *pc* Italmedia (Rome)/Soprofilms (Paris)/Les Films Ariane
(Paris)/FR3 Films (Paris), in cooperation with RAI 2 and FOCINE
(Bogotà) *d* FR *sc* FR, Tonino Guerra *based on the novel by* Gabriel
García Márquez *ph* Pasqualino De Santis *m* Piero Piccioni
ed Ruggero Mastroianni *ad* Andrea Crisanti *cost* Enrico Sabbatini
main cast Rupert Everett (Bayardo San Roman), Ornella Muti
(Angela Vicario), Gian Maria Volonté (Cristo Bedoya), Irene Papas
(Angela's mother), Lucia Bosé (Placida Linero), Anthony Delon
(Santiago Nasar), Sergi Mateu (Cristo Bedoya as a young man),
Carlos Miranda and Rogelio Miranda (Pedro and Pablo Vicario),
Alain Cuny (widower), Carolina Rosi (Flora Miguel), Caroline Lang
(Margot), Silverio Blasi (Colonel Aponte), Leonor Gonzales (Victoria
Guzman), Vicky Hernandez (Clotilde Armenta), Edgardo Roman

(Faustino Santos).
dist Istituto Luce, Italnoleggio Cinematografico

Dimenticare Palermo
The Palermo Connection
aka To Forget Palermo
Italy/France 1990 104m colour 35mm feature
ep Franco Ballati p Mario and Vittorio Cecchi Gori pc Reteitalia/
Cecchi Gori Group Leopard (Rome)/Gaumont Production (Paris)
d FR sc FR, Gore Vidal, Tonino Guerra based on the novel by
Edmonde Charles-Roux, "Oublier Palermo" ("To Forget Palermo")
ph Pasqualino De Santis m Ennio Morricone ed Ruggero Mastroianni
ad Andrea Crisanti, Stephen Graham cost Enrico Sabbatini, Susie
Money, Lisa Frucht
main cast James Belushi (Carmine Bonavia), Mimi Rogers (Carrie),
Joss Ackland (man in power), Philippe Noiret (director of the Grand
Hôtel), Vittorio Gassman (prince), Carolina Rosi (Gianna, the
journalist), Marco Leonardi (boy with jasmines), Harry Davis
(Carmine's father), Tiziana Stella (seductive woman), Giacomo
Giardina (concierge), Ronald Yamamoto (Sam Toy), Marino Masé
(warden), Vyto Ruginis (Ted), Stefano Nadia (doctor in the hospital),
Luigi Laezza (servant), Sal Borgese (coachman), Luigi Maria
Burruano (taxi driver), Gisella Mathews (Carmine's aunt), Egidio
Termine (carabiniere), Terenzio Cordova (florist).
dist Penta Film

Diario napoletano
Neapolitan Diary
Italy 1992 86m colour 35mm documentary and feature
ep Alessandro von Normann pc RAI TV Canale 3 d FR sc FR,
Raffaele La Capria based on a story by FR ph Pasqualino De Santis
m Piero Piccioni ed Ruggero Mastroianni
main cast FR, Pietro Bontempo, Simona Ceramelli, Nino Vingelli.

Francesco Rosi: selected bibliography

Compiled by Carlo Testa and Matthew Stevens

Primary bibliography

A: Published screenplays

Rosi, Francesco and Callisto Cosulich. *Uomini contro* (Bologna: Cappelli, 1970) [in Italian].

Rosi, Francesco, Enzo Forcella, Raffaele La Capria and Enzo Provenzale. "*Le mani sulla città*", *L'Ora* (Palermo) 10 September 1963: 7-10 [in Italian].

Rosi, Francesco and Eugenio Scalfari. *Il caso Mattei: Un 'corsaro' al servizio della repubblica* (Bologna: Cappelli Editore, 1972) [in Italian].

Rosi, Francesco and Lino Jannuzzi. *Lucky Luciano* (Milan: Bompiani, 1973) [in Italian].

Rosi, Francesco and Tullio Kezich. *Salvatore Giuliano* (Rome: Edizioni FM, 1961) [in Italian; partially reprinted in *Cineforum* 15 (May 1962): 429-487; includes filmography].

B: Statements by Rosi

"C'era una volta il cinema", *la Repubblica* 20 April 1994: 33 [in Italian].

"Un débat d'idées, de mentalités, de moralités", *l'Avant-Scène du Cinéma* 169 (May 1976): 6 [in French].

"Dessins originaux du scénario de *Cadavres exquis*", *Positif* 200/201/202 (December 1977/January 1978): 162-174 [in French].

"En travaillant avec Visconti sur le tournage de 'la terra trema'", *Positif* 215 (February 1979): 34-38 [in French].

"Entre 'Le Kid' et 'La terre tremble'", *Positif* 400 (June 1994): 117-119 [in French].

"Francesco Rosi: Cadaveri excellenti [sic]", *Jeune Cinéma* 95 (May/June 1976): 19-21 [in French].

"Francesco rosi parle de carmen", *Cinéma (France)* 304 (April 1984): 49-50 [in French].

"L'histoire de *la Chronique*", *Positif* 315 (May 1987): 14-18 [in French].

"Il était une fois le cinéma", *Positif* 401/402 (July/August 1994): 54-55 [in French; translation of Rosi's article, "C'era una volta il cinema", published in *la Repubblica* 20 April 1994: 33, and published in English in this volume].

C: Interviews with Rosi in journals/magazines

Aprà, Adriano and Luigi Martelli. "Intervista con Francesco Rosi", *Filmcritica* 156-157 (April/May 1965): 235-244 [in Italian].

Bachmann, Gideon. "Francesco Rosi: An Interview", *Film Quarterly* 18: 3 (spring 1965): 50-56.

——————————. "Francesco Rosi: Die soziale Verantwortung des Filmschöpfers", *Film (Germany)* 3: 2 (February 1965): 20-23 [in German].

Baker, Franca Durazzo. "Sono lo psicologo del film e non del personaggio. Colloquio con Francesco Rosi", *Cinema nuovo* 28: 261 (October 1979): 19-21 [in Italian].

Baldassaro, Lawrence. "Francesco Rosi: Intervista", *Annali d'italianistica* 6 (1988): 231-235 [in Italian].

Braucourt, Guy. "Entretien avec Francesco Rosi", *Cinéma (France)* 158 (July/August 1971): 133-136 [in French].

Bruno, Edoardo. "La mia esperienza neorealistica (conversazione con Francesco Rosi)", *Filmcritica* 116 (January 1962): 680-685 [in Italian].

Ciment, Michel. "Entretien avec Francesco Rosi", *l'Avant-Scène du Cinéma* 289/290 (June 1982): 4-13 [in French].

——————————. "Entretien avec Francesco Rosi", *Positif* 349 (March 1990): 12-16 [in French].

——————————. "Entretien avec francesco rosi à propos de lucky luciano", *Positif* 155 (January 1974): 15-24 [in French].

——————————. "Entretien avec Francesco Rosi sur Carmen", *Positif* 278 (April 1984): 7-12 [in French].

——————————. "Entretien avec francesco rosi (uomini contro)", *Positif* 121 (November 1970): 22-33 [in French].

——————————. "Entretiens avec Francesco Rosi sur 'Le christ s'est arrêté à éboli'", *Positif* 215 (February 1979): 24-32 [in French].

Ciment, Michel. "Francesco Rosi's 'Three Brothers'", *Sight and Sound* 51: 1 (winter 1981-82): 46-49.

Ciment, Michel and Bernard Cohn. "Entretien avec Francesco Rosi sur 'l'affaire mattei'", *Positif* 140 (July-August 1972): 24-30 [in French].

Ciment, Michel, Goffredo Fofi and Paolo Gobetti. "Entretien avec Francesco Rosi", *Positif* 69 (May 1965): 4-17 [in French].

Codelli, Lorenzo. "Entretien avec francesco rosi sur trois frères", *Positif* 242 (May 1981): 7-15 [in French].

—————————. "Francesco Rosi talking about Three Brothers", *Films and Filming* 325 (October 1981): 19-24 [English translation of the interview in *Positif* 242 (May 1981): 7-15].

—————————. "Woman of the Ronda", *Stills* 14 (November 1984): ii-iv.

Crowdus, Gary. "Investigating the Relationship Between Causes and Effects: An Interview with Francesco Rosi", *Cineaste* 20: 4 (October 1994): 26-27.

—————————. "Personalizing Political Issues: An Interview with Francesco Rosi", *Cineaste* 12: 2 (1982): 42.

Crowdus, Gary and Dan Georgakas. "The Audience Should Not Be Just Passive Spectators: An Interview with Francesco Rosi", *Cineaste* 7: 1 (autumn 1975): 1-8.

"Débat sur le film et sur la guerre", *Jeune Cinéma* 56 (June/July 1971): 4-7 [in French].

"Entretien avec Francesco Rosi", *Écran* 47 (15 May 1976): 25-28 [in French].

Gauthier, Guy. "Entretien avec Francesco Rosi", *Image et Son* 195 (June 1966): 48-51 [in French].

Gili, Jean A. "Entretien avec Francesco Rosi", *Écran* 83 (15 September 1979): 53-58 [in French].

—————————. "Entretien avec Francesco Rosi", *La Revue du Cinéma/Image et Son/Écran* 362 (June 1981): 27-29 [in French].

—————————. "Entretien avec Francesco Rosi: 'mon ambition a été de faire un film sur le pouvoir dans le monde...'", *Écran* 47 (15 May 1976): 25-28 [in French].

—————————. "Francesco Rosi: 'Mon cinéma n'est en rien un cinéma de documentariste, c'est un cinéma documenté. J'interprète la réalité pour essayer d'atteindre un certain type de vérité'", *Écran* 20 (December 1973): 5-11 [in French].

"Un'immagine della Spagna: colloquio con Francesco Rosi", *Bianco e Nero* 26: 4 (April 1965): 23-48 [in Italian].

Kimmel, Melody. "'Terrorism is murder, and murder is not political...' Francesco Rosi: An Interview", *Films in Review* 33: 5 (May 1982): 303-304.

Lane, John Francis. "Moments of Truth: Francesco Rosi interviewed by John Francis Lane", *Films and Filming* 16: 12 (September 1970): 6-10.

—————————. "Rosi's 'Carmen' more than filmed opera", *Screen International* 460 (25 August 1984): 18.

Langlois, Gérard. "Entretien avec Francesco Rosi", *Cinéma (France)* 168 (July/August 1972): 45-47 [in French].

Piazzo, Philippe. "'Et pourtant, Naples est une ville légère...'", *Télérama* 2320 (2-8 August 1994): 30-32 [in French].

Rémond, Alain. "Entretien avec Francesco Rosi", *Télérama* 26 May 1976: 82-83 [in French].

Robinson, George. "An Interview with Francesco Rosi", *Thousand Eyes* 2: 3 (November 1976): 6, 17 [translation from *Positif* 181 (May 1976)].

Tassone, Aldo. "Entretien avec Francesco Rosi", *La Revue du Cinéma/ Image et Son* 307 (June-July 1976): 76-86 [in French].

—————————. "Francesco Rosi: 'Au cinéma la dénonciation devient vite un prêche...'", *Cinéma 74* 183 (January 1974): 88-99 [in French].

Tournès, Andrée. "Entretien avec Francesco Rosi", *Jeune Cinéma* 95 (May/June 1976): 21-22 [in French].

"Two interviews. One: Francesco Rosi", *Film (BFFS)* 39 (August 1964): 12-14.

Secondary bibliography

A: Monographs devoted to Rosi (on individual films or his work in its entirety)

Bolzoni, Francesco. *I film di Francesco Rosi* (Rome: Gremese Editore, 1986) [in Italian].

Ciment, Michel. *Le dossier Rosi* (Paris: Editions Stock, 1976) [in French].

Coremans, Linda. *La transformation filmique du Il Contesto à Cadaveri Eccellenti* (Berne: Peter Lang, 1990) [in French].

Ferrero, Nino. *Francesco Rosi* (Turin: Edizioni AIACE, 1972) [in Italian].

Gesù, Sebastiano (ed). *Francesco Rosi* (Acicatena: Incontri con il Cinema, 1991) [in Italian].

Giacci, Vittorio (ed). *Francesco Rosi* (Rome: Cinecittà International, 1994) [in English].

Gili, Jean A. *Francesco Rosi: Cinéma et pouvoir* (Paris: Éditions du Cerf, 1976) [in French].

Kezich, Tullio and Sebastiano Gesù. *Salvatore Giuliano* (Acicatena: Incontri con il Cinema, 1992) [in Italian].

Micciché, Lino. *Cadaveri eccellenti* (Acicatena: Incontri con il Cinema, 1991) [in Italian].

Zambetti, Sandro. *Francesco Rosi* (Florence: La Nuova Italia, 1976) [in Italian].

B: Chapters or sections on Rosi and his work in books

Bondanella, Peter. *Italian Cinema: From Neorealism to the Present* (New York: Continuum, 1991).

Bory, Jean-Louis. "Francesco Rosi", in *Dossiers du cinéma: Cinéastes II* (Paris: Casterman, 1971): 169-172 [in French].

Boussinot, Roger. *L'encyclopédie du cinéma par l'image* (Paris: Bordas, 1970) [in French].

Brunetta, Gian Piero. *Cent'anni di cinema italiano* (Bari: Editore Laterza, 1991) [in Italian].

Bruno, Edoardo. "Francesco Rosi e il cinema ideologico", in *Tendenze del cinema contemporaneo* (Rome: Samonà e Savelli, 1965): 68-80 [in Italian].

Buache, Freddy. *Le cinéma italien 1945-1990* (Lausanne: L'Age d'homme, 1992) [in French].

——————. *Le cinéma italien d'Antonioni à Rosi au tournant des années 60* (Yverdon, Switzerland: Editions de la Thièle, 1969): 159-166 [in French].

Buss, Robin. *Italian Films* (London: Batsford, 1989).

Faldini, Franca and Goffredo Fofi. *L'avventurosa storia del cinema italiano raccontata dai suoi protagonisti 1935-1969* (Milan: Feltrinelli, 1979-1981) [in Italian].

——————. *Il cinema italiano d'oggi 1970-1984 raccontato dai suoi protagonisti* (Milan: Arnoldo Mondadori Editore, 1984) [in Italian].

Ferrara, Giuseppe. *Francesco Rosi* (Rome: Editrice Nanni Canesi, 1965) [in Italian].

Ferrero, Adelio, Giovanna Grignaffini and Leonardo Quaresima. *Il cinema italiano degli anni '60* (Rimini-Florence: Guaraldi Editore, 1977) [in Italian].

Gili, Jean A. *Le cinéma italien* (Paris: Union Générale d'Éditions, 1978) [in French].

Grazzini, Giovanni. *Gli anni Sessanta in cento film* (Bari: Editore Laterza, 1977) [in Italian].

——————. *Gli anni Settanta in cento film* (Bari: Editore Laterza, 1976) [in Italian].

Kezich, Tullio. *Il Millefilm. Dieci anni al cinema, 1967-1977* (Milan: Mondadori, 1983) [in Italian].

Leprohon, Pierre. *The Italian Cinema*, translated by Roger Greaves and Oliver Stallybrass (London: Secker & Warburg, 1972).

Liehm, Mira. *Passion and Defiance: Film in Italy from 1942 to the Present* (Berkeley; Los Angeles; London: University of California Press, 1984).

Lizzani, Carlo. *Il cinema italiano: dalle origini agli anni ottanta* (Rome: Editori Riuniti, 1992) [in Italian].

Marcus, Millicent. *Italian Film in the Light of Neorealism* (Princeton, NJ: Princeton University Press, 1986): 339-359.

Miccichè, Lino. *Cinema italiano degli anni '60* (Padua-Venice: Marsilio Editori, 1975) [in Italian].

——————. *Cinema italiano degli anni '70* (Padua-Venice: Marsilio Editori, 1980) [in Italian].

Michalczyk, John J. "Francesco Rosi: The Dialectical Cinema", in *The Italian Political Filmmakers* (Rutherford; Madison; Teaneck: Fairleigh Dickinson University Press, 1986): 19-63.

Perry, Ted. "Francesco Rosi", in Richard Roud (ed), *Cinema: A Critical Dictionary. The Major Filmmakers*, volume 2 (New York: Viking Press, 1980): 886-887.

Sitney, P Adams. *Vital Crises in Italian Cinema: Iconography, Stylistics, Politics* (Austin: University of Texas Press, 1995).

Tassone, Aldo. *Parla il cinema italiano* (Milan: Il Formichiere, 1979): 263-307 [in Italian].

Wakeman, John. "Francesco Rosi", in *World Film Directors 1945-1985*, volume 2 (New York: H W Wilson Company, 1988): 928-932.

Witcombe, R T. *The New Italian Cinema: Studies in Dance and Despair* (London: Secker & Warburg, 1982).

C: Special journal or magazine issues devoted to Rosi

Cinéma (Switzerland) 46 (1966) [in German]
Contents: "Erneuerer des Neorealismus", by Fritz Schaub (621-624); "Soziale Wirklichkeit: Die Struktur von Francesco Rosis Filmen", by Georg Kreis (625-629); "Politik und Stil", by Walter Tecklenburg (630-634); "Il momento della verità", by Karl Aeschbach (635-636).

Cinema (Switzerland) 2/82 (July 1982) [in German]
Contents: "Editorial: Ein exemplarischer langer Marsch", by Martin Schaub (3); "Wechselnde Wirklichkeiten: Rosis Weg vom Problem der Gesellschaft zum Problem des Einzelnen in der Gesellschaft", by Paul Huber (4-24); "Bildbeilage: Augenblicke, Montage", by Thomas Burla (25-53); "Henker und Opfer, ein Kreis: 'Il momento della verità'", by Bruno Haldner (55-67); "Erschaffung von Realität: Notizen zu Rosis filmischer Erzählweise", by Manfred Züfle (69-79); "Treue und Sorge: Rosis 'realistische Haltung'", by Harry Tomicek (80-90); "Jemand führt immer des Mörders Hand: Leonardo Sciascia/Francesco Rosi – 1916 bis heute", by Pierre Lachat (91-100); "Instant Replay: Gegenwart in Rosis Dramen", by Martin Schaub (101-110); "'Vito mio...'", by Corinne Schelbert (110-111); "Filmographie" (113-119).

D: General articles on Rosi in journals, magazines and serials

Alvarez, Luis Alberto. "Profundo sur: El cine de Francesco Rosi", *Cinemateca* 2: 6 (January 1979): 27-39 [in Spanish].

Amengual, Barthélemy. "D'un réalisme 'épique' (sur francesco rosi)", *Positif* 181 (May 1976): 39-44 [in French].

————————. "Rosi in Context", *Thousand Eyes* (November 1976): 17 [translation from *Positif* 181 (May 1976)].

Angell, Roger. "The Current Cinema: A House of Exile", *The New Yorker* 5 May 1989: 165-168.

Benayoun, Robert. "Le cinéaste du centre-gauche", *France Observateur* 14 November 1963: 17-18 [in French].

————————. "Dialectique du clair-obscur chez Francesco Rosi (sur *Chronique d'une mort annoncée*)", *Positif* 316 (June 1987): 12-14 [in French].

"Biofilmographie de Francesco Rosi", *Positif* 69 (May 1965): 31-32 [in French].

"Biofilmographie de Francesco Rosi", *l'Avant-Scène du Cinéma* 169 (May 1976): 32-36 [in French].

"Bio-filmographie de Francesco Rosi", *l'Avant-Scène du Cinéma* 289/ 290 (June 1982): 15 [in French].

Braucourt, Guy. "Gian Maria Volonte Talks About Cinema and Politics", *Cineaste* 7: 1 (autumn 1975): 10-13.

Brèque, Jean-Michel. "Réaliste et lyrique. Carmen dans sa vérité", *Positif* 278 (April 1984): 13-18 [in French].

Bruno, Edoardo. "Poesia e impegno civile", *Filmcritica* 139-140 (November-December 1963): 651-653 [in Italian].

――――――. "'Salvatore Giuliano': ritorno alla verità", *Filmcritica* 116 (January 1962): 677-679 [in Italian].

――――――. "Viaggio in Spagna di Francesco Rosi", *Filmcritica* 156/157 (April/May 1965): 286-288 [in Italian].

Castello, Giulio Cesare. "Cinema Italiano 1962", *Sight and Sound* 32: 1 (winter 1962-63): 31-32.

――――――――――. "Francesco Rosi", *Young Cinema and Theatre* 7 (1965): 3.

Chevassu, François. "L'affaire Mattei; La classe ouvrière va au Paradis", *La Revue du Cinéma/Image et Son* 262 (June-July 1972): 147-149 [in French].

――――――. "Main basse sur la ville", *Image et Son* 167-168 (November-December 1963): 112-120 [in French].

Ciment, Michel. "Au royaume de la lumière", *Positif* 215 (February 1979): 22-23 [in French].

――――――. "Chronicle of a Film Foretold", *Sight and Sound* 56: 1 (winter 1986/87): 18-23.

――――――. "Francesco Rosi, artiste-citoyen", *L'Express* 8-14 September 1975: 16-17 [in French].

――――――. "Neuf propositions pour un éloge de francesco rosi", *Positif* 230 (May 1980): 2-7 [in French].

――――――. "Rosi: à scénario ouvert", *L'Express* 17-23 July 1972: 48-49 [in French].

――――――. "Vivir desviviendose", *Positif* 69 (May 1965): 1-2 [in French].

Ciment, Michel, Lorenzo Codelli and Paul-Louis Thirard. "'L'affaire mattei' sous trois angles", *Positif* 140 (July-August 1972): 12-23 [in French].

Ciment, Michel and Michel Delain. "La Mafia selon Rosi", *L'Express* 22 October 1973: 106-108 [in French].

"Le cinéma est encore un art visuel (trois frères)", *Positif* 244/245 (July/August 1981): 113-114 [in French].

Codelli, Lorenzo. "'Cadavres exquis' sous trois angles", *Positif* 181 (May 1976): 24-33 [in French].

—————————. "Des mots autour des silences", *Positif* 315 (May 1987): 9 [in French].

—————————. "Entretien avec pasqualino de santis", *Positif* 230 (May 1980): 17-25 [in French].

—————————. "Trois notes sur trois frères, de Francesco Rosi", *Positif* 242 (May 1981): 2-3 [in French].

Cohn, Bernard. "Salvatore Giuliano: Une épopée en creux", *Positif* 53 (June 1963): 58-60 [in French].

Cournot, Michel. "Beauté interdite", *Le Nouvel Observateur* 21 June 1971: 48-49 [in French].

Crisanti, Andréa. "De Rosi à Tarkovski", *Positif* 315 (May 1987): 10-11 [in French].

Crowdus, Gary. "Francesco Rosi. Italy's Postmodern Neorealist", *Cineaste* 20: 4 (October 1994): 19-25.

"Débat sur le film et sur la guerre", *Jeune Cinéma* 56 (June/July 1971): 4-7 [in French].

Dell'Acqua, Gian Piero. "Spettacolo con argomenti polemici: 'Lucky Luciano' di Francesco Rosi", *Cinema Sessanta* 94 (November/December 1973): 47-49 [in Italian].

Domecq, Jean-Philippe. "Frisson politique, lucidité poétique. Sur Francesco Rosi", *Positif* 278 (April 1984): 2-5 [in French].

—————————. "Zénith et Nada. Sur *Carmen* de Francesco Rosi", *Positif* 278 (April 1984): 6 [in French].

Durieux, Gilles. "Les choix précis de Francesco Rosi", *Film Français* 13 May 1981: 5-8 [in French].

Elsaesser, Thomas. "Chronicle of a Death Retold", *Monthly Film Bulletin* 54: 641 (June 1987): 164-167.

Fofi, Goffredo. "Une année de cinéma italien", *Image et Son* 190-191 (January-February 1966): 25-26 [in French].

——————. "*I magliari*", *Positif* 69 (May 1965): 18-20 [in French].

——————. "Le sud dans le cinéma italien", *Image et Son* 190-191 (1966) [in French].

Font, Domenec. "Francesco Rosi", *Dirigido por...* 23 (May 1975): 1-17 [in Spanish; includes filmography].

Gardiès, René. "Main basse sur la ville", *Image et Son* 205 (1967): 93-99 [in French].

——————. "Salvatore Giuliano", *Image et Son* 205 (1967): 153-158 [in French].

Ghirelli, Antonio. "Un puritano ostinato", *La Fiera del Cinema* 4: 2 (February 1962): 65-68 [in Italian].

Giannattasio, Sandra (ed). "Infrarosso: I migliori, il linguaggio e le opere a basso costo", *Cinema nuovo* 13: 168 (March-April 1964): 88-99 [in Italian].

Gieri, Manuela. "*Le mani sulla città*. Il cinema di Francesco Rosi a Toronto", *Corriere Canadese* 3 November 1994: 7 [in Italian].

Gili, Jean A. "Cadavres exquis: Vérité, mensonge et révolution", *Écran* 47 (15 May 1976): 24-25 [in French].

——————. "Un cinéma a l'écoute de l'italie réelle", *Écran* 6 (June 1972): 6-15 [in French].

——————. "Un homme contre: Francesco Rosi", *Écran* 20 (December 1973): 2-5 [in French].

——————. "Levi, Rosi, Eboli: Comme s'il y avait deux Italie", *Écran* 83 (15 September 1979): 49-52 [in French].

——————. "Morale et politique", *l'Avant-Scène du Cinéma* 169 (May 1976): 4-5 [in French].

Gillett, John. "Cinderella – Italian Style", *Sight and Sound* 38: 4 (autumn 1969): 214-215.

Goldfayn, G. "La recherche de la vérité", *Art et Essai* 2 (May 1965): 20-24 [in French].

Held, Jean-François. "Francesco Rosi: la Mafia n'a pas de principes", *Le Nouvel Observateur* 29 October 1973: 44-46 [in French].

"Intervention de francesco montemurro, paysan", *Positif* 230 (May 1980): 15-16 [in French].

Jordan, Isabelle. "Le sable et le grain (trois frères)", *Positif* 242 (May 1981): 4-6 [in French].

Jung, Fernand. "Der dokumentarische Spielfilm (I): Francesco Rosi und die realistische Tradition des italienischen Kinos", *Medien + Erziehung* 1 (1977): 43-50 [in German].

Kané, Pascal. "Sur deux films 'progressistes' (L'Affaire Mattei, La Classe ouvrière va au Paradis)", *Cahiers du Cinéma* 241 (September-October 1972): 25-30 [in French].

Kauffmann, Stanley. "Stanley Kauffmann on films: Rosi and Roseland", *The New Republic* 19 April 1980: 26-27.

Klawans, Stuart. "Illustrious Rosi", *Film Comment* 31: 1 (January/February 1995): 60-65.

Lane, John Francis. "Film and politics in Italy: Francesco Rosi's example", *Films and Filming* 22: 8 (May 1976): 16-17.

—————————. "The Law of the Wilds", *Films and Filming* 8: 5 (February 1962): 37-38.

—————————. "Moments de vérité", *Positif* 69 (May 1965): 21-30 [in French; translation of "Moments of Truth", *Films and Filming* 11: 3 (December 1964): 5-10].

—————————. "Moments of Truth", *Films and Filming* 11: 3 (December 1964): 5-10.

—————————. "A Neapolitan Eisenstein", *Films and Filming* 9: 11 (August 1963): 51-53.

—————————. "The New Realists of Italy", *Films and Filming* 7: 4 (January 1961): 46.

Langlois, Gérard. "Francesco Rosi: *L'affaire Mattei*", *Lettres françaises* 17 May 1972: 11ff [in French].

—————————. "Francesco Rosi – *Les hommes contre*: Chercher le véritable ennemi", *Lettres françaises* 9 June 1971: 19-20 [in French].

Legrand, Gérard. "Là-bas et maintenant, autrefois et non loin", *Positif* 230 (May 1980): 8-11 [in French].

Levi, Carlo. "De l'auteur à son éditeur", *Positif* 215 (February 1979): 39-40 [in French].

"Main basse sur la ville: Découpage et dialogue in extenso", *l'Avant-Scène du Cinéma* 169 (May 1976): 7-29 [in French; script of *Hands Over the City*].

Marino, Camillo. "L'ingiusto pessimismo ideologico di Francesco Rosi in 'Cadaveri eccellenti'", *Cinema sud* 61 (September 1976): 15-21 [in Italian].

Masson, Alain. "L'évidence et le paradoxe (sur *Chronique d'une mort annoncée*)", *Positif* 316 (June 1987): 9-11 [in French].

——————. "Là-bas, là-bas, dans la montagne. Carmen", *Positif* 278 (April 1984): 19-21 [in French].

Mastroianni, Ruggero. "A la moviola avec Rosi", *Positif* 315 (May 1987): 12-13 [in French].

Melodia, Andrea, et al. "Incontri critici: 'Il caso Mattei'. Le mani sul petrolio", *Rivista del Cinematografo* 3/4 (March/April 1972): 148-155 [in Italian; comprises "Toccare la coscienza civica", by Claudio Sorgi (149-150); "Visione integralistica", by Andrea Melodia (150-151); "Una casistica donchisciottesca", by Antonio Mazza (151-153); "Più che dire suggerisce", by Aldo Trifiletti (154-155)].

Micciché, Lino. "'Cristo si è fermato a Eboli' di Francesco Rosi", *Cinema Sessanta* 125 (January/February 1979): 48-49 [in Italian].

Michalczyk, John J. "The Political Adaptation: Rosi and Petri Film Sciascia", *Annali d'italianistica* 6 (1988): 220-230 [in Italian].

Mitchell, Tony. "Christ Stopped at Eboli", *Sight and Sound* 47: 4 (autumn 1978): 222.

Morandini, Morando. "Rosi uomo del Sud scava nella realtà", *Il Giorno* 18 November 1975 [in Italian].

Moscati, Italo. "Mattei e l'ideologia del padrone di stato", *Cineforum* 117 (September 1972): 44-50 [in Italian].

Nettelbeck, Uwe. "Politik und Stil: Francesco Rosi", *Filmkritik* 12/64 (December 1964): 628-632 [in German].

Nowell-Smith, Geoffrey. "Salvatore Giuliano", *Sight and Sound* 32: 3 (summer 1963): 142-143.

Overbey, David L. "Rosi in Context", *Sight and Sound* 45: 3 (summer 1976): 170-174.

Padovani, Marcelle. "Con 'Cristo si è fermato a Eboli': il nuovo film di Francesco Rosi", *Cinema sud* 68 (July 1978): 5-6 [in Italian].

——————. "Les damnés du Mezzogiorno", *Le Nouvel Observateur* 5 June 1978: 62-63 [in French].

Pattison, Barrie. "Rosi and Volonte", *Film (BFFS)* 29 (August 1975): 3.

"Propos de Francesco Rosi", *La Revue du Cinéma/Image et Son* 393 (April 1984): 21-22 [in French].

Quaglietti, Lorenzo. "'Cadaveri eccellenti' di Francesco Rosi", *Cinema Sessanta* 107/108 (January/April 1976): 79-80 [in Italian].

—————————. "Fermenti anticonformistici nei film italiani e inglesi", *Cinema 60* 4: 39 (November 1963) [in Italian].

—————————. "Una lucida e appassionata inchiesta: 'Il caso Mattei' di Francesco Rosi", *Cinema Sessanta* 89 (May/June 1972): 63-65 [in Italian].

—————————. "Tre fratelli di Francesco Rosi", *Cinema Sessanta* 140 (July/August 1981): 58-59 [in Italian].

Ravage, Maria-Teresa. "The Mafia on Film: *Salvatore Giuliano*", *Film Society Review* October 1971: 33-39.

Renaud, Tristan. "*Les hommes contre* de Francesco Rosi", *Lettres françaises* 9 June 1971: 18-19 [in French].

Restivo, Angelo. "The Economic Miracle and Its Discontents: Bandit Films in Spain and Italy", *Film Quarterly* 49: 2 (winter 1995-96): 30-40.

Roncoroni, Stefano. "Evoluzione filmica di Francesco Rosi", *Filmcritica* 14: 137 (September 1963): 520-528 [in Italian; includes filmography].

Rubino, María Teresa. "Francesco Rosi completa el mosaico", *Cinemateca* 2: 6 (January 1979): 40-42 [in Spanish].

Sciascia, Leonardo. "Du 'contexte' à 'cadavres exquis'", *Positif* 181 (May 1976): 34-38 [in French].

"La sfida", *Filmcritica* 78/79 (August/September 1958): 140-152 [in Italian; script extract].

Sineux, Michel. "Un réalisme magique", *Positif* 230 (May 1980): 12-14 [in French].

—————————. "Le récit et les images (sur *Chronique d'une mort annoncée*)", *Positif* 316 (June 1987): 15-18 [in French].

St. Jacques, André. "*Il caso Mattei*", *Cinéma/Québec* 2: 8 (May-June 1973): 45-46 [in French].

Strick, Philip. "The Mattei Affair and Lucky Luciano", *Sight and Sound* 44: 3 (summer 1975): 191-192.

Tassone, Aldo. "Le cinéma de Francesco Rosi. Un certain témoignage sur l'histoire italienne, de 1947 à nos jours...", *La Revue du Cinéma/Image et Son* 307 (June-July 1976): 69-75 [in French].

Tassone, Aldo. "Entretien avec Tonino Guerra", *Positif* 215 (February 1979): 41-45 [in French].

Thomas, John. "Salvatore Giuliano", *Film Society Review* September 1966: 18-21.

Tinazzi, Giorgio. "Rosi: la perdita di una cultura", *Cinema e Cinema* 8: 29 (October-December 1981): 84-87 [in Italian].

"Trois frères: Découpage intégral après montage et dialogue in extenso", *l'Avant-Scène du Cinéma* 289/290 (June 1982): 19-58 [in French; script of *Three Brothers*].

Vitoux, Frédéric. "Le pouvoir et ses masques (à propos de lucky luciano) ", *Positif* 155 (January 1974): 25-28 [in French].

Wills, David. "Carmen: Sound/Effect", *Cinema Journal* 25: 4 (summer 1986): 33-43.

Wilson, David. "In the Picture: Tehran Festival", *Sight and Sound* 43: 2 (spring 1974): 88.

Zambetti, Sandro. "Il Caso Mattei", *Cineforum* 117 (September 1972): 51-78 [in Italian].

—————————. "Francesco Rosi: Cadaveri eccellenti", *Cineforum* 152 (March 1976): 111-123, 160 [in Italian].

Zambetti, Sandro. "Il momento della verità di Francesco Rosi", *Cineforum* 45 (June 1965): 373-385 [in Italian].

E: Selected film reviews

The Palermo Connection

Lane, John Francis. "Forget Palermo", *Screen International* 744 (17-23 February 1990): 200-201.

Legrand, Gérard. "Jasmin et jalousie, sirocco et pouvoir (Oublier Palermo)", *Positif* 349 (March 1990): 9-11 [in French].

"Oublier Palerme", *Film Français* 2284 (9 February 1990): 35 [in French].

Roth-Bettoni, Didier. "Oublier Palermo: Un homme contre", *La Revue du Cinéma* 458 (March 1990): 20-21 [in French].

Salachan, Gilbert. "Oublier Palerme", *Télérama* 2319 (22 June 1994): 134 [in French].

Yung. "Dimenticare Palermo (To Forget Palermo)", *Variety* 28 February 1990: 28.

Chronicle of a Death Foretold

Combs, Richard. "Seize the King", *The Listener*, volume 124, 3173 (12 July 1990): 43.

Elsaesser, Thomas. "Cronaca di una morte annunciata (Chronicle of a Death Foretold)", *Monthly Film Bulletin* 54: 641 (June 1987): 163-164.

Gehler, Fred. "Chronik eines angekündigten Todes", *Film und Fernsehen* 10 (1989): 37 [in German].

Lane, John Francis. "Chronicle of a Death Foretold", *Screen International* 599 (9-16 May 1987): 47.

Le Fanu, Mark. "Passionate confusion: *Chronicle of a Death Foretold*", *Sight and Sound* 56: 3 (summer 1987): 222.

Rakovsky, Antoine. "Chronique d'une mort annoncée", *La Revue du Cinéma* 428 (June 1987): 26-28 [in French].

Stanbrook, Alan. "Chronicle of a Death Foretold", *Films and Filming* 393 (June 1987): 30-31.

Walters, Margaret. "Star-crossed macho men", *The Listener*, volume 117, 3016 (18 June 1987): 30.

Yung. "Cronaca di una Morte Annunciata", *Variety* 29 April 1987: 18.

Carmen

Adair, Gilbert. "Carmen", *Monthly Film Bulletin* 52: 614 (March 1985): 79-80.

Amiel, Mireille. "Carmen de Francesco Rosi", *Cinéma (France)* 304 (April 1984): 48-49 [in French].

Canby, Vincent. "¡Ole!" *The New York Times* 20 September 1984: C21 [reprinted in *The New York Times Film Reviews* (1983-1984): 286-287].

——————. "Three New Movies Enrich Their Genres", *The New York Times* 23 September 1984: II 19 [reprinted in *The New York Times Film Reviews* (1983-1984): 289-290].

"Carmen", *Cineinforme* 130 (May 1984): 26 [in Spanish].

Ciment, Michel. "Rosi in a new key", *American Film* 9: 10 (September 1984): 36-42.

Cook, Christopher. "Southern discomfort", *The Listener*, volume 113, 2901 (21 March 1985): 32.

Denby, David. "Movies: Death in the Afternoon", *The New Yorker* 8 October 1984: 85-86.

Goldberg, Robert. "Bizet Would Recognize This New *Carmen*", *The New York Times* 30 September 1984: II 19.

J.-M. B. "Carmen", *l'Avant-Scène du Cinéma* 360 (May 1987): 84-85 [in French].

Kael, Pauline. "The Current Cinema: Mozart and Bizet", *The New Yorker* 29 October 1984: 122-125.

Kauffmann, Stanley. "Stanley Kauffmann on Film: Native Lands", *The New Republic* 1 October 1984: 24-25.

Kerner, Leighton. "Carmen Chameleon", *Village Voice* 25 September 1984: 67.

Kroll, Jack. "Torpid Si, Torpid No", *Newsweek* 17 September 1984: 89.

Len. "Carmen", *Variety* 14 March 1984: 22.

Lucas, Blake. "Bizet's Carmen", in Frank N Magill (ed), *Magill's Cinema Annual 1985: A Survey of 1984 Films* (Englewood Cliffs, NJ: Salem Press, 1985): 98-104.

M.C. "Notes sur d'autres films: Carmen", *Cahiers du Cinéma* 358 (April 1984): 51 [in French].

O'Toole, Lawrence. "A Temptress and a Toreador", *MacLeans* 4 March 1985: 54.

Pintus, Pietro. "*Carmen*: i meriti di Rosi", *Bianco e nero* 45: 4 (October/December 1984): 19-22 [in Italian].

Rinieri, Dominique. "Carmen", *Cinématographe* 99 (April 1984): 47 [in French].

Rubinstein, Leslie. "Carmen Glut", *American Film* 9: 4 (January-February 1984): 10.

——————. "Gypsy", *Opera News* 40 (October 1984): 10-16, 55-58.

Simon, John. "Bizet's *Carmen*, Shaffer's *Amedeus*", *National Review* 19 October 1984: 55-57.

Smith, Ronn. "Not Just Another *Carmen*", *Theatre Crafts* (January 1985): 22ff.

Walsh, Michael. "Bizet's *Carmen*", *Time* 8 October 1984: 82.

Three Brothers

A.Br. "*Tre fratelli*", *Cinema nuovo* 30: 273 (October 1981): 51-52 [in Italian].

Ansen, David. "Politics on Celluloid", *Newsweek* 22 February 1982: 68-70.

Biraghi, Guglielmo. "*Tre fratelli* di Francesco Rosi", *Il Messaggero* 21 March 1981: 13 [in Italian].

Canby, Vincent. "Reserves of Emotion", *The New York Times* 19 February 1982: C8 [reprinted in *The New York Times Film Reviews* (1981-1982): 198].

Cohen, Joan L. "*Three Brothers*", in Frank N Magill (ed), *Magill's Cinema Annual 1983: A Survey of 1982 Films* (Englewood Cliffs, NJ: Salem Press, 1983): 349-352.

Cosulich, Callisto. "Un vecchio e i suoi figli", *Paese Sera* 21 March 1981: 3 [in Italian].

Crowdus, Gary. "*Three Brothers*", *Cineaste* 12: 2 (1982): 41, 43.

de Baroncelli, Jean. "*Trois frères* de Francesco Rosi", *Le Monde* 14 May 1981: 19 [in French].

Forbes, Jill. "The hope of things to come", *Sight and Sound* 51: 1 (winter 1981/82): 62.

Gauthier, Guy. "Trois frères", *La Revue du Cinéma/Image et Son/Écran* 362 (June 1981): 26-27 [in French].

Insdorf, Annette. "Highlights of Cannes Film Festival", *Cineaste* 11: 3 (1981): 27-28.

Kael, Pauline. "The Current Cinema: Francesco Rosi", *The New Yorker* 22 March 1982: 160-164.

Kauffmann, Stanley. "Stanley Kauffmann on films: Good Intentions", *The New Republic* 21 April 1982: 24-25.

Legrand, Gérard. "La flamme d'une chandelle (trois frères)", *Positif* 244/245 (July/August 1981): 111-114 [in French].

McVay, Douglas. "Three Brothers", *Films and Filming* 327 (December 1981): 28-29.

Millar, Gavin. "Fraternal reunion Italian style", *The Listener*, volume 109, 2804 (14 April 1983): 40.

—————. "The larger statement", *The Listener*, volume 106, 2731 (15 October 1981): 448-449.

Pérez, Michel. "*Trois frères* de Francesco Rosi", *Le Matin* 14 May 1981: 24 [in French].

Pisarra, Pietro. "Tre frateli", *Rivista del Cinematografo* 6 (June 1981): 295-296 [in Italian].

Purtell, Tim. "*Three Brothers*", *Films in Review* 33: 5 (May 1982): 305-306.

Quart, Barbara and Leonard. "Three Brothers", *Film Quarterly* 36: 1 (autumn 1982): 53-56.

Ranvaud, Don. "Tre Fratelli (Three Brothers)", *Monthly Film Bulletin* 48: 574 (November 1981): 226-227.

Reggiani, Stefano. "Tre fratelli e un padre in un'Italia confusa", *La Stampa* 5 April 1981: 19 [in Italian].

Rickey, Carrie. "Trinity Holy and Unholy", *Village Voice* 23 February 1982: 52ff.

Sragow, Michael. "*Three Brothers* Rooted in the Earth", *Rolling Stone* 29 April 1982: 32-37.

Tornabuoni, Lietta. "Rosi: Più che denunciare oggi è necessario capire", *La Stampa* 5 April 1981: 19 [in Italian].

Yung. "Tre Fratelli", *Variety* 15 April 1981: 18.

Zambetti, Sandro. "Fratelli d'Italia, l'Italia s'è persa", *Cineforum* 204 (May 1981): 3-7 [in Italian].

Christ Stopped at Eboli

Ansen, David. "Peasant Power", *Newsweek* 31 March 1980: 85.

Argo. "Cristo si e fermato a Eboli", *Variety* 21 March 1979: 24.

Billanti, Dean. "*Christ Stopped at Eboli*", *Films in Review* 31: 5 (May 1980): 313, 317.

Combs, Richard. "Cadaveri Eccellenti (Illustrious Corpses)", *Monthly Film Bulletin* 44: 521 (June 1977): 119-120.

Cowie, Peter. "Cristo si è fermato a Eboli", in Peter Cowie (ed), *International Film Guide 1980* (London: The Tantivy Press, 1979): 200.

de Baroncelli, Jean. "A la recherche d'un monde oublié", *Le Monde* 13 May 1979: 1, 17 [in French].

Erskine, Tom L. "Eboli (Cristo si è fermato a Eboli)", in Frank N Magill (ed), *Magill's Survey of Cinema: Foreign Language Films*, volume 2 (Englewood Cliffs, NJ: Salem Press, 1985): 911-914.

Fox, Julian. "Christ Stopped at Eboli", *Films and Filming* 26: 4 (January 1980): 40-41.

G.P. "*Cristo si è fermato a Eboli*", *Cinema nuovo* 28: 259 (June 1979): 53 [in Italian].

Grelier, Robert. "Le Christ s'est arrêté à Eboli", *Image et Son/Écran* 350 (May 1980): 19-21 [in French].

Hibbin, Sally. "Christ Stopped at Eboli", *Films and Filming* 333 (June 1982): 28.

Maslin, Janet. "Eboli", *The New York Times* 23 March 1980: 54 [reprinted in *The New York Times Film Reviews* (1979-1980): 190].

Ranvaud, Don. "Cristo si è fermato a Eboli (Christ Stopped at Eboli)", *Monthly Film Bulletin* 49: 581 (June 1982): 106-107.

Schickel, Richard. "Way Station: *Eboli*", *Time* 28 April 1980: 76.

Selden, Ina Lee. "Town On Wrong Side of Christ's Path", *The New York Times* 6 June 1978: C5.

Simon, John. "Interior Exiles", *National Review* 30 May 1980: 672-673.

Sterritt, David. "Inside the Peasant Heart", *Christian Science Monitor* 16 April 1980: 22.

Tournès, Andrée. "Le Christ s'est arrêté à Eboli", *Jeune Cinéma* 119 (June 1979): 45-47 [in French].

Trémois, Claude-Marie. "Le Christ s'est arrêté à Eboli...au-delà, les damnés de la terre", *Télérama* 30 April 1980: 102-103 [in French].

Illustrious Corpses

Argentieri, M. "*Cadaveri eccellenti*", *Rinascita* 12 March 1976: 34-35 [in Italian].

Bilbow, Marjorie. "Illustrious Corpses", *Screen International* 88 (21 May 1977): 16.

Canby, Vincent. "Cynical Cinema Is Chic", *The New York Times* 21 November 1976: II 13 [reprinted in *The New York Times Film Reviews* (1975-1976): 287].

—————. "Illustrious Corpses", *The New York Times* 6 October 1976: 34 [reprinted in *The New York Times Film Reviews* (1975-1976): 267].

Coleman, John. "Dead Ends", *New Statesman*, volume 93, 2408 (13 May 1977): 650.

Combs, Richard. "Political paranoia", *The Listener*, volume 114, 2937 (28 November 1985): 37.

Fofi, Goffredo. "Cadaveri eccellenti", *Ombre Rosse* 14 (April 1976): 78-79 [in Italian].

Fougères, Roland. "Cadavres exquis: Un flic intègre seul contre tous", *Ciné-Revue* 56: 21 (20 May 1976): 16-19 [in French].

Gow, Gordon. "*Illustrious Corpses*", *Films and Filming* 23: 10 (July 1977): 34-35.

L.T. "*Cadaveri eccellenti*", *Cinema nuovo* 25: 241 (May/June 1976): 215-216 [in Italian].

Mack. "Cadaveri Eccellenti", *Variety* 31 March 1976: 14.

Millar, Gavin. "Black humour", *The Listener*, volume 97, 2512 (9 June 1977): 757-758.

Rémond, Alain. "*Cadavres exquis*", *Télérama* 27 May 1976: 80-82 [in French].

Salachan, Gilbert. "Cadavres exquis", *Télérama* 2339 (9 November 1994): 149 [in French].

Sinyard, Neil. "Illustrious Corpses", in Frank N Magill (ed), *Magill's Survey of Cinema: Foreign Language Films*, volume 3 (Englewood Cliffs, NJ: Salem Press, 1985): 1466-1470.

Tassone, Aldo. "Les *Cadavres exquis* de Francesco Rosi", *Télérama* 18 March 1976: 86-87 [in French].

Lucky Luciano

a.m. "Lucky Luciano", *Rivista del Cinematografo* 11 (November 1973): 575-576 [in Italian].

Bilbow, Marjorie. "Lucky Luciano", *Screen International* 101 (20 August 1977): 16.

Chevallier, Jacques. "Lucky Luciano", *Image et Son* 279 (December 1973): 108-110 [in French].

Cluny, Claude Michel. "Lucky Luciano: Haute main sur les bas-fonds", *Cinéma (France)* 182 (December 1973): 120-122 [in French].

Combs, Richard. "Black fable", *The Listener*, volume 114, 2939 (12 December 1985): 35.

D.A. "Lucky Luciano", *Cinématographe* 5 (December 1973-January 1974): 4-5 [in French].

Dawson, Jan. "Melting-pot luck", *The Listener*, volume 98, 2522 (18 August 1977): 218.

Erskine, Thomas L. "Lucky Luciano", in Frank N Magill (ed), *Magill's Survey of Cinema: Foreign Language Films*, volume 4 (Englewood Cliffs, NJ: Salem Press, 1985): 1864-1868.

G.P. "*Lucky Luciano*", *Cinema nuovo* 23: 227 (January/February 1974): 46-47 [in Italian].

Milne, Tom. "Lucky Luciano", *Monthly Film Bulletin* 42: 497 (June 1975): 140.

Werb. "Re: Lucky Luciano", *Variety* 14 November 1973: 16.

The Mattei Affair

Baby, Yvonne. "*L'affaire Mattei*, un film de Francesco Rosi", *Le Monde* 7-8 June 1972: 19 [in French].

Cowie, Peter. "Il caso Mattei", in Peter Cowie (ed), *International Film Guide 1973* (London: The Tantivy Press, 1972): 231.

e.b. "Il caso Mattei", *Filmcritica* 221 (January 1972): 53 [in Italian].

Gow, Gordon. "*The Mattei Affair*", *Films and Filming* 21: 11 (August 1975): 41.

Greenspun, Roger. "From Italy, 'Mattei Affair'", *The New York Times* 21 February 1973: 40.

—————————. "*The Mattei Affair*", *The New York Times* 21 May 1973: 40 [reprinted in *The New York Times Film Reviews* (1973-1974): 56].

James, Hugh. "*The Mattei Affair*", *Films in Review* 24: 5 (May 1973): 308-309.

Millar, Gavin. "Italian affair", *The Listener*, volume 93, 2412 (26 June 1975): 850.

Moravia, Alberto. "Machiavelli a cavallo di una bomba: *Il caso Mattei* di Francesco Rosi", *L'Espresso* 6 February 1972: 23 [in Italian].

Reichmann, Vittorio and Goffredo Fofi. "I padroni di stato e i loro cantori (su Rosi)", *Ombre Rosse* 2 (1972): 77-81 [in Italian].

Rosenbaum, Jonathan. "Caso Mattei, Il (The Mattei Affair)", *Monthly Film Bulletin* 42: 497 (June 1975): 131-132.

Sarris, Andrew. "Maverick at the Fall Round-Up (*The Mattei Affair*)", *Village Voice* 4 October 1973: 61ff.

Schickel, Richard. "Italian Crude: *The Mattei Affair*", *Time* 11 June 1973: 70ff.

Tallenay, Jean-Louis. "*L'affaire Mattei*", *Télérama* 18 June 1972: 55-56 [in French].

Werb. "Il Caso Mattei", *Variety* 16 February 1972: 24.

Just Another War

Amiel, Mireille. "Les hommes contre...", *Cinéma (France)* 158 (July-August 1971): 133-137 [in French].

Bruno, Edoardo. "Uomini contro", *Filmcritica* 209 (September 1970): 331-332 [in Italian].

G.L.P. "*Uomini contro*", *Cinema nuovo* 19: 207 (September/October 1970): 382-383 [in Italian].

Jeancolas, Jean-Pierre. "Le film de guerre libéré de l'anecdote", *Jeune Cinéma* 56 (June/July 1971): 1-4 [in French].

Mosk. "Uomini Contro", *Variety* 16 September 1970: 23.

Rolland, Béatrice. "La pesanteur et la cruauté", *Positif* 129 (July-August 1971): 77-80 [in French].

Sorgi, Claudio. "Uomini contro", *Rivista del Cinematografo* 8/9 (August/September 1970): 401-402 [in Italian].

"Uomini contro", *Cinema d'Oggi* 5 October 1970: 10 [in Italian].

Cinderella – Italian Style

Banacki, Raymond. "More Than A Miracle", *Film Quarterly* 21: 3 (spring 1968): 59-60.

Braucourt, Guy. "Les sorcières. La belle et le cavalier", *Cinéma (France)* 131 (December 1968): 125-127 [in French].

Buckley, Peter. "Cinderella – Italian Style", *Films and Filming* 16: 1 (October 1969): 46.

Canby, Vincent. "More Than a Miracle", *The New York Times* 2 November 1967: 58 [reprinted in *The New York Times Film Reviews* (1959-1968): 3711].

"C'era una volta", *Cinema d'Oggi* 6 November 1967: 11 [in Italian].

"C'era una volta", *Intermezzo* 21-22 (30 November 1967): 11 [in Italian].

Croce, Gian Paolo. "Lo straneiro. C'era una volta. In catalessi", *Ombre Rosse* 4 (March 1968): 81-83 [in Italian].

Gambetti, Giacomo. "C'era una volta...", *Bianco e nero* 29: 3/4 (March/April 1968): 166-168 [in Italian].

G.F. "*C'era una volta*", *Cinema nuovo* 16: 190 (November/December 1967): 452-453 [in Italian].

I. "C'era una Volta... (Cinderella – Italian Style)", *Monthly Film Bulletin* 36: 428 (September 1969): 193.

Knight, Arthur. "Once Around the World Lightly", *Saturday Review* 18 November 1967: 57.

Murf. "More Than a Miracle", *Variety* 1 November 1967: 20.

The Moment of Truth

A.F. "Il momento della verità", *Cinema nuovo* 14: 174 (March/April 1965): 135-137 [in Italian].

Alpert, Hollis. "Blood, Sand, and Money", *Saturday Review* 11 September 1965: 51.

Cattani, Richard J. "*The Moment of Truth* on Screen", *Christian Science Monitor* (Western edition) 19 August 1966: 4.

Ciment, Michel. "Le moment de l'illusion", *Positif* 99 (November 1968): 60-62 [in French].

Crowther, Bosley. "The Moment of Truth", *The New York Times* 10 August 1965: 18 [reprinted in *The New York Times Film Reviews* (1959-1968): 3560].

Gill, Brendan. "The Current Cinema: Spilling Blood", *The New Yorker* 14 August 1965: 92.

Hawk. "Il Momento Della Verita", *Variety* 31 March 1965: 6.

"Il momento della verità", *Intermezzo* 20: 7-8 (30 April 1965): 11 [in Italian].

"Il momento della verita", in Peter Cowie (ed), *International Film Guide 1966* (London: The Tantivy Press, 1965): 100.

"Il momento della verità", *Rivista del Cinematografo* 4/5 (April/May 1965): 221 [in Italian].

Jordan, René. "*The Moment of Truth*", *Films in Review* 16: 8 (October 1965): 515-516.

Kael, Pauline. "Bitter Truth From the Bull Ring", *Life* 24 September 1965: 10 [reprinted in *Kiss Kiss Bang Bang* (Boston and Toronto: Little, Brown and Co, 1968): 118-120].

Martelli, Luigi. "Lo spettatore critico: Il momento della verità", *Filmcritica* 156/157 (April/May 1965): 316-317 [in Italian].

P.H. "Momento della verità, Il (The Moment of Truth)", *Monthly Film Bulletin* 34: 401 (June 1967): 89-90.

Roud, Richard. "Festivals 65: Cannes", *Sight and Sound* 34: 3 (summer 1965): 118-119.

Verdone, Mario. "Il momento della verità", *Bianco e nero* 26: 4 (April 1965): 66-68 [in Italian].

Hands Over the City

Casiraghi, Ugo. *"Le mani sulla città"*, *L'Unità* 6 September 1963 [in Italian].

Ciment, Michel. "Main basse sur la ville, ou La question raisonnable", *Positif* 60 (April-May 1964): 36-41 [in French].

Doniol-Valcroze, Jacques. "Un buisson de questions", *Cahiers du Cinéma* 26: 152 (February 1964): 64-66 [in French].

Durgnat, Raymond. *"Hands Over the City"*, *Films and Filming* 13: 1 (October 1966): 18, 53-54.

E.S. "Mani sulla città, Le (Hands Over the City)", *Monthly Film Bulletin* 33: 392 (September 1966): 137-138.

Fofi, Goffredo. "Venise, Secundo Tempo", *Positif* 56 (November 1963): 46-48 [in French].

Hawk. "La [sic] Mani Sulla Citta", *Variety* 11 September 1963.

Monti, Marco. *"Le mani sulla città"*, *Il Secolo d'Italia* 8 January 1964 [in Italian].

Nowell-Smith, Geoffrey. "Le mani sulla citta", *Sight and Sound* 35: 3 (summer 1966): 144-146.

Pranzo, Mario. *"Le mani sulla città"*, *Corriere Lombardo* 12-13 October 1963 [in Italian].

Rondi, Gian Luigi. *"Le mani sulla città"*, *Il Tempo* 6 September 1963 [in Italian].

Schröder, Peter H. "Die Hände über die Stadt", *Filmkritik* 8 (August 1965): 447-449 [in German].

Siclier, Jacques. *"Main basse sur la ville"*, *Télérama* 14 May 1975: 55 [in French].

Sinyard, Neil. "Hands Over the City", in Frank N Magill (ed), *Magill's Survey of Cinema: Foreign Language Films*, volume 3 (Englewood Cliffs, NJ: Salem Press, 1985): 1330-1334.

Thompson, Howard. "Hands Over the City and Salvatore Giuliano", *The New York Times* 18 September 1964: 28 [reprinted in *The New York Times Film Reviews* (1959-1968): 3490].

Zambetti, Sandro. "Le mani sulla città di Francesco Rosi", *Cineforum* 3: 30 (December 1963): 954-977 [in Italian].

Salvatore Giuliano

A.F. "Salvatore Giuliano", *Cinema nuovo* 11: 156 (March/April 1962): 138-139 [in Italian].

Baby, Yvonne. "*Salvatore Giuliano*", *Le Monde* 6 March 1963: 13 [in French].

Combs, Richard. "Love's Labour Lost", *The Listener*, volume 119, 3059 (21 April 1988): 38.

d'Yvoire, Jean. "*Salvatore Giuliano*", *Télérama* 17 March 1963: 58 [in French].

Hawk. "*Salvatore Giuliano*", *Variety* 27 December 1961: 6.

Mardore, Michel. "Le marxisme, pour quoi faire?", *Cahiers du Cinéma* 24: 142 (April 1963): 41-47 [in French].

Martin, Marcel. "Salvatore Giuliano", *La Revue du Cinéma* 435 (February 1988): 48 [in French].

Nowell-Smith, Geoffrey. "Salvatore Giuliano", *Sight and Sound* 32: 3 (summer 1963): 142-143.

P.J.D. "Salvatore Giuliano", *Monthly Film Bulletin* 30: 353 (June 1963): 80.

S. "Salvatore Giuliano", *Film Français* 984 (5 April 1963): 18 [in French].

"Salvatore Giuliano", *l'Avant-Scène du Cinéma* 26 (15 May 1963): 60 [in French].

Sinyard, Neil. "Salvatore Giuliano", in Frank N Magill (ed), *Magill's Survey of Cinema: Foreign Language Films*, volume 6 (Englewood Cliffs, NJ: Salem Press, 1985): 2613-2617.

Thompson, Howard. "Hands Over the City and Salvatore Giuliano", *The New York Times* 18 September 1964: 28 [reprinted in *The New York Times Film Reviews* (1959-1968): 3490].

The Swindlers

Bruno, Edoardo. "Lo spettatore critico: *I magliari*", *Filmcritica* 90 (October 1959): 293-294 [in Italian].

Fofi, Goffredo. "I magliari", *Positif* 69 (May 1965): 18-20 [in French].

F.V. "I magliari", *Cinema nuovo* 9: 143 (January/February 1960): 49-50 [in Italian].

Hawk. "I Magliari", *Variety* 16 December 1959: 6.

Lane, John Francis. "The Italian Look", *Films and Filming* 6: 3 (December 1959): 31.

Legrand, Gérard. "Profession: magliari. Tailler, bâtir et coudre", *Positif* 291 (May 1985): 69-70 [in French].

"I magliari", *Intermezzo* 14: 19-20 (31 October 1959): 6 [in Italian].

RPK. "Auf St. Pauli ist der Teufel los", *Filmkritik* 6 (June 1961): 305-306 [in German].

Trémois, Claude-Marie. "Profession: magliari. Les débuts de Rosi", *Télérama* 1829 (30 January 1985): 13 [in French].

The Challenge

Bruno, Edoardo. "Rassegna critica dello spettacolo: La sfida", *Filmcritica* 81 (November 1958): 260-261 [in Italian].

Hawk. "La Sfida", *Variety* 17 September 1958: 18.

Jones, G & P. "La sfida", *Brighton Film Review* 16 (January 1970): 14.

K.C. "La sfida", *Sight and Sound* 28: 1 (winter 1958/59): 23.

Mardore, Michel. "Pour des tomates. Le défi", *Positif* 34 (May 1960): 45-47 [in French].

Marinucci, Vinicio. "'The challenge'", *Il film italiano* 24 (September 1958): 28-30 [in Italian].

Siniscalchi, Vincenzo M. "La sfida di Francesco Rosi", *Primi Plani* 9-10 (September-October 1958): 20-21 [in Italian].

T. "Le défi (La sfida)", *Film Français* 847 (26 August 1960): 16-17 [in French].

Index

195

Notes on contributors

Salvatore Bizzarro is Professor of Spanish, Italian and Latin American Studies at the Colorado College in Colorado Springs. He has published extensively on Italian cinema and has worked especially on and with Lina Wertmüller, Franco Brusati and Ettore Scola. He is the author of the *Historical Dictionary of Chile* (1972; 2nd edition, 1987) and *Pablo Neruda: All Poets The Poet* (1979), and has contributed to the book, *Latin America During Nixon's Second Term* (1978). He was also a contributor to the *Hispanic American Report*, and a member of the editorial board of the *Latin American Yearly Review*.

Manuela Gieri is Associate Professor of Italian and Cinema Studies at the University of Toronto. She received a *Laurea in Lettere* at the University of Bologna, Italy, and a PhD in Italian and Film Studies at Indiana University. She is the author of several articles on Italian cinema, contemporary Italian women writers, and Luigi Pirandello. Among her publications are *La Strada: Federico Fellini, Director* (1987), *Contemporary Italian Filmmaking: Strategies of Subversion* (1995) and *Luigi Pirandello: New Critical Perspectives* (forthcoming).

Ben Lawton is Chair of Italian Studies at Purdue University. He has taught Italian film, literature and language for over twenty years. His *Literary and Socio-Political Trends in Italian Cinema* was one of the first texts to be widely used by Italianists in North America. In addition to his various studies on Italian cinema, he is perhaps best known for his translation of Pier Paolo Pasolini's *Empirismo eretico*, as organiser of international conferences on literature and film, and as co-editor of the Purdue University *Film Studies Annuals* and *Romance Languages Annual*.

Harry Lawton graduated from the University of Oxford with a degree in French and Italian. Since the late 1960s he has been teaching Italian literature and film at the University of California at Santa Barbara.

Millicent Marcus is currently Professor of Italian at the University of Texas at Austin. She has written *An Allegory of Form: Literary Self-*

Consciousness in the Decameron (1979), *Italian Film in the Light of Neorealism* (1986) and *Filmmaking By the Book: Italian Cinema and Literary Adaptation* (1993), as well as numerous articles on Italian literature and film. She is presently working on a collaborative, interdisciplinary project entitled *Italy 1919*.

Claudio Mazzola is currently the director of the Institute of European Studies in Milan, where he also teaches Italian cinema and literature. He received his PhD in Comparative Literature from the University of Washington, and completed his film studies at the Scuola del cinema in Milan. He has published articles on Bertolucci, Salvatores, Pasolini, and on a number of contemporary Italian writers.

Carlo Testa teaches Italian at the University of British Columbia. His work on the European 19th and 20th centuries includes *Desire and the Devil: Demonic Contracts in French and European Literature* (1991), and a number of articles in English, French and Spanish, centring on the question of the self, the Utopian issue and marginality. His interest in the area of Italian film covers filmmakers from both the older and the younger generations (Rosi, Fellini, Moretti, the Tavianis, Archibugi, Nichetti, Zaccaro). He is currently completing *Diagonal Contexts: Italian Cinema and European Intellectual History, 1970-1990*.